4th Edition

Negotiating the Special Education Maze

A Guide for Parents & Teachers

Winifred Anderson
Stephen Chitwood
Deidre Hayden
Cherie Takemoto

Woodbine House ■ 2008

Fourth Edition

All rights reserved. Published in the United States of America by Woodbine House, Inc., 6510 Bells Mill Rd., Bethesda, MD 20817. 800-843-7323. www.woodbinehouse.com

Library of Congress Cataloging-in-Publication Data

Negotiating the special education maze : a guide for parents and teachers / Winifred Anderson ... [et al.]. -- 4th ed.
     p. cm.
  Includes index.
  ISBN 978-1-890627-46-1
  1. Children with disabilities--Education--United States. 2. Children with disabilities--Civil rights--United States. 3. Home and school--United States. I. Anderson, Winifred.
  LC4031.A66 2008
  371.910973--dc22

                                                                      2007045827

Manufactured in the United States of America

10   9   8   7   6   5   4   3   2   1

To Daniel Reed Chitwood, whose life inspired us all, and Pete Scampavia, who continues to guide us.

TABLE OF CONTENTS

Acknowledgements

We have endeavored to write a practical guide based upon the experiences of hundreds of parents, and those advocates, both legal and educational, who continue to strive to obtain appropriate services for children and youth with disabilities. This book represents the work of many people working together—the group brain—as we like to call it. In particular, we would like to express appreciation to the staff and friends of the Parent Educational Advocacy Training Center, the Goss family, the Houston family, Irene Moore, Judy Dunbar, Pierre Ames, and Rosalia Fajardo, who brought reality to the examples we used in this book.

We especially want to thank our editors at Woodbine House, Beth Walker, for her help in giving the book a fresh perspective, and Susan Stokes, for her painstaking attention to detail. And finally the rest of the staff at Woodbine House for their vision and perseverance in creating and distributing the SPECIAL NEEDS COLLECTION of which this book is a part.

We express admiration and appreciation to those parents and professionals who work together to teach the process of educational advocacy to others across the country, especially to those in Virginia, West Virginia, Maryland, and Illinois. These team members use NEGOTIATING THE SPECIAL EDUCATION MAZE to guide and inform their work with parent groups and have provided us with valuable comment. To the thousands of parents who have participated in our training courses in educational advocacy, we say THANK YOU—for teaching us as you shared your experiences with us.

PREFACE

The first edition of *Negotiating the Special Education Maze* was published in 1982, following the signing of the ground-breaking Education for All Handicapped Children Act. The authors, Winifred Anderson, Steve Chitwood, and Deidre Hayden, wrote the book knowing that parents were mandated by the new law to help school personnel plan individual programs for their children. But at that time neither parents nor school people had had much experience working closely in educational planning. The notion of parents as equal partners in the education of their children was a novel and somewhat controversial notion. Yet the law required what best practice and research have continued to show: children succeed in school when parents and professionals share information and work together.

Nearly thirty years later, one would think that families and school personnel are at last working collaboratively and that the promise of The Education for All Handicapped Children Act, now called the Individuals with Disabilities Act (IDEA), has been fulfilled. As the U.S. Congress noted in 2004 as they reauthorized IDEA, however, that is not the case. Congress stated:

> *"The promise of special education has been impeded by low expectations of students with disabilities, and insufficient focus on applying replicable research on proven methods of teaching and learning for children with special learning needs…"*

Almost thirty years of research and experience have demonstrated that effective education of students with disabilities relies, among other things, on "strengthened roles and responsibilities of parents so that they have mean-ingful opportunities to participate in the education of their children at school and at home."

The 2004 revisions to IDEA ensure that strong parent participation is ad-dressed through the legislation and its regulations. The new law requires many new procedures that schools must follow and parents must understand in order to participate fully in decisions about their children's education.

The fourth edition of *Negotiating the Special Education Maze* has been ex-panded and reorganized to address the changes made in IDEA. It focuses on strengthened roles for parents. It emphasizes high expectations for all students. It shares the belief that with the right supports and services in place, all students with disabilities can have access to, and experience success within, the general education curriculum. The authors underscore the importance of students with disabilities taking an active part in their own educational plans as early in their school careers as possible.

Each reauthorization of IDEA has produced additional, often confusing, rules and regulations, thus creating an increasingly complex special education process. And yet, the original principle that informed the first edition of *Negoti-ating the Special Education Maze* has remained true: Parents are their child's first and best advocate. By knowing children's strengths and needs, understanding the basic special education process, and being able to work collaboratively with school people, parents can be instrumental in shaping a successful experience for their children in school, and help prepare them for life as full members of their communities.

Cherie Takemoto, current Executive Director of the Parent Educational Advocacy Training Center (PEATC), has joined the original authors in writing the fourth edition of this book. Cherie brings a wealth of experience as a pro-fessional educator and as the mother of Peter Scampavia, a recent high school graduate who is finding success as an advocate for himself and other young people with disabilities.

It is the hope of the authors that this new and updated edition of the book helps both new and experienced parents find their way, changing the world for their own children as well as others who will follow.

Winifred Anderson
Steve Chitwood
Deidre Hayden
Cherie Takemoto

March 2008

INTRODUCTION

Parents of children with disabilities face a confusing array of information and service systems. Those who have just learned that their children might have special needs may have heard of laws or programs that can help them. Yet, they wonder how and where to begin. Who should they call? Are special services really necessary?

Parents whose older children are already in the school system may be aware of the Individuals with Disabilities Education Act (IDEA), a strong federal law that provides for special education for all children with disabilities. Yet they, too, have many questions. For example, when talking with school professionals, a father might wonder what educational jargon such as "scaled scores," "least restrictive environment," and "response to intervention" mean. What have they to do with his lively, lovable child?

Parents of young people who are nearing graduation from school and from special education have other concerns. They ask, "Will our son have a job when he graduates?" "Are there further opportunities to go to college or learn a trade?" "Are there laws that guarantee him services and benefits as an adult?"

These and many other common concerns of parents of children with disabilities are addressed in IDEA. It can be easy, however, to become confused or lost in the maze of the legislation, of state and federal regulations, and of local interpretations of IDEA. In this complex law, what is most important for you to focus upon? Your child's strengths, special learning needs, and aspirations for the future will help you to sort out your priorities and sharpen your focus.

Negotiating the Special Education Maze discusses those parts of IDEA most relevant for you to know as you make your way through the special education process. The main chapters give primary attention to the part of IDEA which covers special education for children ages three to twenty-one (Part B of IDEA). Chapter 11 is written especially for parents of very young children and covers Part C of IDEA, which provides early intervention for infants and toddlers. If you are just beginning this process with an infant or young toddler, that chapter will be most helpful to you.

Chapter 2 will help you become more familiar with the people and processes you will encounter as you travel through the special education maze. In Chapters 3 through 6 you will learn how to be a keen observer of your child and what he[1] needs to be successful so that you can be an equal partner with others who will evaluate your child and help determine whether he is eligible for services.

In Chapters 7, 8, and 9 you learn how to use the provisions in IDEA and the information you have gathered to become an effective advocate in developing your child's educational plan. Chapters 12 and 13 help you plan through the teen years and prepare for life after high school.

The skills and knowledge you gain from this book are valuable no matter what the age of your child. The emphasis on this plan is to *individualize*—to write a unique program for the education of your unique child. What if, despite all these efforts, things don't go as you would like? Chapter 14 discusses both formal and informal ways to resolve disagreements and Chapter 15 will help you understand more about nondiscrimination protections your child has through IDEA and other civil rights laws.

Where appropriate, chapters end with a short list of actions you can take right now. As it is important to encourage students to learn to be advocates for themselves, the list may include actions that involve your child or his opinions.

Everywhere you go in the maze you may be faced with unfamiliar language. The glossary in the back of the book should help you understand the terms as you are reading and in discussions you have with professionals and other parents. You can refer to the Resources section for organizations and websites that can provide further information about the topics covered in the book.

As you journey through the special education maze, use the rights, responsibilities, protections, and procedures that are a part of the special education law. Combined with your unique, understanding of your child, the special education rules and procedures can help you create the program your child needs to progress and learn in school.

---

1. *To avoid sexist use of pronouns, the masculine gender is used in even-numbered chapters; the feminine gender, in odd-numbered chapters.*

Parents as Educational Advocates

As you will discover through reading this book, IDEA empowers parents to become *educational advocates* for their children. An advocate is one who speaks on behalf of another person or group of persons in order to bring about change. There are consumer advocates, working to influence regulatory agencies to bring about change in the quality of products we purchase. Political advocates seek to bring about social and economic change through state and national legislatures. Legal advocates use the court system to bring about change in the interpretation of laws that affect our lives. An educational advocate is one who speaks knowledgeably for the educational needs of another person.

You, the parent, know your child best. It is you who can speak most effectively on your child's behalf to secure his educational rights under the law. This book was written to assist you in your role as educational advocate by helping you gain the knowledge required to be an effective educational planner for your child. You will learn how to present your child's strengths and needs, cope with your feelings, and gain insights and understanding of the complex maze of special education.

Many school systems and interest groups have written manuals to assist parents and teachers understand and fulfill their roles under IDEA. Most of these books or brochures describe the legal requirements for special education, the procedures of the school system, the characteristics of various disabilities, and regulations prescribed by the state and local school systems. The terminology is often confusing and includes legal terms that are bewildering to many who are new to special education. Many other manuals are limited in that they stress what the school system knows—its rules and regulations—and seem to overlook the parent and the child.

This book is different. It begins with what you know better than anyone—your own child. *Negotiating the Special Education Maze* is a practical step-by-step guide based upon the experience of thousands of families as they have worked to secure special education services that meet the *individualized needs* of their children. These parents have increased their knowledge of school systems' procedures, learned skills in organizing and presenting observations of their children, and become more assertive and effective in their role as educational advocates for their children. The understanding these parents have gained of the value of active participation in educational planning is shared with you; indeed, their experience is the basis for *Negotiating the Special Education Maze*.

This book alone may provide you sufficient information to become an influential educational advocate. You can do this by working with the school or with the special education coordinator to identify other parents, then organizing a group of parents and locating someone to lead the group as you all read and talk about the book, chapter by chapter. This lets you work through the steps outlined in this book with help from others. This book points the way toward additional sources of assistance—books, resource groups, and other training courses.

Whether you read this alone or with a group, *Negotiating the Special Education Maze* was written with you, the parent, in mind. You may read it all at once, but you will probably focus on the step in the special education maze you are about to enter. Some of you have already spent many years working to get appropriate school services for your children. Others of you are just embarking on the road through the special education maze. Whatever the stage of your journey, the authors hope this road map will help you give others a clear understanding of your child's abilities and needs. At the end you should find your child making progress, because you and school personnel are partners in his well-being.

1. Beginning the Journey
A Plan for the Trip

As you enter the special education maze, the primary question for you is, "How do I help my child?" The answer is refreshingly straightforward. You begin the journey with what you know best, your child. You, of all people, know her special ways of learning, her strengths, things that impede her learning, and things that make her want to learn. You and your family have many hopes and dreams for her life and future.

But as you enter the maze, you can easily become confused or intimidated as you encounter special education laws, regulations, policies, and procedures. Even when you think you understand the written rules of the road, the ways your local school system interprets and implements the federal and state rules might seem different. Yet, powerful special education laws promise your child an equal opportunity for success in school. Your perspectives and unique knowledge of your son or daughter are the key ingredients to making those important laws work for you.

Building on your knowledge of your child, this book can serve as a guide for you as you proceed through the maze of special education laws and procedures. The book's primary focus is on Part B of the Individuals with Disabilities Act, IDEA, which covers special education for school-aged children. So before you embark on your own journey, it may be helpful to gain an overall understanding of IDEA.

What is Special Education?

Before children with disabilities had the broad protections of the law, many parents in the United States were told, "We are sorry, your child cannot go to school here because she is too severely disabled." Parents had no recourse. Since 1975, however, federal and state laws have been enacted that require schools to provide education for all children with disabilities. The Individuals with Disabilities Education Act, IDEA, mandates that all children with disabilities in the U.S. receive a free, appropriate public education.

Special education is defined in IDEA as specially designed instruction, at no cost to parents, to meet the unique needs of a child with a disability. Special education instruction is provided by teachers who are trained in methods that address the learning needs of children with disabilities. These special methods, coupled with the individualization of instruction, promise that each child will be given the opportunity to travel successfully through her developmental pathways.

Six Principles of the Individuals with Disabilities Education Act

The foundation of special education rests on the six principles of IDEA. Understanding these principles can help you understand the big picture of special education.

1. All children will be served.

Congress intended that no child in need of special education will be excluded from receiving services, even children with the most severe disabilities, and those who have been suspended or expelled. States provide services for children with disabilities from birth to age 18, and most states extend special education through age 21.

2. Children will be tested fairly to determine if they will receive special education services.

Before children can be declared eligible for special education services, a team of professionals must evaluate them. Schools and other agencies are required to give tests to children that show both their strengths and their weaknesses. All tests must be given to children in their own language and in such a way that their abilities and their disabilities are accurately displayed. This is called nondiscriminatory testing. Children will be placed in special education based upon several tests, not upon one single test or test score. Nondiscriminatory testing ensures that children who do not need special education will not be placed there, and that children who need special school services will get them.

3. Schools have a duty to provide individually designed, appropriate programs for every child at no cost to their parents.

IDEA requires public schools to provide a *free, appropriate public education* to all children who have been identified as needing special education. The appropriateness is determined by a group of people, including parents and educators, who work together to design a program that addresses the child's individual educational problems. This program is called an Individualized Education Program (IEP). Your child has a right to a full range of educational services, which may include such related services as special transportation, assistive technology, interpreting services, speech/language therapy, counseling, occupational or physical therapy, or other services necessary to enable her to benefit from special education. To the extent feasible, these services and supports must be based on research-based practices.

4. Children with disabilities will be educated with children who do not have disabilities.

Before IDEA, our schools almost always segregated children with disabilities from children without disabilities. Now, however, our nation has legal requirements that all students have equal access to education and have access to the general education curriculum. As a result, increasing numbers of children with disabilities are being integrated into their communities' schools. Under IDEA, students with disabilities are guaranteed services in the *least restrictive environment*. That is, when the IEP is written, a determination is made regarding the amount of time each student with disabilities will *not* participate with non-disabled peers both in classroom and all other school activities. The assumption is students will be educated with peers who do not have disabilities. Students are to be educated in a separate classroom or school only when the nature and severity of their disabilities makes it impossible to meet their educational needs in a less restrictive environment.

5. The decisions of the school system can be challenged by parents.

Prior to the passage of IDEA and the laws that preceded it, parents had little or no recourse if they disagreed with the decisions made by the school authorities. Under IDEA, parents and students have a right to *due process*. Under these due process rights, there are provisions for settling disputes by an impartial third party, through a formal due process hearing or mediation. Parents have the right to challenge decisions made about their children in the areas of inclusion or exclusion from special services, testing in a nondiscriminatory manner, the appropriateness of the education as written in the IEP, the placement of their child in the least restrictive educational environment, and other related areas.

In addition to guaranteeing the right to challenge, IDEA provides parents with the right to notice. When any change is to be made with regard to testing, provision of new services, the withdrawal of services, the IEP, or the amount of time the child will be with nondisabled children, the parents must first be notified. In many situations, the consent of parents is also required before school personnel can make changes.

6. Parents of children with disabilities participate in the planning and decision making for their child's special education.

The basic premise of this book is that parents are their child's first and best advocates. Who else can possibly know your child in the ways that you do? Your love and caring were seen by the Congress of the United States to be a vital contribution to educational planning for your child. Therefore, IDEA mandates the partnership between parents and school personnel. You, as parents, will be working with school and other professionals to see that a free, appropriate public education in the least restrictive environment is provided for your child. That is your child's right. And the school system has a duty to provide it. At each step along the way, the partnership ideally will ensure that your hopes, visions, and expertise will be combined with the commitment and the specialized training of professionals to educate your child.

Each of the six principles of IDEA involves you, the parents. The continuing importance of your involvement in the special education process has been reflected in numerous Congressional actions and court decisions. Since the passage of the law in 1975, Congress has made several changes strengthening the rights of parents and their children. Understanding the special education law and parental rights has never been so important.

The Evolving Picture of IDEA

Special education laws introduced the concept of delivering education that is tailored to the individualized needs of students. Now this concept is increasingly applied to all students. Previously there was often only one way to measure success. Many educators were limited in the tools they had to teach children with diverse strengths and needs. Research has demonstrated that while "one size fits all" approaches work for some students, for many other students it does not work. Teachers have found that by analyzing the individual learning strengths and needs of children and understanding that there are multiple ways of looking at intelligence, they can be much more successful in educating all children.

Increasingly, students with disabilities are being taught the same curriculum and mastering the same subjects that were previously only open to students without disabilities. Schools are being held accountable for showing how students with disabilities are making similar progress in school as their peers. As schools have paid attention to the special learning needs of students with disabilities, they have found that many more of their "at risk" students are also learning and thriving.

Special attention and response to the educational needs of students with disabilities have led to technological and educational improvements in special education and other areas. For example, assistive technology can change what is written in text or pictures into speech so that people can communicate and be understood more easily. Activities that were previously impossible to do independently or places to go that were impossible to get to are now accessible for many people with disabilities.

Studies about learning and successful practices have led to innovative and effective ways to teach many more students to read, write, learn, and behave in ways that help them to flourish in school and in life. These new technologies, as well as information about effective ways to teach, have never been more attainable. Yet, too many students still do not have access to these tools, services, and approaches that might make a difference in their lives and futures.

Along with new possibilities have come higher expectations for students with disabilities. Previously, many children and adults with disabilities lived at home or in institutions throughout a lifetime of dependency. Now many people with disabilities are not only surviving, but also thriving. They continue to disprove old notions about limitations. In fact, the greatest obstacle to success is not necessarily a person's disability. It is the idea or perception that a person with a disability cannot be successful. These unwanted, unneeded attitudes have stifled hope and kept many people with disabilities from reaching their potential.

Your Child's Role as a Self-Advocate

Over the years, a great evolution in IDEA is the law's attention to the importance of the key role played by the student. The ways that people with disabilities view themselves and speak on their own behalf is called self-determination. The advancement of self-determination has been one of the most striking changes in society in the past ten years. Disability rights and advances in special education have encouraged children, young people, and adults with disabilities to speak up for themselves and to seek opportunities for more fulfilling lives and promising futures.

Part of your role as your child's educational advocate is to help her as she thinks about what she needs to be successful and determine her own future. Your child can contribute to, or complete, many of the activities in this book. Often, you will find that your child has been thinking about some of the perplexing problems you and her teachers may be trying to resolve. She may very well have ideas about what she needs to learn and master new achievements. Of course, parents of children with physical or communication challenges learn to "listen" carefully to what their children are saying through subtle cues or other behavior.

Sometimes you may not agree with your child's perspectives or priorities. This may be frustrating to both of you, but is a natural part of growing and learning for you and your child. As you support your child as a self-advocate, she will be able to understand her abilities and disabilities and let others know what she wants, thinks, and feels. Together, you can be formidable, successful advocates.

WHAT YOU CAN DO NOW

1. Write down the questions you have about special education.
2. Talk with your child about your role as an educational advocate.
3. Encourage your child to advocate for herself and communicate to you what is most important.
4. If your child is under three years old, skip to Chapter 11 to learn about early intervention services.

2. PEOPLE AND PROCEDURES
Charting Your Course

Your knowledge of the school system's procedures and your skills in communicating information about your child are essential to becoming an effective educational advocate. This chapter introduces the important people and processes you will come to know as you travel through the maze.

Preparing Yourself to Work in Partnership with the School

Thinking back on times you have worked with various teachers and other professionals, you may find that you, like many other parents, experienced feelings similar to those listed below:

- inadequate
- fearful
- tentative
- anxious
- enthusiastic

- hopeful
- intimidated
- challenged
- overwhelmed
- friendly

- exhausted
- confused
- worried
- prepared
- proud

Although these feelings are shared by many parents, some of these feelings may make it difficult to communicate your hopes, plans, and expectations for your child's school life. But these feelings are natural. As a parent going into school meetings, you are moving into a situation where the people you meet use a language you may not understand completely. They are familiar with routines and regulations you know little or nothing about. Everyone carries some remnants of their own school experience—good and not so good—into school buildings. Your perceptions of school professionals and your own school experiences may cause you to question your ability to say the right thing at the right time and to convey your cares, hopes, and opinions about your child's best interests and needs.

To overcome feelings of anxiety or confusion it helps to learn about the special education process and the people involved. This helps you be more comfortable in your role as advocate for your child. To help your child, you need as much information as possible, both about your child and about the school system, to be effective.

Remember, as you work with the school staff and routines, you will gain skills in presenting your view of your child to the school. This will help to ease any negative feelings, so you can be an effective partner in planning for your child's education. This chapter helps you understand how the system works and who is involved.

The Special Education Planning Cycle

Almost as important as understanding **how** schools make decisions about your child is understanding **when** they make those decisions. Often, one of the first sources of conflict between parents and schools is the sequence and timing of the major decisions in the special education process. As the following case study shows, differences in how and when the parents make plans for their child can lead to problems and frustrations on both sides.

Jessica Lee: A Case Study

During Jessica Lee's year in kindergarten, her parents became concerned when they noticed that she could not use pencil and paper as well as the other children. Jessica's crayon pictures were mainly scribbles, and toward the end of the school year, she was still unable to copy the letters in her name. Jessica was also restless. During group and story time she often jumped up and moved about the room, playing with objects on other children's desks or in the storage cabinets. She didn't listen to the story. When her teacher called her back to the group, she would roll around the floor, twisting her hair, apparently off in her own world.

For the first few months of the school year, the teacher said Jessica would soon learn what was expected of her in the classroom and that her skills and behavior would improve. Mr. and Mrs. Lee continued to worry, but listened to the teacher's suggestions. Finally, late in the year, the kindergarten teacher recommended that Jessica be referred, then tested by the school psychologist. This testing would help to determine whether or not she needed special education during the coming school year. Mr. and Mrs. Lee readily consented to the testing and worked with a group of professionals to decide on the kinds of tests that would best help everyone understand educational areas where Jessica needed additional attention. The Lees felt relieved that something was finally being done to see if Jessica had a learning problem.

Since most of the school psychologists were away during the summer, Jessica's testing had to be postponed until early in September. Reluctantly, the Lees waited. When September came, the testing began. But in the meantime, Jessica was having an even harder time in the first grade. She noticed that other children could easily do many things she couldn't, and she was getting in trouble at school and at home. The Lees were angry that the school system was not giving Jessica the special help they were now sure she needed. The school administrators, on the other hand, defended themselves by citing the regulations they were required to follow before declaring a child eligible for special education. Everyone was frustrated and angry.

The parents' cycle looks like this:

Parents' Cycle

The Parents' Cycle

The Lees' **awareness** of problems in Jessica's school life came early in her kindergarten year. They began to **gather information** that might help them to understand and to help Jessica. They talked with the pediatrician, observed other children Jessica's age, read books on child development and learning problems, and talked frequently with the kindergarten teacher. On the basis of their observations of Jessica and the knowledge they gained through other sources, the Lees gradually came to an **acceptance** of their original hunch. They concluded that Jessica did indeed have some problems needing special education at school. At this point, they talked again with the school principal and kindergarten teacher, hoping that **planning** for her special needs would begin. They were ready early in Jessica's kindergarten year for Jessica to have special education services.

The School System's Cycle

The school system, on the other hand, was reluctant to refer Jessica for special services so early in her school life. The kindergarten teacher at first adopted a "wait and see" attitude. Toward the end of the school year, though, the teacher realized the Lees' concerns were valid and activated the school system's planning cycle. She made a **referral** to the school principal, requesting that Jessica be considered for special education testing.

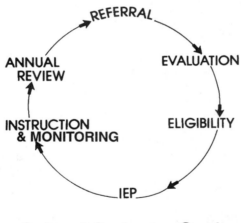

School System's Cycle

The principal convened the local screening committee, sometimes called the child study committee, to discuss Jessica's problems and consider whether her difficulties could be addressed through alternative teaching methods. They tried some alternatives for thirty days, but saw little change in her behavior and skills so decided that Jessica's problems warranted a full **evaluation**. This set in motion the evaluation process of psychological, educational, and other testing. A teacher, the school psychologist, the school health nurse, and a social worker were a part of the multidisciplinary team that sought to understand Jessica and her educational problems. This evaluation process, interrupted by summer vacation, was completed in the fall. The results of the series of tests were presented to a committee of school professionals and Jessica's parents. They determined that Jessica needed special services and qualified, or was **eligible** for special education.

Following the eligibility decision—that is, once the committee decided that Jessica qualified for special education services—the Lees and the school personnel, including a special education teacher, met together to plan an **Individualized Education Program (IEP)** for Jessica. The IEP included long-range educational goals based on Jessica's needs, as well as the special services she would require to help her reach her goals. At the same time, the team decided where Jessica would receive services to meet her educational goals. Only at this time did the parents' planning cycle and the school system's planning cycle come together.

At this point, some of the tension and frustration were alleviated. The Lees had been ready for Jessica to receive special education instruction several months before the school system had completed the required cycle of referral, evaluation, eligibility, and Individualized Education Program. Once the two cycles meshed, cooperative planning for Jessica's learning and appropriate behavior became possible. Subsequently, Jessica began to have a more successful time in school.

Jessica Lee's case illustrates only one type of conflict that can arise when parents' and school's planning cycles differ. Not all parents realize as early as the Lees did that their child needs special services. For example, the Okinski family didn't anticipate their son's referral:

Sam Okinski: A Case Study

Sam was a cheerful boy who daydreamed often; he could focus for long periods on a single project, but then have problems remembering to do his chores. His parents knew that he wasn't like his brothers, who had been quick to catch on to reading and simple math, and had more or less kept up with their classmates. But Sam's parents weren't overly concerned. They thought he was maturing at a different rate.

Sam's fourth grade teacher, however, saw Sam tuning out when the class worked together on reading and math. He didn't interact with the other children much, and he seemed to have a hard time understanding what the teacher asked him to do.

After meeting with the parents and watching Sam for a few months, the teacher thought that Sam might need some extra attention, and referred him for an evaluation.

Sam's parents were very surprised that Sam was referred and might be eligible for special education services. They hadn't realized how far off the track Sam had drifted, although both parents were very much involved in Sam's life. They made sure he finished his homework. He received pass-ing grades and they hadn't had any bad reports about his behavior.

In this case, the school personnel had recommended a formal evalu-ation of a child whose parents were unaware of significant problems. Sam's parents believed that he would outgrow any difficulties in school, and they struggled with the decision about whether to give the required permission for the next step—a formal evaluation.

Sam's parents decided to talk about Sam with others, including their family doctor and a child psychologist, before they would permit the evaluation.

In Sam's case, the school is ahead of the parents in the cycle. While the parents are barely, if at all, in the first stage of their planning cycle—the awareness phase— the school system is ready for the second step in its cycle—evaluation. This means that before the school and parents can work together as a team, school personnel must first thoroughly explain their concerns to the parents and convince them that significant problems may exist. Other times, as described in the example with Jessi-ca, parents see the problems before the school does and must advocate for testing.

Repeated Planning Cycles

Planning cycles for parents and for school systems aren't just one-time events. If a child is evaluated and enters the special education process, subse-quent evaluations are done to track whether the child is being helped with the plan, needs other plans, or no longer requires special education services. Understanding the planning cycles and the evaluation, along with the kinds of help your child can receive, removes any stigma associated with special educa-tion, and helps you focus on what's important: your child.

You may want to gain a better understanding of the types of services your child's school may have to offer. These are briefly reviewed in Chapter 8.

Your Role

An understanding of the school system's cycle can help to clarify your par-ticipation as your child's educational advocate. The school system's cycle is described in the rules and regulations published by the school system in your community. These rules and regulations must comply with the requirements set forth in the federal law, the Individuals with Disabilities Education Act (IDEA). The following two activities will help you understand how your school's special education process works. The understanding you gain will help to change any feelings of inadequacy and uncertainty you may have into ones of competency.

Activity #1: Rules of the Road

Every school system in the country has a set of regulations governing special education. The complexity of these regulations varies, however, from locality to locality. Some large school systems have documents of a hundred or more pages outlining their procedures. Other school systems have no more than a page or two of printed regulations. The first part of Activity #1 is to contact your school superintendent, director of special education, or special education advisory committee and ask for a copy of your local school system's procedures and regulations for special education. Rules and regulations as well as parent handbooks are often available through the Internet.

Schools are required to make this information available to all citizens. Most schools provide parents with a handbook summarizing their special education procedures. Having a copy of your school system's policies and procedures will help you gain confidence in your ability to be an advocate for your child.

When your local school system wrote its procedural guidelines, it had to follow the regulations of your state department of special education. So a second part of Activity #1 is to look on the Internet for the state special education regulations or write your state director of special education to request a copy.

Because you are a citizen and because special education regulations are public documents, you should have easy access to this information. At the very least, these documents will be available in either your public library or a public school library. If you have trouble locating regulations, contact your state parent training and information center (PTI) or the office of your state legislator for assistance. The Resource section in the back of this book tells you how to find your state's PTI and your telephone book will tell you how to contact your state legislator.

Obtaining state special education regulations is especially important if your school system's policies and procedures are not highly structured and developed. Your school system, like many local school systems, may simply follow what the state has written with no elaboration. While you are requesting a copy of your state regulations, ask for, or search the Internet for, parent handbooks describing the special education process in your state and locality.

Procedural Safeguards

An important part of the rules and regulations is the set of procedural safeguards that make sure your rights, and your child's rights, are respected. Procedural safeguards describe your rights and your child's rights to have the special education process conducted in a specific way—notifying you in writing when the school is proposing to evaluate your child, for example, and explaining how you can dispute any actions the school is proposing to take. Here are some of the basic procedural safeguards that IDEA requires every state to have:

- Schools must give reasonable written notice to parents before they evaluate or place a child, change his special education placement, or refuse to take such actions. The notice must contain a full explanation for the school's decision and be communicated to the parents in their native language and in a manner they can understand.
- Schools must obtain parent consent before any evaluation is conducted and before the child is first placed in a special education program on the basis of the IEP.
- Schools must make available to parents for inspection and review all records used in the evaluation, placement, and IEP processes as well as those records that are a part of the child's official school file. These records must be maintained in strict confidentiality. Chapter 14 includes information about your rights to your child's school records.
- Schools must provide for the child to have an independent evaluation at public expense if the parents disagree with evaluation results obtained by the school system. Chapter 5 provides information on when you might want to consider an independent evaluation.
- Schools must explain to parents the requirements for placement in private schools. When parents believe the school cannot provide an appropriate education for their child, they can place the child in a private school, but the school has specific rules that parents must follow. Chapter 8 includes information about placement options.
- Every year, your child's school is obligated to provide you a copy of the procedural safeguards. Schools must also give parents a copy when a child is to be evaluated for the first time; the first time parents file a complaint; and whenever parents request a copy. Chapter 14 tells you about procedural safeguards.

More information on the procedural safeguards developed by the U.S. Department of Education is available on the IDEA website listed in the Resources.

Activity #2: Key People

Key individuals are involved in every phase of the educational planning process. Among others, these typically include:

- the principal of the school, who may chair the committee that decides whether your child should have special testing
- the school psychologist who conducts some of the testing
- a teacher who knows your child particularly well

Make your own personal directory of school personnel, including names, addresses, office and cell phone numbers, email addresses, and fax numbers. This saves time later in remembering who might be able to help you when you need assistance. On the next page you will find an example of a Key People Chart.

You may find that terminology used and titles of key positions in your school district differ from those in the example. Generally, however, titles will be similar. Using your parent handbook and state and local regulations as a guide, you can change the Key People Chart, as found on pages 16-18, to reflect the terminology used in your school system.

Many parents find it very helpful to keep a Contact Record such as the one on page 19 to keep track of the people with whom they talk and notes about the conversation. Some parents and school people prefer email. Keep copies of email and all written correspondence to document your communication with school personnel. In addition, because you cannot always be assured that email is received or read, you may want to follow up important information such as that dealing with timelines and meeting dates with a written letter.

Chapter 3 provides you with some helpful hints on keeping track of all of the information you will be gathering during your trip through the special education maze.

This chapter has introduced you to the cycle of referral, evaluation, eligibility, IEP, and placement that your school system must complete before your child can begin special education. You have also obtained the rules and regulations describing and guiding the special education process in your school system. Along the way, you have identified key people who can help you secure appropriate services for your child. Now you are ready to begin developing the picture and the understanding of your child you wish to convey in school meetings.

WHAT YOU CAN DO NOW

1. Get a copy of the state and school rules on special education. You can look on the Internet or call the central office of your school district.
2. Check for parent handbooks specific to your school district and state.
3. Ask about parent support groups in your area.
4. Call your state's Parent Information and Training Center to learn about their services. You can find their number by contacting the Technical Assistance Alliance for Parent Centers Office at 888-248-9000, or on the Internet at www.taalliance.org.

KEY PEOPLE CHART

School Jurisdiction:

| **Director of Special Education:** | Phone: |
| | Email: |

I. Referral Child Study Committee

Principal or designee:	Address:
	Phone:
	Email:
Referring Person:	Address:
	Phone:
	Email:
Teacher(s)/Specialist(s) (as appropriate):	Address:
	Phone:
	Email:

II. Evaluation Team

Evaluation Team Coordinator:	Address:
	Phone:
	Email:
School Representative qualified to provide or supervise special and general education services:	Address:
	Phone:
	Email:

Teacher(s)/Specialist(s) (with knowledge of suspected disability):	Address:
	Phone:
	Email:
Therapists:	Address:
	Phone:
	Email:
Classroom Teacher:	Address:
	Phone:
	Email:
Psychologist:	Address:
	Phone:
	Email:
Social Worker:	Address:
	Phone:
	Email:
Others:	Address:
	Phone:
	Email:

III. Eligibility Committee

School Representative:	Address:
	Phone:
	Email:

Evaluation Team Member(s) (presents evaluation findings):	Address:
	Phone:
	Email:
Others:	Address:
	Phone:
	Email:

IV. Individualized Education Program (IEP Team)

School Representative qualified to provide or supervise special and general education services:	Address:
	Phone:
	Email:
General Education Teacher(s):	Address:
	Phone:
	Email:
Special Education Teacher(s):	Address:
	Phone:
	Email:
Therapists:	Address:
	Phone:
	Email:
Others, at your or your school's request:	Address:
	Phone:
	Email:

CONTACT RECORD

Who: _____ Date: _____

_____ Phone: _____

_____ Email: _____

Notes: _____

_____

_____

Follow up? ____ No   Who: _____

____ Yes   When: _____

Who: _____ Date: _____

_____ Phone: _____

_____ Email: _____

Notes: _____

_____

_____

Follow up? ____ No   Who: _____

____ Yes   When: _____

Who: _____ Date: _____

_____ Phone: _____

_____ Email: _____

Notes: _____

_____

_____

Follow up? ____ No   Who: _____

____ Yes   When: _____

3. You and Your Child

Strengthening Exercises for the Journey

You have invaluable information that you can use to identify the special education needs of your child. This chapter helps you capture the unique knowledge you have of your child, understand the importance of that knowledge for educational planning, and learn ways to communicate that critical information clearly to professionals working with your child.

Preparing for Your Journey through the Maze

How do you prepare for your journey through the maze? You begin by carefully looking at the central figure in the whole planning process—your child. This book suggests a number of activities, or "strengthening exercises," to help you observe your child and to clarify and organize what you know about your child. These exercises are useful at any stage of the planning process, whether you are preparing for your baby's first infant assessment, your school-age child's first formal evaluation, or your child's IEP meeting. You can find your way through the maze without completing the strengthening exercises, but they will make your trip more productive—you will be less likely to go up blind alleys in the maze. The exercises build on each other, each preparing you for the next.

How Your Child Learns: Exercise #1

To help you focus on your child, start by filling out a Learning Style Questionnaire, Strengthening Exercise #1, on page 36. Take some time to write your responses to the five questions. It may help to look at the examples of completed questionnaires on pages 37 and 38. If you get stuck, you might want to move on to the next section, and fill out the learning style questionnaire later.

After you fill out the questionnaire, save it. Your responses will help you pinpoint specific information about your child and discover keys that make it easier for her to learn.

Observing Your Child in a Systematic Way: Exercise #2

You might have trouble answering the questions in the learning style exercise. You know a lot about your child, but your knowledge is often "felt" in a general sense rather than in the specific terms needed to answer the questions. Yet while you are absorbed in the routine of everyday living, you are constantly and automatically gathering information about your child. Perhaps you do not realize how much you do know!

Since planning an appropriate program for your child requires specific, documented facts rather than generalized impressions and concerns, your first step is to collect your own facts. To convey personal knowledge of your child to school personnel—people accustomed to dealing with specific behaviors, test scores, goals, and objectives—written, concrete facts and documented behavior communicate information about your child most effectively.

One way to collect these facts is to observe your child in a formal way. "Observe!" you say. "How? And when am I going to find the time?" Some days, you may barely have enough time and energy to brush your teeth before turning in for the night. How are you going to fit one more thing into your overcrowded day?

You can do it, because it's something you already do. Use any of the natural, spontaneous opportunities during the day to watch your child. Gathering and organizing information is a vital part of becoming an effective educational advocate for your child.

For example, family uproar occurred almost every morning in Sara's house because she was so slow getting dressed. Sara's mom wondered if the reason was her difficulty in using her hands to fasten buttons and zippers, or if it was her indecision about what to wear. As a result, Sara's mother decided to observe her getting ready for school one morning.

Another family was worried about their son, Tony, falling down and getting hurt as he learned to climb the stairs. Tony's parents decided to observe their son carefully as he attempted to go up and down the stairs. They decided to watch Tony at a distance that was still safe enough to catch him if he fell as he climbed the stairs alone. They hoped to get ideas about what seemed to motivate him to do this independently, identify their concerns for his safety, and learn what might help him climb stairs safely and more readily. The next section offers suggestions to help you develop and sharpen your observation skills.

Becoming a Skilled Observer

Step Back

Suspend for a brief time (three to five minutes) your normal role in family life. Step back from your family situation to put some distance between you and your child. By not intervening where you normally would, you may see your child's abilities and problems in a new light. For example, to understand why Sara was so slow getting ready for school, her mother decided not to push and prod her as usual. She asked her husband to prepare breakfast that morning so that she would be free to observe Sara.

Start Fresh

Try to be open to new aspects of behavior you may have overlooked before. Observe behaviors occurring in the present. Although reports on the past are important in describing a child's development, school personnel are interested in fresh, up-to-date information on what she can do now. Start fresh, also, in how you view your child. For example, Tony's parents could stand a short distance from the stairs and observe rather than holding Tony's hands every step of the way. In this way, they noticed new things about how Tony had a strong and sturdy grip on the rail going upstairs, but seemed to be less steady going down the stairs.

Be alert and relaxed, yourself, as the observer. A preoccupied observer cannot record what is happening as accurately as one who can concentrate.

Get Focused

Decide upon a specific behavior or skill to observe. How should you make this decision? The best rule is to look at those areas that trouble you or your child. You may want to examine one of the problem behaviors you have listed in Strengthening Exercise #1, or you may want to ask a professional to suggest behaviors to observe. For example, your pediatrician might suggest you watch your child as she prepares to do homework or other chores independently to see how she organizes or attends to the task.

You can plan your observation to include various factors: *who* will be with your child, as well as *where* and *when* you will observe her. Concentrate on the one skill you have chosen, ignoring as best you can other aspects of behavior.

Go with the Flow

As you watch your child's activities, record what you see actually happening, not your interpretations of your child's actions. You should become a "candid camera," waiting until later to reflect upon what you see. For example, Tony's dad observed that he had a big smile on his face when he successfully got to the top of the stairs, but started to frown and wanted to stop when he tried to go down the stairs. Tony's dad wrote down both of these observations, waiting until later to interpret them.

Write down specific observations only—not your reaction to what you are observing. Write down detailed, factual information. You will find this is easier if you observe for only a short time—perhaps less than five minutes. Short, frequent observations let you record facts—exactly what happens. You can go back at another time, review your collection of observations, and then interpret the data.

When parents observe their children carefully and systematically, they can offer specific information to teachers and other professionals to help in educational planning. One mother noticed that her daughter's friends used complete sentences when they talked. She was concerned because her child's language seemed less advanced. She wrote down exact words and phrases her daughter used as she played with a friend. At another time she used a tape recording as the children played. These specific examples were very useful when it was time to talk with her child's teacher.

In another family, the occupational therapist suggested the mother watch her child, who was having trouble learning how to write, to see how she used her left or right hands in different activities (writing, eating, picking things up, throwing objects). When they next met, the mother was able to share her observations so that she and the occupational therapist could compare notes in deciding how to best help the child. The guidelines listed below, and the section on "Other Sources of Information" on page 32, show people, places, and activities you might include as you plan to observe your child.

Guidelines for Planning an Observation

Before you begin to observe your child, some guidelines are presented on the next page to help you.

Now! Actually observe your child with a specific behavior or skill in mind. Children behave differently, with different people, in different places, and at different times. In order to understand more fully your child's strengths and problems, you may want to observe your child for a specific behavior in a variety of situations.

The information you gather by observing will add to the specific data necessary in planning an educational program to meet your child's unique needs.

Strengthening Exercise #2, Parents' Observation Record on page 39, provides you with a sample form to assist you in keeping a log of your observations. Examples of the Parents' Observation Record completed for children of different ages can be found on pages 40-42.

The first time you observe, simply write down what you see. Then you can review the next section, which talks about how to organize the notes you've

Elements of an Observation	Example
What will you be looking at in the observation? What skill or behavior do you want to observe?	■ How your child solves disagreements or problems. ■ How your child moves her arms and legs when crawling. ■ What distracts your child; what holds her attention. ■ How your child dresses or feeds herself. ■ Which toys or games your child prefers. ■ What happens when your child is frustrated.
Who, if anybody, will be interacting with your child? (Optional—if social interaction helps you gain insight into the behavior/skill.)	■ parent ■ relative(s) ■ brothers or sisters ■ stranger ■ best friend ■ several friends ■ teacher(s) ■ unfamiliar children ■ professionals
Where will you observe your child—in what setting? Where is this behavior or skill most likely to occur?	■ Home (your child's room, TV room, dinner table, homework area) ■ Neighborhood (neighbor or friend's house, playground, store, church) ■ Family events (picnics, car trips, birthdays, visits to relatives) ■ School (classroom, therapy session, playground, field trip, evaluations, vocational classroom, cafeteria)
When will you observe your child? Which time is most likely to show the behavior or skill? What time would work for you, as the observer, so you are fresh?	■ At meals ■ At bedtime ■ At work or homework ■ Under stress ■ When sick ■ Playing board games, card games, or video games

made describing your child's actions. After you complete this exercise once, you'll have a better idea of how to observe your child with fresh eyes, while still noting actions that may be focused on one category, such as social interaction or movement.

Here are some examples of behaviors parents recorded in their observations in Strengthening Exercises #1 and #2:

- Jason does homework best in a quiet, uncrowded place.
- Fred can recite the alphabet.
- May Lin can put two words together to speak in phrases.
- Virginia has learned to catch herself with her arms as she falls.
- Enrico can write a short paragraph with the ideas in proper sequence.
- Jamie puts on her shoes and socks by herself.
- Henry can find the grocery list items at the store.
- Tyrone shares his toys with Sandra.
- Lee eats with a spoon.
- Michael makes his own lunch to take to school.
- Steve writes capital and lower-case letters in cursive.
- Shantell learns best when she is with one or two good friends.
- Denise can copy a pattern of colored beads strung together.
- Maria shows off her school work with pride and excitement.
- Margaret understands thirty-two words in sign language.
- Susie recognizes the right bus to ride to her after-school job.
- Silvia does her homework assignments in the same order each day.
- Andrew can play a multilevel video game for 90 minutes.
- Orin catches and throws a large ball.
- Barbara can use a computer keyboard to do her homework
- Henry can manipulate his power wheelchair.

Organizing Your Observations

After you collect records from several observations, you can compare and contrast them, looking for trends, consistencies, inconsistencies, or changes in your child's behavior. Organizing your observations is a vital step in preparing yourself to meet with school personnel.

Organizing your observation records into general areas of child development will help you think about and discuss your child in language similar to that used by educators. To use your observations to your child's best advantage, you can group the bits and pieces of observed behavior into developmental categories like those used by school staff.

The preceding list of behaviors parents have observed can be organized into six broad developmental areas:

1. Movement
2. Communications
3. Social relationships
4. Self-concept/independence
5. Thinking skills
6. Senses/perception

Definitions of Developmental Areas

Movement: The ability to use muscles to move the body and to control small and detailed movements. Professionals may use terms like "fine motor" to talk about using small muscles especially in the hand to make small movements, such as write, pick up things, use a keyboard, eat, or dress. The term "gross motor" is used to describe activities that involve larger muscles, such as walking, jumping, swinging, throwing, and catching.

Communication: The ability to understand and respond (verbally or non-verbally) to spoken language, gestures, or written symbols, and to express oneself clearly and with meaning. Professionals may use the term "expressive language" to describe how a child communicates her thoughts or feelings with others. The term "receptive language" refers to how the child understands language.

Social Relationships: The ability to relate to others—for example, to play with other children or to develop attachments to family members and friends.

Self-Concept/Independence: The ability to distinguish oneself from others and to care for one's own needs. Some professionals may use the term "self-help" to describe skills a child has to care for her own needs. It can also include the ability to respond to difficult situations.

Thinking Skills: Often called cognitive skills, they include the ability to reason and solve problems, to classify, to make associations, to understand similarities and differences, and to comprehend cause-and-effect relationships. School skills such as reading, arithmetic, and spelling can be placed in this category.

Senses/Perception: The ability to use eyes, ears, and the senses of touch, smell, and taste to learn about the environment. This may refer to hearing, the need to use glasses to read, or a child's extra sensitivity to sound, touch, or one of the other senses.

There are many ways to classify development; essentially, these classifications can help you structure observations about growth and development. Some people may encourage you to learn the terminology of physicians, educators, therapists, and other specialists. *This guidebook's view is that your language about your child is the best language.* So, for purposes of educational advocacy in this book, very generalized developmental categories are suggested. The categories will fit well into those used by your child's teachers and specialists. If you are meeting with a specialist, however, and don't know a term that is used, write down the term or phrase, and either ask for a definition or look it up later.

Your Child's Learning Style

In addition to having different abilities in the various developmental areas, every child has a particular learning style. *A learning style is the combination of unique personal characteristics that determine the way in which a person learns best.* For instance, some people learn best through reading or writing; others, through listening or talking. Often a talent in one area—drawing, music, or athletics, for example—can help you identify how a person learns. Characteristics such as neatness, sensitivity to noise, accuracy, and distractibility will also affect learning. Think for a minute about the way you learn best, your learning style. For example:

- You may learn best by reading information.
- Perhaps you understand things better when you have participated in group discussions.
- You may need to work in a neat environment, or you may feel more comfortable having a messy desk.
- You might need absolute quiet when you concentrate, or you might prefer music as background to your thinking.
- You may need to draw pictures, diagrams, or charts to help you analyze a problem.
- You may take frequent, short breaks while working, or you may concentrate until the task is finished.
- You may have to do something, in practice, to understand how it works.

Thinking about your own learning style can help you become aware of your child's special ways of learning. Remember, there are no right or wrong ways, only different ones. In addition, most people learn using different aspects of their learning style in various situations. Sharing information about your child's individual ways of learning with those who are teaching her can help to create the best setting to meet her needs. Good teachers make adaptations to the classroom and to their teaching methods in order to accommodate children's various learning styles. Children can often give personal insight about what helps them to learn and master new accomplishments and information. It may help to ask your child for this information or check out your assumptions with her.

Analyzing Your Observations

The following section shows how to analyze your observations from Strengthening Exercises #1 and #2 so that you can communicate effectively with school personnel. The recorded observations parents have made of their children, found on page 26, can be placed within the areas of development and learning style on pages 30-31.

Perhaps you are puzzled by the way some of these behaviors have been organized into developmental categories. No single behavior falls exclusively into one category or another. For example, you might think that Jamie's ability to put on her shoes and socks fits into the areas of *movement* and *thinking skills*, as well as *independence*. Jamie's movement skills are not a problem. Physically she is able to put on her shoes and socks. The emphasis she needs is in developing her independence. Therefore, her parents place "putting on shoes and socks" under *Independence/Self-Concept*.

Think about the developmental areas you believe are particularly important to your child's growth now, and put your observations of her accomplishments into that category. Remember, there need not be only one "right" category.

To organize your observations about your child's development and learning style, transfer your work on the first two Strengthening Exercises into a Developmental Achievement Chart (page 43). Developmental Achievement Charts completed for children of different ages are found on pages 43, 44-46.

Notice that Question #1 on the Learning Style Questionnaire provides information for the column *Can Do*. Question #3 on the Learning Style Questionnaire coincides with the second column, *Working On*. Question #5 corresponds with the column *To Accomplish in 6 Months*. Questions #2 and #4 give information about your child's *learning style*. These observations about learning style can be recorded in the bottom row of the chart.

If your observations have not given you a complete picture of your child's development, repeat Strengthening Exercise #2, targeting the specific developmental areas about which you want more information. For example, if you are satisfied with what you know about your child's movement skills, but want to know more about her social skills, you can arrange to observe that area of her development.

Recording Other Notes and Thoughts

As you have time, you can continue to make observations to see what your child does well, what is frustrating, and what is motivating. These observations offer valuable information and insight that can help you figure out what will help your child learn and do well at home and at school.

Child	Observation	Notes	Category
Jason	*What:* Getting homework finished *With Whom:* No one *Where:* His room, by himself *When:* Around 4pm	Jason does homework best in a quiet, uncrowded place.	Learning style
Fred	*What:* Counting and letters *With Whom:* Family *Where:* Living room *When:* After dinner	Fred can recite the alphabet.	Thinking skills
May Lin	*What:* How well May Lin talks *With Whom:* Friend *Where:* Playdate *When:* Morning on a weekend	May Lin can put two words together to speak in phrases.	Communication
Virginia	*What:* How well she walks. *With Whom:* Family *Where:* Living room *When:* After dinner	Virginia has learned to catch herself with her arms as she falls.	Movement
Jamie	*What:* How much can Jamie do for herself? *With Whom:* no one *Where:* Her bedroom *When:* Before breakfast	Jamie puts on her shoes and socks by herself.	Independence/self-concept
Tyrone	*What:* How Tyrone gets along with other children *With Whom:* Sandra, Kim, and Lee *Where:* His playroom *When:* Saturday morning	Tyrone shares his toys with Sandra.	Social Relation-ships
Michael	*What:* Michael has a hard time getting things done *With Whom:* No one—I'll give him more time and see if he can do it himself *Where:* Kitchen *When:* Before breakfast	Michael makes his own lunch to take to school.	Independence/self-concept
Shantell	*What:* How does Shantell learn best? *With Whom:* All her class-mates at preschool *Where:* The playground *When:* After lunch	Shantell learns best when she is with one or two good friends.	Learning Style

Child	Observation	Notes	*Category*
Denise	*What:* Making sense of colors and shapes *With Whom:* By herself *Where:* Her bedroom *When:* Saturday morning	Denise can copy a pattern of colored beads strung together.	Perception/ Senses
Margaret	*What:* How much does Margaret understand? *With Whom:* Family *Where:* Dining room *When:* Sunday at dinner	Margaret understands thirty-two words in sign language.	Communication
Susie	*What:* Can she get around by herself? *With Whom:* By herself *Where:* Street by her school *When:* After school, at 3:05	Susie recognizes the right bus to ride to her after-school job.	Perception/ Senses
Silvia	*What:* Organization *With Whom:* By herself *Where:* In her bedroom *When:* After dinner	Silvia does her homework assignments in the same order each day.	Learning Style
Andrew	*What:* How quick and perceptive is Andrew? *With Whom:* His friend Joe *Where:* In the computer room *When:* Saturday morning	Andrew can play a multilevel video game for 90 minutes.	Thinking skills
Orin	*What:* Orin's coordination *With Whom:* No one *Where:* Backyard *When:* After breakfast	Orin catches and throws a large ball.	Movement
Barbara	*What:* How coordinated is Barbara? *With Whom:* No one *Where:* In the computer room *When:* After school	Barbara can use a computer keyboard to do her homework	Movement
Henry	*What:* How well can Henry get around? *With Whom:* Classmates at school *Where:* In the school *When:* Lunchtime	Henry can manipulate his power wheelchair.	Independence/ Self-concept

In addition, many parents find it useful to supplement their observational data by keeping a general record of their thoughts and reflections on a form such as "Notes and Thoughts," below.

Date	Notes and Thoughts
2/3	Jennie "read" *Green Eggs and Ham* by looking at the pictures and remembering what most of the words said.
3/5	Mrs. Lanzano said that Jennie has made friends with Maria. They eat lunch together and like to draw pictures during free time.
3/7	Jennie threw a tantrum when she woke up and found out there was no school today. She kept insisting that we get in the car to make sure that Maria and her classmates were not there. I called Maria's mother and arranged for her to come over and play this afternoon. Jennie calmed down and was excited about having her friend come over.
4/10	Jennie wrote her name by copying what I had written on a blank piece of paper. I can't tell whether she favors her left or right hand yet.

Other Sources of Information

Your child may be your best source of information. You can help her think through what she likes to do, what she is good at, how she learns new things, or how she has solved a problem. Talking with her gives her skills as she encounters new learning opportunities and challenges. Similar to your journey to becoming a successful educational advocate, she will improve her own understanding of her abilities and disabilities, and will be better able to advocate for herself.

Often people outside of your immediate family can offer fresh perceptions of your child and new insights into her growth and development. Bear in mind, too, that when your child participates in activities outside of the home, opportunities may arise to observe skills and behavior she does not demonstrate at home.

Family documents and projects can also provide a wealth of information as you build a complete picture of your child. One family brought pictures of their son to show in a meeting with school officials; another mother made tape recordings of her child's language while they were riding in the car. Your imagination will tell you many ways to use your daily routines to increase your observations of your child.

There are many times, places, and ways that you can collect information about your child's growth and development. Here are some sources other parents have found useful—add your own to the lists:

People

Relatives	Playmates	Brothers, sisters
Bus drivers	Scout Leaders	Teachers
Coaches	Doctors	Neighbors
Employers		

Places

Restaurants	Church	Family camping
Grocery store	Doctor's office	Scout troop
Car pools	Swimming pool	Sport events
Museums or theme parks		

Family Documents & Projects

Photos	Art projects	Examples of school work
Tape recordings	Gardening	Preparing for holidays
Home videos	School report cards	Writing samples
Computer-based presentation by child		

Gather any family history of disability, such as attention deficit disorders (AD/HD), depression, or anxiety. This may be important, especially if others in the family have similar symptoms. If it's hereditary, you may be able to more quickly identify precisely what will help your child, because you know what helped others in your family with those symptoms. Medical records that include information about medically related conditions, disabilities, or recommended treatments can offer insight into what may be needed to help your child.

What Other Information Helps Round Out a Picture of My Child?

To make the best use of the information you have gathered through observation, you may want to understand the bigger picture—the expected skills and behaviors for a child at her age. This is where reading, communicating with other parents, your doctor, your child's teacher, and, especially, your child can help. You may want to consider the following:

- Take notes on what other children your child's age learn and do. This helps you track, in a timely way, areas where your child doesn't seem to be on the expected developmental path. To find out more about expected developmental milestones, talk to your doctor or pediatrician or your child's teacher.
- Take notes on how your child is doing in school—for example, whether she is keeping up with other students, and which areas are hard for her. To find out whether she is keeping up, check your child's papers and grades, and talk to the teacher. Also, observe your child doing homework, and see which assignments are the most frustrating for her.
- Ask the teacher whether you can help in some way—maybe with extra homework, flashcards, playing a word game, or reading aloud.

- Ask your child about her thoughts about school, how she's doing, and what might help.

Keeping Track

You have observed, taken notes, and completed the learning style questionnaire and observation records. You have organized your information by filling out the developmental achievement chart. Now what? To communicate effectively with professionals and to help your child learn and grow, you will want to keep track of the valuable records and information you have collected. Some parents find it helpful to keep information in a three-ring binder. This way all the information is in one place and will not be misplaced when they need it. When sharing information, they can tell that it came from their notebook by the three holes on the page. Other parents like a large file folder with smaller folders inside, using different colors for school, medical, and home information.

Below are examples of how several parents organized their information.

Joyce Klein sorted the complicated medical records and tests in chronological order with a summary of dates, doctors, and findings in the front so that doctors and others would not have to wade through reams of records to find important information. She also kept a separate record of dosages of all medications and a log of all contacts with medical personnel with follow-up dates. Because of the large number of papers and sensitivity of the information, she kept the medical records in a separate notebook from the school records.

Ray Andrews put everything in a file box with folders for observation records, learning styles and developmental achievement charts, relevant evaluation reports, and Individualized Education Programs (IEPs). He also kept photos of his child at special events or doing favorite activities. He kept samples of his child's work that showed what she did well and her progress over time. By doing this, he was able to provide a picture of his child as a unique and special individual, whose disability was only one part of her rather than her defining characteristic.

Elena Gomes made a scrapbook of mementos and pictures as her child participated in everyday activities, reached milestones, and celebrated important events. She also had separate plastic sleeves to show off her child's school projects, poetry she had written, report cards, and awards.

Mrs. Gomes's daughter made a computer presentation complete with pictures to document who she is, what she likes to do, her life at home, school, and in the community, her hopes for the future, and how she would like people to help her achieve her goals.

As you think about an information system that is right for you, you may wish to think about other types of information you want to collect. Below are some examples that may be helpful to you as you think about gathering information about your child:

- Medical records,
- Family history,
- Evaluations,
- Notes to/from teachers,
- Samples of work or projects,
- School progress reports, and
- Your thoughts, work, and observations collected on forms like those in this book.

Conclusion

Throughout your child's school years, you will need to make new observations of her growth and development. Collecting fresh observations prior to meetings with teachers and other professionals can help you provide specific recommendations for her special education program. By completing the first Strengthening Exercises, you gain a better understanding of your child's unique strengths and needs. By having this valuable information at your fingertips, you will feel confident as you participate in the special education planning process.

WHAT YOU CAN DO NOW

1. Get a box or a notebook, or clear an area for everything you might need that describes your child. You might want some sticky notes, notebooks, file folders, and pens, too.
2. Think of an area your child might need help in, or that you want to understand or communicate about clearly. Then select a situation in which you can observe your child and gather information that might help school staff understand your child.
3. Observe your child and take objective notes.
4. Analyze your observations as well as you can, using the charts in this chapter or something like them.
5. Write down your own thoughts and ideas, especially of situations that might help others understand your child.
6. Compare your understanding of your child to what other children her age are doing.
7. If you are using a computer, find a way to keep email and other digital data together; print out anything important and put it with the other papers.
8. As your observations and other records accumulate, keep them together.
9. Talk to your child about how she sees herself and what she wants to do. (And of course, write notes about the conversations!)

STRENGTHENING EXERCISE #1

Learning Style Questionnaire

1. List three things your child has recently learned or accomplished.
   1.

   2.

   3.

2. Choose one of the items in question#1. What about your child helped him/her learn this?

3. Think of three things your child is working to learn now.
   1.

   2.

   3.

4. Choose one of the items in question #3 that your child is having trouble learning. What is causing him/her trouble?

5. What one thing would you like your child to learn within the next six months?

STRENGTHENING EXERCISE #1 – Example 1

Learning Style Questionnaire

1. List three things your child has recently learned or accomplished.

   1. Loading the dishwasher.

   2. How to properly answer the telephone.

   3. Bass fishing—he caught a huge catfish a couple of days ago.

2. Choose one of the items in question #1. What about your child helped him/her learn this?

   Bass fishing; it's one of the few things he loves as much as video games. He says that he can "think like a fish." ☺

3. Think of three things your child is working to learn now.

   1. How to ride a bike.

   2. How to do laundry from start to finish

   3. How to have a two-way conversation with one of his friends.

4. Choose one of the items in question #3 that your child is having trouble learning. What is causing him/her trouble?

   Riding a bike: Bryan is 12 years old and is very aware that his peers can already ride a bike. He continues to have difficulty keeping his balance while on his bike.

5. What one thing would you like your child to learn within the next six months?

   How to ride a bike. It will boost his self-esteem and give him the opportunity to spend time with his friends while outdoors.

STRENGTHENING EXERCISE #1 – Example 2

Learning Style Questionnaire

1. List three things your child has recently learned or accomplished.
   1. Now uses action figures appropriately in pretend play.

   2. His teacher reported that he recognized a few simple words like "the, and" in print

   3. He can put his shoes and socks on.

2. Choose one of the items in question#1. What about your child helped him/her learn this?
   He has a very good imagination and will remember something he saw in a movie and then act it out later with some of his toys.

3. Think of three things your child is working to learn now.
   1. Be more independent putting on his clothes.

   2. Remember bathroom skills and refasten clothing.

   3. At school he is working on money recognition and use.

4. Choose one of the items in question #3 that your child is having trouble learning. What is causing him/her trouble?
   Mike is highly and easily distractible. Even if he is reminded to lift the toilet seat by the time he gets in the bathroom he has forgotten what you told him. This is made worse if there is something going on he'd rather be doing like watching a movie.

5. What one thing would you like your child to learn within the next six months?
   Consistently remember to zip up his pants and use the bathroom completely independently without my husband or me being present.

STRENGTHENING EXERCISE #2

Parent Observation Record

Observer: _____ Date of Observation: _____

Beginning Time of Observation: _____ Ending Time: _____

Who Was Observed? _____

Where? _____ When? _____

What was the focus of the observation? _____

_____

_____

_____

Why was this focus chosen? _____

_____

_____

_____

What occurred during the observation? _____

_____

_____

_____

_____

_____

Reflections on the observation? _____

_____

_____

_____

_____

_____

STRENGTHENING EXERCISE #2 – Example 1

Parent Observation Record

Observer: __Carmen__   Date of Observation: __May 15__

Beginning Time of Observation: __10:00 am__   Ending Time: __10:15 am__

Who Was Observed? __Elena__

Where? __At home__   When? __At breakfast__

What was the focus of the observation? __How Elena eats her Cheerios.__

_____

Why was this focus chosen? __I want Elena to improve her eating skills.__

_____

What occurred during the observation? __Elena grabbed the spoon with her fist and licked the applesauce. She got it near her mouth and pushed it into her mouth with her other hand. She grabbed her Cheerios with her fist and stuffed them into her mouth.__

_____

Reflections on the observation? __Elena gets the concept of using a spoon, but is not coordinated enough to eat independently. Her tongue does not work the same as most people's and it is thrusting out more.__

_____

STRENGTHENING EXERCISE #2 – Example 2

Parent Observation Record

Observer: __Irene__ Date of Observation: __July 8__

Beginning Time of Observation: __10:00 am__ Ending Time: __10:10am__

Who Was Observed? __Bryan__

Where? __Family Living Room & Kitchen__ When? __Morning__

What was the focus of the observation? __Bryan wanted to contact his best friend via telephone to ask how to get past a certain point in a video game.__

Why was this focus chosen? __He usually asks me to make the phone call and then hand the phone to him whenever he wants to speak to his best friend. He needs to take that step of independence to initiate the phone call without assistance.__

What occurred during the observation? __Bryan picked up the phone, and then asked where I keep his friend's phone number. I showed him the phone list next to our phone in the kitchen. He knew how to dial out. He reached his best friend's father and said, "Uhm, hi. Is Jared there?" He and his friend continued to talk for several minutes and then Bryan hung up after saying, "Bye."__

Reflections on the observation? __Bryan needs a little practice on how to ask an adult if his friend is home. (e.g., "May I speak to Jared, please? This is Bryan.") He will also benefit from role-playing how to leave a message if he reaches someone's voice mail. This will include leaving his phone number along with his name.__

STRENGTHENING EXERCISE #2 – Example 3

Parent Observation Record

Observer: __Judy__   Date of Observation: __July 11, 2007__

Beginning Time of Observation: __7 am__   Ending Time: __7:15 am__

Who Was Observed? __Mike__

Where? __His bedroom__   When? __Wake-up/Getting dressed__

What was the focus of the observation? __Helping him to get up and dressed__
__for the day.__

Why was this focus chosen? __He traditionally has trouble getting__
__motivated on his own without help. This is an important skill for__
__him to know and be able to do.__

What occurred during the observation? __He needed physical assistance__
__getting the proper clothing out of the dresser. Needed__
__reminders to put dirty PJs in the hamper rather than the floor__
__and to go to the bathroom appropriately (turn on light, lift seat,__
__go in toilet completely, flush). Needed help to orient his__
__underwear properly.__

Reflections on the observation? __Mike needs many prompts and redirec-__
__tions to accomplish simple dressing skills and bathroom tasks.__
__When I tried to give the direction only once he would forget__
__what I'd said. Frequently he needed help to get clothes oriented__
__properly and on straight.__

Developmental Achievement Chart

	Can Do	Working On	Accomplish within 6 months
MOVEMENT			
COMMUNICATIONS			
SOCIAL RELATIONSHIPS			
SELF-CONCEPT/ INDEPENDENCE			
THINKING SKILLS			
LEARNING STYLE			

DEVELOPMENTAL ACHIEVEMENT CHART – Example 1 (Young Child)

	Can Do	Working On	Accomplish within 6 months
MOVEMENT	Creeping	Crawling	Walking with assistance
COMMUNICATIONS	Lets people know what she wants by her beautiful smile. Says a few words.	Increasing her vocabulary	Be able to let people know what she wants
SOCIAL RELATIONSHIPS	Plays with others at day-care. Lets them know that she likes them by smiling.	Saying "hi" and "bye;" sharing toys	Pretend play with a playmate
SELF-CONCEPT/ INDEPENDENCE	Drinks from a sippy cup	Eating with a spoon	Eat with a fork and spoon; drink from a cup
THINKING SKILLS	Looks at picture book	Identifying and saying what she sees	Identifying and saying what she sees in the picture book
LEARNING STYLE	Elena wants to do things that make other people smile.		

DEVELOPMENTAL ACHIEVEMENT CHART – Example 2 (Middle School)

	Can Do	Working On	Accomplish within 6 months
MOVEMENT	Walk, run, skip, swim	Balance (riding a bike)	Ride bike independently
COMMUNICATIONS	Uses concrete words and phrases	Tone of voice when speaking	Use appropriate tone of voice
SOCIAL RELATIONSHIPS	One best friend; plays video games with older neighborhood kids	Building on expanding his number of close friends to 3; learning about "small talk" and how to use it properly	Have a reciprocal conversation without prompts
SELF-CONCEPT/ INDEPENDENCE	Gets his own breakfast in the morning; prefers mom or dad to make the other meals. Insists on dressing himself, but won't initiate picking out his own clothes	Picking out clothes for himself; accepting more responsibility with making lunch for himself on a consistent basis.	Get dressed completely without any prompting or assistance. Know what age appropriate meals he can make for himself for lunch (summertime and school year weekends).
THINKING SKILLS	Writes creative, humorous stories	Writing paragraphs on subjects that he perceives as not "fun to write about"	Complete stories and/or essays on topics that are least preferred without any adult prompts
LEARNING STYLE	Visual/concrete/prefers structured activities	Being able to get through unexpected transitions without feeling too overwhelmed	Feel comfortable with transitioning between his middle school classes from one part of the school to another

DEVELOPMENTAL ACHIEVEMENT CHART – Example 3 (High School)

	Can Do	Working On	Accomplish within 6 months
MOVEMENT	Walks, runs (independently)	Balance and coordination	Improve ability on stairs
COMMUNICATIONS	Uses single words to express needs	Improve articulation so more people can understand what he is saying	Greater articulation / less echolalic
SOCIAL RELATIONSHIPS	Is a very sweet young man; he enjoys being with others	More appropriate ways to interact with others	Independently initiate peer interaction
SELF-CONCEPT/ INDEPENDENCE	Feeds himself	Dressing / bathing	Independent dressing and decreased assistance with bathing
THINKING SKILLS	Works with prompting	Staying on task	Increase attention to 5 minutes
LEARNING STYLE	He needs to use all his senses (visual/auditory/ hands on) to be able to learn a new skill	Needs frequent redirection	

4. REFERRAL AND EVALUATION
Which Way to Go?

You have collected important information describing your child's educational and developmental achievements and learning style. By systematically observing in a variety of situations, you have developed a picture of his present strengths and needs in a way that will help others understand him. You have also collected school and other records that may help others understand your child.

The next step is to use that information.

Chapter 2 briefly introduced the special education cycle. This chapter examines in detail the first two of these phases: *referral* and *evaluation.* Each phase is described in terms of its purposes, activities, and participants, along with pointers on how you can actively participate in these phases.

IDEA gives you and your child's teachers the right to ask the school to evaluate your child to determine whether he needs special education services. This is called a "referral." The rules and regulations of both your local school system and your state division of special education specify how to make a referral for special education services.

Identifying Children with Disabilities

Every school system is required by IDEA to conduct a public awareness campaign, often called "Child Find," to inform the public of the rights of children with disabilities to an education that meets the child's individual needs and is provided at no cost to the parents. School systems must also tell parents in the community about the availability of special education services. Additionally, each school system is charged with identifying, locating, and evaluating all eligible children. It includes children who are not failing but who are struggling in school. In most states, children are eligible from ages three through twenty-one.

Child Find is also required to identify infants and toddlers with developmental delays, from birth through two, and their families. If you are reading this book and have a child under the age of three, contact your local school district or ask your child's doctor about the early intervention program in your community. Early intervention provides services designed specifically to meet the individual needs of a child and his family, to enhance the development of the young child, and to minimize the need for future special education. These services are jointly selected by the parents and a team of service providers. In working with the team of specialists, you will use the techniques described in this book. For more specific information on early intervention, refer to Chapter 13.

First Steps to Evaluation

When a child is having problems at school, parents and teachers begin to explore what is causing the child's difficulties. If you are concerned, often, the first action is to talk to your child's teacher, then write a letter requesting that the school consider evaluating whether your child needs special education services. You can address your letter to the principal at your child's school or to a special education administrator at the school or the district.

In the letter, list the reasons you believe your child needs special education. If professionals other than school personnel have identified your child's disability and those findings seem accurate to you, include information about their findings in the letter. For example, if your child has been seeing a private speech therapist, it can be useful to include the therapist's diagnosis, identified developmental issues, and any progress the therapist has made with your child.

This is an opportune time to let the school know that you plan to be very involved in your child's education and are interested in establishing a collaborative partnership with your child's teachers and other providers. The tone of the letter you send and the first conversations you have with your child's school can lay the groundwork for positive future relationships that can benefit your child throughout his school career.

If your child is identified as needing extra help, a committee comprised of you and other school professionals may be formed. This committee might be called a screening committee, a child study committee, a pre-referral committee, or other similar name. The committee's major purpose is to

■ Discuss your child's learning and developmental needs.

- Consider adaptations or alternative strategies to address those needs. For example, your child may need intensive help with reading, and may qualify for time with a reading specialist.
- Determine whether your child's learning and developmental needs are significant enough to require a formal evaluation.

To prepare for the meeting, observe your child as described in Chapter 3 and develop a presentation of information you believe would help the committee reach its decision.

Alternative Routes-Getting Help Early

IDEA encourages schools to identify and address problems before a child *needs* special education. The committee will discuss alternative strategies with you that might help your child get back on track. Some formal terms for these processes may be "early intervening services" or "response to intervention" approaches. If your child is in such a program, make sure the strategies are clearly defined and a timeline is in place to assess your child's progress.

Ideally your child will do well. If, however, you believe the strategies are not working, or disagree with the committee's decision, you can always refer your child directly to your school system's special education director, who will determine whether an evaluation is needed.

Referral: Getting the Special Education Process Started

If the committee believes a full evaluation is needed, they send the necessary recommendation to the school's special education director. The committee's decision must be made in writing and include the information leading to the committee's conclusions. You are formally notified with a letter including an evaluation consent form. Federal IDEA regulations require schools to make a decision about evaluation in 60 calendar days from the date of the written referral. States are allowed to have different timelines specified in their regulations.

Recommendation to Deny an Evaluation

If the committee does not believe your child needs special education, you can agree to continue the alternative strategies for a while longer to see if your child begins to make progress. Make sure that the school monitors your child's progress and establishes a timeframe to reconsider the decision if your child continues to have problems. The school may have special programs and supplemental services for students who are struggling in school, and who are not doing well, or are at risk of not doing well, on statewide tests and assessments. You may also want to work more closely with your child's teacher to understand the curriculum and help him learn.

While trying these strategies, be sure to continue to observe your child's strengths, difficulties, and learning style. You may also request that the school provide your child with accommodations that can help him learn in the classroom.

If the committee does not recommend that your child be referred for a formal evaluation, you can send your referral directly to the special education director. If the director agrees with the committee not to evaluate, you can challenge the decision through dispute resolution channels. Chapter 14 describes the procedures you may use to challenge this and other decisions made by school officials.

If you aren't sure what to do, continue reading to find out more about the evaluation process and about the kinds of special education services that are available through the IDEA that can help your child.

Surprised?

If you started the process and have spoken with your child's teachers about his difficulties, then you are prepared in some way for the special education process.

If you didn't start the referral process and you find out in a letter or conversation that the school wants to look into whether you child needs special education, you may be taken off-guard. What should you do when faced with the school's request to evaluate your child's learning needs? Maybe, you think, the school knows best. So you sign the form, grant permission for your child's evaluation, and then wonder if you did the right thing. You may be relieved the school is finally going to do something. Or maybe you refuse to grant permission for evaluation and again wonder if you made the right decision.

Neither of these responses may be the most helpful to you or your child. What you need is a greater understanding of the evaluation process and a knowledge of specific actions you may take in response to the request to evaluate your son or daughter. You need some information about the rights and responsibilities of the people involved in your child's evaluation. Knowing what to do will reduce your feeling of helplessness and begin to let you and your child "do" something about evaluation, as opposed to being "done in" by evaluation.

Notification and Consent Are Required

Under federal and state laws, the school system must notify you of its wish to evaluate your child for purposes of receiving special education services. It must explain to you what tests will be done and the reasons your child is being evaluated. Further, you must give your permission before the testing begins. Your consent for the evaluation does not mean that you are consenting to special education and related services; it is the first step in the process. The school must also obtain your consent to provide special education services after the IEP is written.

If you refuse to give consent for the initial evaluation, the school system is no longer responsible for identifying your child as needing special education. This could have an impact on your child later. See Chapters 8 and 15 for information about the rights of children who are suspended or expelled from school.

A sample notification and consent letter can be found on pages 52 and 53.

The Evaluation Process

There may be many reasons why a child's physical, social, or intellectual development is slower than others his age. Some children merely mature more slowly than their peers; time will find them "catching up." For some children, the language spoken at home or a lack of access to early childhood education may have influenced their progress. Others may have physical conditions that interfere with their development. Perhaps they have a visual or hearing problem. Still other children may have developmental delays, intellectual disabilities, learning disabilities, or emotional problems. Any of these conditions could interfere with a child's academic and developmental progress.

The purpose of the school's evaluation process is to determine if a child has a disability that requires special education services in order to succeed in school. In doing so they identify:
- Present levels of academic achievement;
- Any existing disabling conditions that effect learning or development;
- What will help the child academically and developmentally.

You have a very important role to play in the evaluation process. IDEA specifically requires that parents be part of the team that reviews existing data and information and decides what additional information is needed. Existing information to be reviewed includes:
- Evaluations and information provided by the parents;
- Performance on local or state assessments;
- Current classroom assessments and observations; and
- Observations by teachers and specialists.

Based upon the review of the above information, you and the school then decide what additional information is needed. While there are no requirements in IDEA for specific evaluation components, the school should gather enough

Mr. & Mrs. Austin   RE   Evaluation

1519 S. West Street   SCHOOL   Westview Elementary

Alexandria Va. 22355   ID NO.   10094

Dear   Mr. & Mrs. Austin:

As we have discussed, the following individual evaluations are essential in understanding your child's particular needs.

Audiological	X
Educational	X
Psychological	X
Sociocultural	X
Speech and language	
Vision	X
Medical	X

The evaluations may include conferring with your child, testing of general ability and educational achievement, and/or an evaluation of feelings.

If you have any questions about the evaluations or why they are necessary, please call __Ms. Pilerton__ at __624-5525__. When the evaluations are completed, an opportunity will be provided for you to discuss the results. You also may have access to these and any other educational records pertaining to your child.

We are not able to proceed with these evaluations until we have your permission to do so. Please return the attached form to me, at the above address, within ten working days after receipt of this letter. You do have the right to refuse to give your permission. Should you refuse to give permission, the _____ County Public Schools has the right to appeal your decision.

If a recent medical examination is required, the examination may be scheduled through a private physician—at your own expense—or through the _____ County Department of Health Services—free of charge. If you wish to schedule a free medical examination for your child, please contact __County Health Dept.__ at __524-6660__.

If you would like to be informed of the time, date, and place of subsequent meetings held to discuss your child's educational needs, contact __Ms. Pilerton__ at __624-5525__ who will inform you of the local screening and eligibility committee meetings.

Sincerely,

Marcia J. Pilerton
Principal
/ct

Attachment

cc: Cumulative File

EVALUATION CONSENT FORM

Student's Name: _____ Notice Date:_____

TYPE OF ASSESSMENTS: A variety of assessment tools and strategies should be used to gather information that determines the educational needs of this student.

____ **Assessment in All Areas Related to the Suspected Disability(ies)—** describes the student's performance in any area related to the child's suspected disability(ies).
Recommended assessment(s):_____
_____
_____

____ **Educational Assessment**—includes the history of the student's educational progress in the general curriculum and includes current information on the student's performance

____ **Observation of the Student**—includes the student's interaction in the student's classroom environment or in a child's natural environment or an early intervention program.

____ **Educational Assessment**—includes the history of the student's educational progress in the general curriculum and includes current information on the student's performance.

____ **Health Assessment**—details any medical problems or constraints that may affect the student's education (including hearing, vision, attention, etc. as relevant.)

____ **Psychological Assessment**—describes the student's learning capacity and learning style in relationship to social/emotional development and skills.

____ **Home Assessment**—details any pertinent family history and home situations that may affect the student's education and, with written consent, may include a home visit.

I understand that I have the right to review my child's school records and to be informed of the results of these evaluations. I understand that no change will be made in my child's educational program as a result of these evaluations without my knowledge. I understand that I have the right to refuse to give permission Please indicate your response by checking at least one (1) box and returning a signed copy to the school district. Please keep one copy for your records. Thank you.

❑ I accept the proposed evaluation in full.
❑ I reject the proposed evaluation in full.
❑ I accept the proposed evaluation in part and request that only the listed assessments be completed:

I additionally request the following assessment(s):
❑ assessment(s) listed above: _____
❑ other assessments: (specify) _____
❑ I will be providing information from my child's physician or other evaluation reports (specify) _____

_____   _____
Signature of Parent or Student 18 and Over*   Date
*Required signature once a student reaches 18 unless there is a court appointed guardian for these evaluations.

information to assess your child in all areas related to the suspected disability, including health, vision, hearing, social and emotional status, general intelligence, academic performance, and communication and movement skills. Schools use many different tests and materials to evaluate children. In fact, IDEA requires that the evaluation include a variety of assessment tools and strategies, including information provided by the parents.

Legal Requirements that Shape the Formal Evaluation

All school systems are required by IDEA and by state laws to follow certain procedures when evaluating a child.

1. Parents must be fully informed.

The administrator of special education must inform you in your native language and primary means of communication—verbal, sign language, or Braille—of:

- the school's intent to evaluate your child;
- your rights as parents pertaining to special education for your child;
- a list of anticipated tests to be used; and
- the need for your consent prior to initial evaluation and re-evaluations

2. The school system must ensure its evaluation procedures provide for the following:

- your written consent prior to any evaluation;
- the assignment of surrogate parents if you are not available to protect the interests of your child;
- confidentiality of all evaluation results;
- an opportunity for you to obtain an independent evaluation of your child if you believe the school's evaluation is biased or invalid;
- an opportunity for you to have a hearing to question evaluation results with which you disagree;
- an opportunity for you to examine your child's official school records;
- testing that does not discriminate against your child because of racial or cultural bias or because the tests are inappropriate for a person with your child's disabilities;
- a reevaluation at least every three years, unless the evaluation team notifies you that it doesn't need further testing or other information to de-

termine continued eligibility. (They can only waive the evaluation with your consent. If you want the school to re-evaluate it must do so.);

- an opportunity for you to request a reevaluation, if your child is not improving academically or developmentally (if it has been less than one year, a school may deny your request);
- a re-evaluation before ending special education services.

3. The school system must make sure its tests and evaluation procedures meet these requirements:

- The tests are administered in the language and form most likely to yield accurate information on what your child knows or can do.
- The tests are not discriminatory on a racial or cultural basis.
- The tests are professionally approved for the specific purposes for which they are used.
- The tests are given by trained professionals according to the instructions of the publishers of the tests and materials.
- Tests and evaluation materials identify a broad range of your child's characteristics, strengths, and needs, including social development, cognitive development, emotional, and behavior characteristics. They also should identify physical, sensory, or developmental concerns.
- Tests are selected and administered to ensure that they accurately assess the child's potential, accomplishments, and other aspects they are designed to measure, rather than simply focusing on the child's disabilities.
- The evaluation is undertaken by professionals from multiple backgrounds, including at least one teacher or other specialist with knowledge in the area of your child's suspected disability. Your child should be assessed in all areas related to the suspected disability, including, where appropriate, health, vision, hearing, social and emotional skills, general intelligence, academic performance, communication skills, and motor abilities.
- No single test is used as the only criterion to determine if your child is eligible for special education services.
- The evaluation must take place within 60 calendar days of the parent's consent—or within the period of time established by your state.

These are the minimum requirements school officials must meet when evaluating your child's need for special education services. The regulations of your state and local school district may include additional procedures. For example, your school may provide for a conference between you and the evaluation team members to discuss the results of your child's testing. Before proceeding with the evaluation for your child, review your school's rules and regulations carefully. Remember, if you believe your school system has not fulfilled the evaluation requirements as stated above and in your school's regulations, you can take various steps to protect your child's right to a thorough, accurate evaluation. Chapter 14 outlines these requirements in detail.

Parent Action-Steps for Evaluation

Now you have some understanding of the evaluation process and can make the decision about whether to have your child evaluated.

The following list of action-steps suggests activities other parents have found helpful when entering the evaluation phase of the special education process. Some of the actions and steps are applicable to testing conducted by private or public agencies outside the school system rather than in a school setting. Other steps are appropriate for young children rather than older students. You will want to undertake only those actions and steps that:

1. make sense to you;
2. are appropriate to the age and developmental level of your child; and
3. will help you make a confident decision.

Whether to Evaluate: Giving or Refusing Permission to Evaluate

After the school system has notified you in writing of its intent to evaluate your child, you must decide whether to give or refuse permission for this evaluation. Deciding whether to have your child evaluated is a big decision. To help you decide, you may wish to:

ACTION A: Explore your feelings about this evaluation by:

- talking to your spouse, a friend, or a helping professional such as a teacher, counselor, or advocate;
- if you have already been through an evaluation process with your child, recalling what was difficult and what was helpful in previous evaluations.

ACTION B: Consider the kinds of services your child may be eligible for by:

- understanding fully the areas in which the referral committee thinks your child should be evaluated;
- learning more about the services available through your school and how those can help your child;

- considering possible benefits and drawbacks as comprehensively as you can;
- thinking about all the ways you can help your child, if you feel that he needs some special attention but aren't sure whether to have him evaluated.

ACTION C: Learn more about your local evaluation process by:

- asking the director of special education or your school principal to identify the person in the school system most responsible for your child's evaluation;
- getting copies of and reviewing all relevant written policies and procedures from the person responsible for the evaluation, the school's public information officer, or the department of special education;
- obtaining and reviewing parent handbooks and pamphlets on special education and evaluation;
- making a list of all your questions;
- meeting with a knowledgeable person such as an experienced parent, a school representative, or an advocate to discuss evaluation.

ACTION D: Learn more about the evaluation planned for your child by:

- requesting in writing from school officials the reasons for this evaluation;
- requesting a detailed plan of the evaluation proposed or that could be proposed for your child. Make sure the plan includes:
    - ❏ areas to be evaluated (for example, communication skills and movement skills),
    - ❏ tests or portions of tests to be used,
    - ❏ reasons for selecting these tests,
    - ❏ qualifications of individuals who are giving the tests,
    - ❏ a statement as to how the evaluation will be adapted to compensate for your child's suspected disability,
    - ❏ all other data that the committee will use; for example, additional information may include observations by teachers or other service providers.

ACTION E: Explore the independent evaluation alternative by learning about your right to an independent educational evaluation (see Chapter 14);

- learning your school's procedures for providing (and paying for) independent evaluations;

- talking with parents whose children have had independent evaluations;
- consulting with a psychologist, diagnostician, or other professional in private practice.

ACTION F: Consider the consequences of refusing to give permission for the evaluation by:

- talking to the principal and teachers about alternatives to special education at the school;
- discussing your concerns with the person in charge of the evaluation;
- learning your school's procedures when parents refuse evaluation;
- consulting with a knowledgeable advocate or attorney about the effects of refusing evaluation on your child's continued rights to special education services;
- talking with knowledgeable professionals about your child's learning needs and the reasons you are considering refusing the school's evaluation.

Reevaluation

If you are reading this book as you and your child are just beginning the special education process, you may be preparing for your very first evaluation. If your child is already receiving special education services, you may be aware that IDEA requires the schools to conduct a reevaluation at least every three years. One exception to this rule is if the IEP team decides they have enough information to continue providing specialized instruction and services to your child so further testing is not necessary. If this is the case, however, they must send you a letter informing you of their decision, and you must give consent.

You can request a reevaluation if your child is not improving academically or developmentally. If it has been less than one year since your child's last evaluation, the school may deny your request.

The school must also conduct a reevaluation before deciding to end special education services for your child, unless he graduates or leaves school at age twenty-one.

Conclusion

Ultimately, the decision as to whether to have your child evaluated is up to you and your sense of what is best for your child. If you aren't sure whether to continue, consult with experts and family, investigate the services your school may have, and learn more about how an Individualized Educational Program might help your child.

WHAT YOU CAN DO NOW

1. Collect any medical records and notes you have that support your belief that your child requires (or doesn't require) special education.

2. Complete additional observations of your child to help document any area of disability.

3. Talk to your physician or another professional about your concerns, and consider any advice they can give you. For example, you may be referred to a book for more information about a specific condition or general child development.

4. Try to find other parents with similar concerns so you can talk with them about the steps you are about to take.

5. Make a list of the pros and cons of consenting to the evaluation.

6. Talk to your child about getting extra help and how he feels about that.

7. If you aren't sure whether to consent to the evaluation, read the next few chapters about the evaluation process and the kinds of help your child may receive.

5. The Evaluation Process
Navigational Survival Tips

Now you are ready to move ahead with the evaluation. After you give permission to proceed with the evaluation, what comes next? This chapter describes three phases of action steps for you to consider:

1. Before the evaluation
2. During the evaluation
3. After the evaluation

Information about ways to organize and analyze the evaluation reports in preparation for the rest of your trip through the maze is included.

The following suggestions are a compilation of action-steps that families have used and found helpful as they moved through the evaluation process. Note that some actions and steps apply only to testing conducted by private or public agencies outside the school system rather than in a school setting. If you are not pursuing testing outside of the school system, skip those actions. Some steps are appropriate for young children rather than older students.

As mentioned in the previous chapter, take only actions and steps that:

1. make sense to you;
2. are appropriate to the age and developmental level of your child;
3. may help you make a confident decision.

You need not take all the actions and all the steps outlined. Look over the list and choose the actions and steps to follow that will be most helpful to you and to your child in assuring that the evaluation is fair and thorough. In making your selection, you will want to keep in mind your family's needs, and your child's age, disability, and past experience with evaluations.

Phase I: Before Evaluation

ACTION A: Plan for your child's evaluation with a representative of the evaluation facility or school's psychological services by:

- asking for additional or alternate assessments or evaluations, if you think these are necessary;
- arranging for a meeting or a phone conference;
- providing information about your child that may determine the choice of evaluation that will be used;
- listing your questions and concerns in priority order;
- asking for more information about, or clarification of, the evaluation process;
- sharing your plans for your involvement;
- raising concerns you might have over keeping the experience a positive one for your child.

ACTION B: Anticipate your child's needs in this evaluation by:

- talking with your spouse, your child's therapist or teacher, or an earlier evaluator about how your child handles tests and evaluations. Consider her:
  - ❑ reaction to strangers,
  - ❑ tolerance for testing demands,
  - ❑ ability to sit still for long periods,
  - ❑ response to doctors and other professionals,
  - ❑ fatigue threshold—how long until she gets too tired to work at her best,
  - ❑ need for an interpreter if she doesn't speak English or uses sign language, and
  - ❑ high and low points in the day;
- reading pamphlets or articles on children and evaluations;
- talking with your child about this evaluation and about prior evaluations, if any.

ACTION C: Prepare yourself for this evaluation by:

- talking to other parents about their experiences;
- seeking tips on rough spots and how to work around them from an organization for parents of children with disabilities;
- listing your practical concerns about the evaluation, such as:
  - ❑ schedules,

    ❑ costs,

    ❑ child care,

    ❑ transportation,

    ❑ obtaining an interpreter

- learning the evaluation facility's or school's expectation for your involvement;
- choosing among various roles you may take, such as:

    ❑ observer of your child,

    ❑ supporter of your child,

    ❑ information source about your child.

ACTION D: Participate in the evaluation planning process by:

- reviewing past report cards and other school progress reports;
- gathering examples of your child's school work;
- along with your child, creating a portfolio that describes and illustrates her strengths and needs.

ACTION E: Prepare your child for the evaluation by:

- talking together about the reasons for this evaluation;
- giving your child opportunities to express her feelings and ask questions;
- visiting the place where the evaluation will be conducted so your child will be familiar with the people and the surroundings;
- planning together for a special activity when the evaluation is completed.

Phase II: During Evaluation

    During the evaluation process itself, the actions and steps you select will be strongly influenced by your child's age and her past experience with evaluations. In many instances your child will be tested in school, during school hours, making it difficult or inappropriate for you to be present during the evaluation. When it is appropriate for you to be present, especially with a young child, you may want to consider some of the following actions and steps. Keeping in mind your child's age, personality, and disability, you may wish to:

ACTION A: Ease your child into the situation by:

- making sure she is well rested;
- allowing her to become familiar with the areas in which she will be tested;

- introducing her to the people who will be giving the tests;
- reviewing the day's plan with her;
- reassuring her that you will be available to her;
- encouraging her to ask questions and share worries.

ACTION B: Monitor the evaluation process by:
- requesting that the evaluation start on time;
- inquiring as to any changes in personnel or tests to be used;
- observing testing of your child whenever appropriate;
- recording your impressions of your child's performance;
- recording your impressions of each evaluator's interactions with your child.

ACTION C: Monitor your child's performance by:
- keeping an eye on her fatigue and stress levels;
- staying with her during medical procedures—shots, blood tests, EEG;
- asking for explanations of unexpected procedures.

ACTION D: If you are not with your child during the evaluation, make sure you are calm when you see your child by:
- keeping an eye on your own fatigue and stress levels;
- doing what you can to relieve tension and stress, such as taking time for a cup of tea or going for a walk;
- keeping track of time so that the schedule is uninterrupted and you are able to pick her up on time.

Phase III: After Evaluation

Parents and children usually need to feel that the evaluation is truly completed. There are a number of ways you and your family can wrap up the evaluation experience and begin to use the information gained from the evaluation for educational planning. You may wish to:

ACTION A: Help your child round out the experience on a positive note by:
- encouraging her to review the experience through storytelling, drawing pictures, or dramatic play;
- discussing with her the people and activities she liked and disliked;
- sharing your own feelings and perceptions of the experience;

- informing her of the evaluation results—what was learned about her strengths and needs;
- doing one of her favorite things with her!

ACTION B: Help yourself complete the experience by:

- recounting the experience to a friend or parent support group;
- checking the actual evaluation experience against what you had planned or anticipated;
- writing a letter to the evaluation facility describing your sense of the strengths of the process and areas that should be changed;
- doing something special for yourself!

ACTION C: Prepare for the next step:

- finding out when the next meeting is scheduled and whether that includes a decision about whether your child is eligible for special education and/or an IEP meeting;
- asking when you will receive results of this current evaluation (make sure you are to receive them in time to understand them before an eligibility meeting);
- noting your concerns in the form of questions that you can ask at the next meeting;
- talking directly to the evaluator about your questions and concerns;
- organizing your notes, observations, and examples of your child's work to contribute to the discussion of the evaluation;
- starting work on the Four-Step Record Decoder described below.

To help you systematically negotiate the evaluation phase of the special education maze, a Parent Action—Steps for Evaluation Chart follows on pages 66-67. The chart has space for writing each action and step you will take in the evaluation phase. At the end of the chart is a section for names, phone numbers, and dates related to those actions and steps. The chart allows you to plan steps you choose to take in your child's evaluation, to monitor the progress of the evaluation, and to maintain a record of how and when the evaluation was conducted and completed—all useful information.

Evaluation Results

Before proceeding on to any meetings where your child's eligibility for special education is discussed, make sure you understand the evaluation team's perspective of your child's current abilities and problems. Request and review

PARENT ACTIONS–STEPS
FOR EVALUATION CHART
(WORKSHEET)

Phase I: Giving/Refusing Permission to Evaluate

Action: _____

    Step: _____

    Step: _____

Action: _____

    Step: _____

    Step: _____

Action: _____

    Step: _____

    Step: _____

Phase II: Before Evaluation

Action: _____

    Step: _____

    Step: _____

Action: _____

    Step: _____

    Step: _____

Action: _____

    Step: _____

    Step: _____

(CONTINUED NEXT PAGE)

Phase III: During Evaluation

Action: _____

    Step: _____

    Step: _____

Action: _____

    Step: _____

    Step: _____

Action: _____

    Step: _____

    Step: _____

Phase IV: After Evaluation

Action: _____

    Step: _____

    Step: _____

Action: _____

    Step: _____

    Step: _____

Action: _____

    Step: _____

    Step: _____

Important Telephone Numbers   Important Dates

_____   _____

_____   _____

_____   _____

_____   _____

_____   _____

a copy of the written reports, and make sure you understand them thoroughly, preferably by working closely with someone who is knowledgeable about the tests given to your child during the evaluation. Chapter 13 describes your rights to obtain, review, and challenge your child's school records.

Once you have all the reports in hand, you may wonder what you've got. The language of the educators, psychologists, educational diagnosticians, and other school professionals often can be extremely difficult to understand. If this is the case for you, all you need to do is ask someone to help you. IDEA requires school personnel to explain the reports to you when you do not understand them. Or you may take a friend or a knowledgeable professional with you to help review the records and explain confusing parts. When you do this, however, you will be asked to sign a form giving that person permission to see your child's records. Once you clearly understand the reports themselves, it's time to make them useful to a wide range of school professionals—including your child's teacher.

The Four-Step Record Decoder

When you have obtained the school's records, often a stack of documents an inch or more thick, what will you do with them? How can you begin to make sense of all this material written about your child? You have already organized your home observations of your child into the framework of the Developmental Achievement Chart; now you will organize the school's observations of your child by employing the Four-Step Record Decoder. The decoder helps you organize, read, analyze, and evaluate your child's school records.

Organize

1. After obtaining the complete set of records from the school system, separate the documents describing your child (teacher reports, psychological evaluations, social history, IEPs, etc.) from other documents or correspondence of an administrative nature (the minutes of an eligibility committee meeting, consent forms, etc.). The other documents and correspondence help you keep track of your contacts with the school system.
2. Make an extra copy of the records and set the original aside, away from the work area. This way you will have an original and also a copy you can mark, cut, paste, and use however it will help you.
3. Arrange each set—descriptive reports and other documents—in chronological order.
4. Secure the pages in a folder with a clip or in a loose-leaf notebook so that if you drop them you won't have to back up three steps.

5. Starting with the reports file you put together: number each report and make a chronological list that can be added onto as new records are generated. The list might look like this:

Educational Reports of Jessica Lee

REPORT	DATE	REPORTING PERSON	NOTES
1. Psychoeducational evaluation	5/3/07	Angelica Connor	■ Reading at 5th grade level ■ Easily frustrated ■ Word comprehension an area of strength
2. Teacher's report	5/8/07	Cathy Lambert	■ Trouble with homework ■ Often tardy ■ Helps others in class
3. Social history reports	5/8/07	Pat Roberts	
4. Psychiatric evaluation summary	5/12/07	Dr. Maria Ortiz	■ Attention issues ■ Tired easily
5. IEP	5/13/07		
6. Psychological evaluation summary	1/9/08	Angelica Connor	■ Limited attention ■ Disorganized ■ Gave up quickly
7. Teacher's report	1/18/08	Chuck Morris	■ Reading at 5th grade level
8. Psychologist's memorandum	1/22/08	Angelica Connor	■ Recommendations for accommodations

Read

1. Read through the entire record to get an overall impression of the school's view of your child.
2. In the margins of your working copy, put a question mark beside the statements or areas of the reports you do not understand or with which you disagree.

Analyze

1. Now reread the reports and underline the phrases or sentences you feel best describe your child's strengths and problems. Put an "S" in

the margin opposite a description of your child's learning strengths; a "P" opposite the problems. When you come to a phrase or sentence reporting your child's learning style, write "LS" in the margin.

2. Using a worksheet similar to the one on pages 72-73, place these phrases or sentences about your child's strengths and problems within the developmental categories of movement, communications, social relationships, self-concept/independence, perception/senses, thinking skills, and learning style.

3. After each piece of data, put the source and date. Often you will find trends beginning to emerge. The same observation, said in similar language, may occur in several reports over a period of time.

4. List recommendations made by each evaluator or teacher in the last section of the analysis sheet. Recommendations might include services needed, classroom environment, class size, type of school setting, further testing needed, specific teaching materials, or equipment.

Evaluate

Using the question-mark notations you have made in the margins and your overall sense of the records from your analytical work with them, evaluate them against the following criteria:

Accurate. Do the reports and portions of the records correspond with your own feelings, perceptions, observations, and assessments of your child?

Complete. Are all the documents required by the school system for the eligibility, Individualized Education Program (IEP), and placement decisions available in the file? For example, medical report, social history, psychological examination, educational report, and others as may be required by your local or state guidelines.

Bias Free. Are the reports free from bias due to culture, race, ethnicity, disability, or socio-economic levels? Do they take into consideration the effect your child's disability might have had upon the outcome of the results of the tests? Was it given in your child's language or mode of communication (including sign or cued speech)?

Nonjudgmental. Do the reports reflect a respect for your child and your family? Do they avoid the use of language that judges rather than describes? Examples of judgmental statements include: "She is fickle." "She is stubborn." Examples of descriptive statements include: "He is inconsistent in stating what he likes and dislikes." "He will not respond to directions to stop disruptive behavior."

Current. Are the dates on the records recent enough to give a report of your child's present behavior and functioning? Records generated within the past three years are generally useful for making good decisions. Older ones should be used with caution.

Understandable. Is the language used meaningful, clear, and understandable to you? If technical terms (jargon) are used, have they been defined or made understandable to the nonspecialist? (Example of an unclear statement: "She appears to have a psychological learning disability, calling for treatment involving a moderation of the special focus on interpersonal sensitivity she has received so far." What does that mean?)

Consistent. Is there consistency among the descriptions of your child given by each evaluator or teacher? Or do you find contradictions and differences of opinion? Considering the record as a whole, does it make sense and lead to the given recommendations?

An example of the analysis sheets of the Record Decoder Elena's parents worked out are found on pages 74-75.

By completing your own Record Decoder analysis sheets, you will become thoroughly familiar with your child as seen through the close-up lens of her evaluation reports and other school records. The information in these records provides the basis upon which crucial decisions will be made concerning your child's education. The importance of organizing, reading, analyzing, and evaluating your child's school records cannot be overemphasized. Therefore, before continuing to the next phase of the maze, make sure the information in your child's file paints an accurate picture of her.

Evaluation Troubleshooting

After you have reviewed your child's latest evaluation reports and examined past evaluations in the school file using the Record Decoder, you will conclude one of two things. Either you agree that the evaluation results are accurate, complete, consistent, and up to date; or you believe they are deficient in some respect. If you believe the evaluation materials are satisfactory, you move to the next corridor of the special education maze—eligibility determination. But what if you think the evaluation findings are inadequate? What steps do you take next?

You can select one of two paths in attempting to correct the defects you find with the evaluations. One path is informal; you informally ask school officials either to remove the faulty evaluation from the record, undertake additional evaluations, add materials you provide to the file, or possibly just clarify for you the deficiencies you see in the evaluation findings. Should this approach fail, you can seek to resolve your difficulties through a more formal approach.

Independent Educational Evaluations

If your problem involves earlier evaluations that are now a part of your child's official school file, you can seek to amend the records through the formal process

FOUR-STEP RECORD DECODER

Data	Source	Date
MOVEMENT Strengths: Problems:		
COMMUNICATIONS Strengths: Problems:		
SOCIAL RELATIONSHIPS Strengths: Problems:		
SELF-CONCEPT/INDEPENDENCE Strengths: Problems:		

SENSES/PERCEPTION

Strengths:

Problems:

THINKING SKILLS

Strengths:

Problems:

LEARNING STYLE

Strengths:

Problems:

RECOMMENDATIONS

FOUR-STEP RECORD DECODER

Data	Source	Date
MOVEMENT **Strengths:** Beginning to crawl, not quite ready to stand, picking things up by grabbing them **Problems:** Not quite ready to stand	Ms. Nelson Peabody	Feb. '07
COMMUNICATIONS **Strengths:** Says words like "wat dat?" and has about a 20-word vocabulary **Problems:** Pronunciation of words is delayed, not clear if she understands move than she can talk	Ms. Granger HELP 13-18 mos.	Feb. '07
SOCIAL RELATIONSHIPS **Strengths:** Plays with other children **Problems:** Difficulties initiating play. Cries if someone takes her toy.	Ms. Granger HELP 2-3 years	Feb. '07
SELF-CONCEPT/INDEPENDENCE **Strengths:** Helps with dressing, finger-feeds self, looks at books **Problems:** Has difficulty making eye contact and does not like transitions	Ms. Granger HELP 2-3 years	Feb. '07

	Dr. Martinez	March '07
SENSES/PERCEPTION		
Strengths: No sensory delays are identified at this time		
Problems:		

	Ms. Granger HELP 2-2½ years	Feb. '07
THINKING SKILLS		
Strengths: Knows colors, can complete tasks with some attention and reinforcing. She can count to the number 12, but does not match quantity with numerals. She recognizes 5 letters of the 26 letter alphabet.		
Problems: She does not match quantities with numerals.		

	Ms. Granger progress report	Feb. '07
LEARNING STYLE		
Strengths: Elena likes routines. When she understands what is coming next, she is much calmer and especially likes music.		
Problems: When things do not go as regularly scheduled, or if Ms. Granger is absent, Elena is much more fussy and more difficult to handle.		

RECOMMENDATIONS

In six months, Elena will be able to recognize the alphabet and recognize a few words. She will expand her vocabulary (learning sign language and verbal language), so that she can communicate and understand language at a 3-year-old level.

for correcting records described briefly above and more thoroughly in Chapter 14. If your concern is the inadequacy of the school's most recent evaluation, you can request that an independent evaluation of your child be made at public expense.

Independent Evaluations Paid for by the School

Both federal and state laws provide parents the opportunity to obtain an Independent Educational Evaluation (IEE) of their child when they believe the school's evaluation is inadequate. An independent evaluation is one made by professionals not employed by the school system. Some local school systems maintain a list of professionals or organizations whose personnel meet the licensing criteria for conducting independent evaluations. However, the parent may also select evaluators not on the list as long as they meet the licensing criteria and fees are reasonable. Sometimes the county or state departments of health or mental health may conduct these evaluations. The steps you should follow to secure an independent evaluation are outlined in your state regulations. But remember! An independent evaluation paid for at public expense does not mean that you, the parent, can choose whomever you wish to evaluate your child. The evaluators must meet the licensing criteria of the school system.

Will school officials agree to pay for an independent evaluation? Not always. Before they can deny your request, however, they must hold a due process hearing as described in Chapter 14 and must prove to the hearing officer the appropriateness of their evaluations. Otherwise, the school system cannot deny your request for an independent evaluation. Remember! You don't have to prove that the school's evaluation results are incorrect before asking for an independent evaluation—you are entitled to an independent evaluation if you merely believe the school system's findings are inadequate. If school professionals don't wish to pay for the independent evaluation, they must initiate the hearing procedure to justify denying the request.

Paying for an Independent Evaluation Yourself

An alternative to the independent evaluation at public expense is the independent evaluation at private expense. If you can obtain an independent evaluation at public expense, why would you ever want to pay for one out of your own pocket? There are several reasons. First, you can personally choose the professionals who will make the evaluation. This often gives you greater confidence in the findings and allows you to select the specialist most appropriate for working with your child. Second, when you pay for your own evaluation, you can control who sees the results. When an independent evaluation is made at public expense, the findings must be considered by the school system in making educational decisions regarding your child.

Further, the independent, publicly financed evaluation may be presented as evidence in a due process hearing. If you feel that the independent evaluation is also incorrect, you have no way to stop its being used by the school system or the hearing officer. In contrast, if you pay for the evaluation of your child, you determine how those results are used and who gets to see them. Thus, if you conclude that the results accurately describe your child, you may submit the results for consideration by the school system or a hearing officer. If you are not confident of the findings, you do not have to submit them to the school or at a hearing unless required to do so by the hearing officer.

Although there are many benefits to paying for your child's evaluation, you must weigh these benefits against several potential costs before deciding to have your own evaluation. One major cost is the dollar outlay itself. Complete educational evaluations may cost $3000 or more. Check with your health insurance company to see if it covers the type of evaluation you are considering. When the evaluation merely confirms the school's findings, it may still be beneficial—it gives more reason to believe the initial testing results—but it is an expensive procedure for securing such confirmation. Still another cost occurs if you introduce findings from your own specialists, and these findings are given little or no significance by school officials or the hearing officer.

The reason sometimes given for downplaying the importance of private evaluation data is reflected in the comments made by one school official in a due process hearing. According to that school administrator, "Parents can shop around until they find a psychologist or other professional who will say exactly what they want to hear." If the school official or hearing officer with whom you are working has this attitude, the benefits of the evaluation you pay for may not equal their costs.

One last word about obtaining your own evaluations: never have the evaluation results sent to school officials before you have examined them. On more than one occasion parents have done this to save time, only to discover that the evaluation results worked to their child's disadvantage. Therefore, discuss the evaluation findings with the professionals who developed them first. Then, and only then, decide whether you want the results sent to the school or the hearing officer.

What Happens Now?

At the next meeting—the eligibility meeting—the committee decides whether or not your child qualifies for special education services, and makes recommendations for the types of services that would help your child.

Conclusion

All of the action steps listed in this chapter may seem overwhelming. Evaluations can be stressful. By being prepared, understanding the process and your rights, you can look ahead to the good part—helping your child succeed.

WHAT YOU CAN DO NOW

1. Prepare for the evaluation by following the action-steps in this chapter that make sense for you and your child.
2. Collect evaluation results as soon as they are available.
3. Analyze the records using the School Record Decoder.
4. Consider the possibility of independent testing, if you think that is appropriate. List the pros and cons of proceeding with independent tests.
5. After the evaluation, take some time to relax—if you can find the time!

6. The Eligibility Decision

A Turning Point

You have passed through the educational planning cycle's first two phases—referral and evaluation. You have gathered data at home and examined your child's school records with the Record Decoder. Now comes phase three—eligibility. This is the part of the special education process where you and a group of qualified professionals determine whether your child's disability affects his learning to the extent that he will need special education.

Who Decides a Child Is Eligible?

IDEA requires that the eligibility decision is made by a team, which includes parents. The team is known by different names in different states; for example, IEP Team, Eligibility Committee, Multidisciplinary Team (M-Team), or Admission, Review, and Dismissal (ARD) Committee. The exact name for this team, its composition, and procedures will be found in your local or state regulations. The meeting where this team decides whether a child is eligible also may have different names depending on your state's procedures for determining eligibility and where you are in the special education process. For example, it may be referred to as an evaluation meeting, a referral/qualification meeting, an IEP meeting, or a triennial meeting.

The eligibility team's role is to consider all of the data from the evaluation—including the results of the assessments and other evaluation measures as described in Chapter 5. The team uses this data to determine whether your child has a disability as defined by state and federal laws, and the nature of his educational needs.

Definition of Eligibility Categories

The procedure followed by the team to determine your child's eligibility for special education is simple to describe in theory, and often impossible to describe in practice. In theory, here is how the team operates. State regulations for special education include a series of definitions of disabilities. These definitions vary from state to state, but generally follow the federal definitions as outlined in IDEA. Children who receive special education services are those:

1. who are evaluated as having
   - mental retardation (sometimes called intellectual or cognitive disability);
   - hearing impairment including deafness;
   - speech or language impairment;
   - visual impairment including blindness;
   - serious emotional disturbance (sometimes called emotional disability, behavioral disorder, or mental illness);
   - orthopedic impairment (sometimes called physical disability);
   - autism (sometimes includes pervasive developmental disorder (PDD) and Asperger's syndrome);
   - traumatic brain injury;
   - other health impairment, including ADHD and Tourette syndrome;
   - specific learning disability;
   - developmental delay (a category used in some states for children ages 3 through 9 who have problems with the development of their physical, cognitive, communication, social/emotional, or adaptive skills)

AND

2. because of their disability require special education in order to benefit from their educational program.

There are three additional important considerations for eligibility specifically mentioned in IDEA.

1. Schools are to ensure they have not over-identified children in terms of race or ethnicity;
2. A child cannot be determined eligible for special education solely because of a lack of instruction in reading or math or because of limited English proficiency.
3. Unlike in the past, IDEA offers alternatives to identifying a specific learning disability based on an IQ test. Children no longer have to

demonstrate a severe discrepancy between ability and achievement in order to be found eligible for special education. If you would like to learn more about how schools determine that a child has a specific learning disability, contact or visit the websites of the learning disabilities organizations in the Resources section.

The definitions of disabilities found in federal and state regulations are not always easy to understand. You may be surprised to learn that school personnel are themselves sometimes uncertain as to the exact meaning of the definitions. You may also discover that the local, state, and federal definitions of specific disability categories may differ. In addition, you may find that your school district uses phrases such as educable mental retardation, trainable mental retardation, or severe mental retardation. These terms are no longer used in the professional field because they limit how others view a child's potential and therefore the services to the child. Many states now use the preferred term of an "intellectual disability" or a "cognitive disability" instead of mental retardation.

If you are unsure of the definition of disability being discussed in relation to your child, keep asking until you find someone who can explain the definition to your satisfaction. This way you can ensure that your child's learning problems are accurately identified.

The glossary defines each eligibility category as written in the IDEA regulations.

Matching Evaluation Data with Eligibility Categories

Each member of the team, including you as the parent, receives copies of the evaluation reports and other relevant information contained in your child's official school file before the team convenes. The evaluation reports either identify the presence of one or more disabilities or suggest the absence of conditions severe enough to require special education services. The job of the team is to compare the results and conclusions of the evaluation against the definitions of the disabilities that qualify for special education services. If the team agrees that the evaluation results: 1) correspond with one or more of the definitions, and 2) your child needs special education, your child will be found eligible for special education services. If the team concludes that the results of the evaluation do not meet the eligibility criteria, your child will be found ineligible for special education. The team must give you a copy of the report documenting the eligibility decision.

Remember, the team's job is to decide whether your child has a disability that adversely affects his ability to learn *and* whether he needs special services in order to progress in school. For example, a child who has a physical disability who is succeeding in school and doesn't require specialized services would not automatically be eligible for special education. Or, a child with AD/HD whose symptoms are under control may also not be eligible for specialized services. The disability must always be paired with the child's ability to make progress in the general education curriculum.

It is possible that others on the team and the school may make a determination that you do not agree with. If this happens, you can resolve your disagreement or appeal the team's decision as described in Chapter 14.

If your child is found ineligible for special education services under the criteria for special education under IDEA, he may still be able to receive some services under Section 504 of the Rehabilitation Act or the Americans with Disabilities Act. See Chapter 15, which discusses the requirements of Section 504 and ADA.

Eligibility in Action: A Case Study

Roberto Herrera is seven years old. When he was two, his parents first noticed that his development was slow. Roberto always has taken longer and expended much more effort to learn most of the things his brothers and sisters seem to pick up with ease. He has speech problems and uses only short, simple sentences. Roberto's teacher put him in a special reading group for students who were having reading difficulties. The reading teacher used a reading program that had been validated by research to make sure that all the students in this group had proper reading instruction. Though Roberto made some progress, he still was behind his peers in reading. Because of Roberto's continuing problems in school, his teacher suggested he be evaluated for special services. Mr. Herrera agreed with the recommendation and signed permission for the evaluation to take place.

Tests of general intelligence showed Roberto to have an IQ of 105. Other tests showed him to have difficulties in coordinating his eyes and hands when copying geometric figures; problems coordinating his hands to catch a ball and his feet to stand on one leg; and difficulty in remembering things he had heard or read. Academic achievement tests found Roberto to be more than two years behind his peers in reading and arithmetic.

In the state where Roberto lives, the regulations governing special education define specific learning disability as:

"a disorder in one or more of the basic psychological processes involved in understanding or in using language, spoken or written, which may manifest itself in an imperfect ability to listen, think, speak, read, write, spell, or do mathematical calculations which adversely affect the child's educational performance. The term includes such conditions as visual-motor disorders, dyslexia, and developmental aphasia. The term does not include children who have learning problems which are primarily the result of visual, hearing, or motor disability, of mental retardation, of emotional disturbance, or of environmental, cultural, or economic disadvantage."

When the team compared Roberto's evaluation reports with the preceding definition, they found that the results matched the definition. He displayed problems with reading and arithmetic. The evaluation results indicated he had difficulty copying various shapes and was unable to distinguish left from right. These and other results showed he had perceptual impairments, as well as problems with his movement or motor control. None of these problems could be explained by mental retardation. His IQ, at 105, was in the normal range. Emotional problems, visual or hearing deficits, or environmental, cultural, or economic disadvantages were not found to be the source of Roberto's problems. All the signs of the evaluation pointed to perceptual difficulties. Roberto was therefore declared eligible for special education services because of his specific learning disabilities.

In the preceding case, the child was found to have only one major disability. But what happens if evaluation results indicate that a child has two or more disabilities; for example, specific learning disabilities and emotional problems? Usually the team will try to identify the primary disability responsible for inhibiting the child's educational growth. If both conditions contribute to the child's learning problems, the team may list the disabilities or decide to declare that the child has multiple disabilities.

Consider carefully any eligibility category assigned to your child. It should not drive services or placements. In practice, however, it often happens that students with similar eligibility categories are educated in the same groups and receive the same services. For example, children with emotional disabilities may receive services in special classes that don't address their learning disabilities. Some students with intellectual disabilities may not routinely be assigned to classes where academics are stressed. Talk to other parents to find out if and how eligibility categories may affect placement and services in your school system.

Your Role as an Educational Advocate during the Eligibility Meeting

As a parent, you have an important role to play at the eligibility meeting. Remember that you are a member of the team that is coming together to make this important decision for your child.

You have now collected useful and insightful information about your child that can help the rest of the team gain a better understanding of your concerns along with your child's strengths, abilities, and needs. As a member of the team, your information is to be considered along with other assessments. What can you do to organize this information in a way that the team can best understand and digest it? You may wish to prepare your own parent statement to be considered at this meeting and included in your child's record of this meeting. Most of the material for your presentation may be drawn from the analyses you made using the Developmental Achievement Chart and the Four-Step Record Decoder.

The parent statement that follows is an example of what you can give to the team in advance of the meeting or can distribute and present at the meeting.

Action Steps Before the Eligibility Meeting

Action Steps Before the Eligibility Meeting

1. Read your state regulations and local policies and procedures that your school system uses and the timelines it must follow.
2. Review eligibility categories defined in the regulations, and determine which best describes your child. Find out the kinds of services given to children who fit into this category or categories, and consider whether these services will best help your child (see next chapter). If they won't, examine the categories further. Work with professionals to select an appropriate category and find out services typically given to similar students. Your school special education coordinator or the director of special education can help you in your investigations.
3. Find out if the eligibility determination and the development of the IEP occur at the same meeting. If so, you will want to be prepared for the IEP meeting, as suggested in subsequent chapters of this book. You may also request that the IEP meeting be scheduled for a later date.
4. Find out who is the designated contact person or case manager coordinating the meeting. Most likely a specialist in a certain disability area, the coordinator of special education, or one of the professionals who tested your child will be designated the case manager.
5. Ask for a copy of the evaluation reports that will be used to determine your child's eligibility.
   a. Review Chapter 14 for information on school records and reports.

PARENT STATEMENT

Related to the eligibility of: _____ Date: _____

Proposed Eligibility Category: _____

Child's Learning Style: _____

Strengths and Needs Related to Disability: _____

_____

_____

_____

_____

Reporting Person/Role	Date	Information that supports eligibility category

Other relevant issues and comments related to evaluations: _____

_____

_____

_____

_____

  b. Make sure that you understand and agree with the information in the evaluation reports.
  c. Ask for clarification from the person who conducted the evaluation or ask that changes be made when there are inaccuracies, if needed.
6. Prepare your Parent Statement that you will share for inclusion with the evaluation reports and for discussion at the meeting.
  a. Analyze the information using the Developmental Achievement Chart on page 43 and the Four-Step Record Decoder on page 72.
  b. Put your information in writing in your own words or using the Parent Statement form above.
7. Plan for your child's active inclusion at the meeting.
  a. Determine whether your child will attend all or part of the meeting. For example, if the meeting will be long, and your child is very young, he may not be good at sitting still for very long.
  b. Prepare for how your child may advocate for himself through a verbal presentation, written statement that he or another person reads, a personal video, or other means.
8. Determine who else needs to be at the meeting
  a. In many instances you may wish to bring to the meeting professionals, teachers, and others who have worked with and know your child. Prior to the meeting, talk with these people to find out how their opinions and views would add to your case. Ask them to come if you think it would help.
  b. Get another person—family member or friend—to attend the meeting with you. At the eligibility meeting you will find anywhere from four to ten school officials in attendance. If you attend by yourself, you may feel overwhelmed. You should acquaint the person accompanying you with your plans for the meeting. Your partner can monitor your list of agenda items and bring to your attention any important points you may have missed.
9. Let your contact person know how you plan to take an active role in the eligibility process.
  a. Submit your Parent Statement as a formal part of the evaluation reports to be considered and discussed at the meeting.
  b. Let the contact person know who else you are bringing to attend the meeting.
  c. Find out what to expect at the meeting. If an IEP meeting follows this meeting, you may wish to prepare for that meeting

by combining action steps from this chapter and from Chapter 9: The Individualized Education Program Meeting.

   d. Consider alternative means to allow your key people (doctors, therapists, family member) to participate. For example, if they cannot attend in person, consider teleconferences or use of speaker phones.

Action Steps During the Eligibility Meeting

1. Help the team to understand your child as a unique individual. You want the team to know that this is a real person—your son or daughter—whose educational needs are in their hands. This can be an opportunity for your child or you to present the information prepared in advance of the meeting.

2. Ask the chairperson what procedures will be used to make an eligibility determination. This step is very important since it assures that everyone will proceed with the same expectations for the meeting, thus eliminating potential confusion.

3. Present your information to the team using your Parent Statement.
   a. Respond to questions from team members so that they can understand your information and perspective.
   b. Ask that your Parent Statement be included in the record of the meeting in its entirety.

4. Listen carefully to the team's presentation and discussion.
   a. Ask questions if you need clarification or if you think that other information is needed for the rest of the team to understand the report.
   b. If you have invited other teachers or professionals to present at the meeting, ask the team to include their information or materials.
   c. If team members appear to be using biased, inaccurate, incomplete, or out-of-date material or to be making incorrect statements, intervene and explain your concerns.
   d. Always remember that diplomacy and tact throughout the meeting will serve you well.
   e. Take notes throughout the meeting. It is amazing how much information is presented—notes will help you capture it all.

5. Be an active partner in the eligibility decision.
   a. Consider making concluding remarks summarizing the discussion and relating it to the information you have shared at this meeting.

Action Steps After the Eligibility Meeting

1. Make sure that you have an accurate copy of all the information related to this meeting and review your child's official record to ensure that the correct information (including any information you or your child shared) is there.
2. If you agree with the decision of the rest of the team, ready yourself for the next step—either active involvement in the IEP by moving on to Chapters 8 and 9 of this book, or to Chapter 15 for information about Section 504 of the Rehabilitation Act.
3. If you disagree with the decisions made at the eligibility meeting, review the next section.

When Parents Disagree with the Eligibility Decision

Two major points of contention can arise between parents and school systems as a result of eligibility meetings:

1. The team finds the child ineligible for services and the parents believe the child is eligible.
2. The team finds the child eligible, but says the child's disability is something different from what the parents believe it is.

For example, the team may conclude that a child's primary disability is emotional disability, but the parents feel that it is a learning disability. Or the team may conclude that the child has autism, while the parents believe his hearing impairment is the major cause of his learning problems.

For parents and children, either of the preceding problems is serious. Both could possibly lead to ineffective educational programming that does not address the child's unique needs and strengths. Therefore, parents should participate actively in the eligibility meeting and not wait for such difficulties to occur before entering the special education maze. By following the suggestions made to this point, you will often be able to head off conflicts. And if that is accomplished, you are halfway through the maze. If, despite your active participation, either of these problems does occur, you may request additional evaluations that may clarify your child's special needs through an Independent Educational Evaluation at your own expense or at the school's expense. You may also challenge the eligibility team's findings through the procedures described in Chapter 14. Don't forget, if your child is declared ineligible for services, or if you feel the team has classified your child incorrectly, you do not have to accept these results.

A Final Look at Evaluation and Eligibility

Evaluation and eligibility determination are key phases in the special education cycle. An accurate, perceptive evaluation will pinpoint your child's specific learning problems and often may identify the causes of those difficulties. A valid evaluation, therefore, is essential to a fair and reliable determination of your child's eligibility to receive special education services.

Evaluation results, unfortunately, do not always provide clear, precise insights into your child's learning problems and their causes. When this is the case, the eligibility meeting takes on an even greater importance in your child's educational future. During this meeting, school professionals will review evaluation results, other records, and verbal testimony. They will then interpret what this often confusing information means for your child's future educational placement. You cannot allow this meeting and these decisions to take place without your active participation. By following the previous suggestions for obtaining and in-

WHAT YOU CAN DO NOW

1. Gather up the evaluation results and decode them.
2. Use this information to investigate eligibility categories, and select one or more that best describes your child and offers services you think will help him the most.
3. Prepare a parent statement, and include information you feel must be presented so the committee has the best opportunity to understand your child's needs.
4. Consider whether your child should participate, and if so, how. You may choose to talk to him about it and discuss his role in the meeting.
5. If he plans to attend the meeting, talk with him about what you can both do if the meeting becomes uncomfortable—perhaps you don't agree with the interpretation given to the evaluation results.
6. Take notes at the meeting.
7. If you don't understand the definition of the disability your child is believed to have, ask to have the definition clarified. Keep asking until you understand it well enough so you can summarize it yourself.
8. If you disagree with the committee's recommendations and want to challenge them, read through Chapter 14. You may also want to investigate whether a 504 Plan, described in Chapter 15, would meet your child's needs.

terpreting school records, for evaluation troubleshooting, and for participating in the eligibility meeting, you will be able to exert maximum personal influence in the decision-making process. You will have an active voice in your child's educational planning, and, even if your opinion does not prevail, your systematic planning for the meeting will lay the groundwork for seeking a remedy through the procedures described in Chapter 14, or for investigating an alternate route, such as a 504 Plan, introduced in Chapter 15.

7. THE INDIVIDUALIZED EDUCATION PROGRAM
Road Maps, Sign Posts, One-Way Streets

Congratulations! You are well on your way toward navigating the maze. You are now ready to help develop your child's Individualized Education Program (IEP). The first step is to understand the parts and purposes of the IEP.

The Individualized Education Program describes the special education and services specifically designed to meet the needs of a child with disabilities. The program is developed at one or more IEP meetings, and its provisions are detailed in writing in an IEP planning document. In other words, the IEP is a map that will direct special education services and supports that will help your child succeed in academics, develop socially, and be equipped with necessary day-to-day living skills.

The IEP Written Document

You play a vital role in developing the IEP —the written description of the program tailored to fit your child's unique educational needs. The IEP is developed *jointly* by parents, educators, and, often, the person for whom the plans are being made, your *child*. It includes:

- Goals for your child, based on her current levels of functioning; these are developed by everyone involved in planning and providing services;
- Where your child will be educated, sometimes referred to as educational placement;
- The services necessary to reach the goals listed in the IEP. The IEP also includes the date services will begin and end, how long they will last, and how often they are provided;

■ How the curriculum may be modified to fit your child's individualized needs, and what accommodations and supports will make it easier for your child to learn and demonstrate what she can do;

■ The way in which your child's progress will be measured.

The IEP serves multiple functions:

■ It is an outline of, and management tool for, your child's special education program.

■ It defines your child's needs, what will be provided to meet those needs, and how to tell if those needs are met.

■ It is the official agreement you have with the school system and includes the resolution of any differences you and the school system may have had.

■ It is the commitment in writing of the resources the school agrees to provide.

For all of these reasons, the Individualized Education Program—both the document and the process through which it is developed—is the cornerstone of special education.

The sections of an IEP are:
1. A Description of Your Child—Present Level of Performance
2. Hoped-for Achievements—Measurable Annual Goals
3. Checking Up—Reviewing Your Child's Progress
4. What Services Will Help Your Child: Special Education and Related Services
5. Duration of Services: Who, Where, When, How Often, and How Much?
6. Where Your Child Receives Services: Placement/Least Restrictive Environment
7. Everyone Gets Tested: Participation in State and District-wide Assessments
8. Preparing for Graduation: Transition Planning
9. Just for Your Child: Consideration of Special Factors

IEP Part 1: A Description of your Child— Present Level of Performance

The first component of the IEP answers the question "Who is this child?" After all, everyone involved in your child's education must come to know the person described in her written program. Basic identifying information, such as name, age, and address, is included. This section of the IEP also contains a description of your child as she is right now. The Present Level of Performance includes a description of:

- the child's current level of educational and behavioral performance,
- the child's academic and functional needs,
- the effect of her disability on academic and nonacademic achievements,
- the child's learning style.

This information is written in a space on the IEP document labeled *Present Level of Functioning and Academic Performance,* or simply *Present Level,* or something similar, depending upon your local school system's IEP format.

You have already collected information necessary to contribute to a description of your child's present level of performance. In Chapter 2, Strengthening Exercise #2, you filled out a column in the Developmental Achievement Chart labeled *Can Do* in each of the developmental areas. In Chapter 5, in the Four-Step Record Decoder, you recorded *strengths* and accomplishments in each developmental area. The *Can Do* and *Strengths* are the information sources for your child's present level of functioning. The following chart presents examples parents have gathered from each source.

Development Achievement Chart
CAN DO ■ sets the table completely and correctly ■ catches the school bus, transfers to the subway, and gets to school on time ■ follows a recipe to bake a cake ■ rolls over from front to back ■ skips rope when others turn the rope
Four-Step Record Decoder

STRENGTHS
■ follows two commands
■ knows the multiplication table through the 5's
■ consistently uses the "m" sound to indicate the need for "more"
■ on Peabody Individual Achievement Test (PIAT):
    Reading recognition 2.3 grade level
    Reading comprehension 1.6 grade level
    Math 2.0 grade level
■ uses a head pointer on the typewriter to spell words

Besides providing information about your child's development, in Part 1 of the IEP you have the opportunity to contribute your very important information about your child's unique learning style. Be sure to include written descriptions of your child's way of approaching a learning situation. A new teacher may need weeks or months to discover the way in which your child learns best. You can help the teacher and your child avoid some frustrations by including in the "present level" such descriptions as:

- He needs a quiet, secluded place for concentrated work.
- She learns quickly when working in a small group of children.
- He understands and learns better what he hears rather than what he sees.
- She imitates other children and learns from them.

These descriptions of *Can Do, Strengths, and Learning Style* are the substance of the first part of the IEP. Just listing test scores, numerical attainment of grade level, IQ score, age equivalent, or simply naming your child's disability is insufficient. Descriptive statements are required in order for everyone involved in teaching your child to know her. The description of her present level of performance must be as complete and accurate as possible, for it is the foundation upon which the second part of the IEP, goals and objectives, is built.

IEP Part 2: Hoped-for Achievements—Measurable Annual Goals

In the second section of the IEP, you and the other members of the IEP team set measurable annual goals that will help your child master the knowledge, skills, or behaviors you believe she should attain. These goals—and objectives, when used—are based upon her present level of performance.

Before thinking about specific goals for your child, it's important to understand the process of setting goals—specific goals. We set goals for ourselves and for others all the time. What are goals? Simply stated, goals are results to be achieved. You set goals for what you would like to do. You might set a goal to buy a new car, to lose ten pounds, to take a family vacation, or to plant a vegetable garden. To set specific goals, you have to answer many questions. For example, to plan a vacation you might consider:

Who will go with you? The whole family? Should we invite the grandparents?

What will you do? Go camping? Visit relatives? Swim in the ocean?

How will you get there? By car? By bus?

Where will you go? To the mountains? To the beach?

When will you go and how long will you stay? Early summer? Late summer? To stay forever?

After you and your family have made these decisions, you could write the following goal for your vacation plans:

Goal: My family will drive to the mountains to camp for one week beginning August 4.

This goal for a family vacation contains five necessary ingredients or parts. It answers *who? will do what? how? where?* and *when?* These five basic parts are necessary for all clearly stated goals.

Goals for an IEP are structured in much the same way. Goals are an expression of results to be achieved in the long run. Annual measurable goals state what your child is expected to do in one year. Each goal must be written as:

    1. a positive statement that . . .

    2. describes a measurable and observable skill.

A well-written goal not only tells what skill your child will achieve but also is written in such a way that you and others can observe the achievement. Many IEPs contain vague goals whose outcomes are not observable or measurable.

Poorly Written Goals:
- Eduardo will communicate better.
- Nina will improve in reading.
- Isabel will improve in math.
- Tom will know what will help him do better in school.

None of these poorly written goals fulfills both criteria of being:

    1. a positive statement that

    2. describes an observable skill.

None of these poorly written goals contains all five essential parts:

    Who? . . . will achieve?

    What? . . . skill or behavior?

    How? . . . in what manner or at what level?

    Where? . . . in what setting or under what conditions?

    When? . . . by what time? an ending date?

A well-written goal contains all five parts.

Well-written Goals:
- Eduardo will increase his sign language vocabulary to 300 words as described in the sign language notebook that travels between home and school by June 30.

Short-term Objectives

In the past, IDEA required that a student's IEP include short-term objectives or benchmarks for each goal. IDEA 2004 eliminated this requirement for most students with disabilities. Short-term objectives are now only required for students who are being tested on a different basis than students in the general education curriculum. (See the section below on "IEP Part 7: Everyone Gets Tested: Participation in State and District-wide Assessments.") However, many parents and school personnel find that including short-term objectives can be helpful in understanding how to implement the IEP and reviewing for progress.

If you believe that the measurable annual goal is sufficient, or if your child's school does not include short-term objectives because they are not required, it is even more important for the IEP to contain specific ways for your child's progress to be measured in the IEP.

Objectives are intermediate steps taken to reach the long-range goal. Just as there are specific interim tasks necessary to make your vacation run smoothly, there are small steps or accomplishments your child needs to make in order to reach the annual goals written on her IEP. Short-term objectives are the steps to be taken between the "present level of performance" and the "annual goal." Short-term objectives contain the same five basic parts as annual goals—the who, what, how, where, and when.

An example of a well-written goal, based upon the present level of performance, with appropriate short-term objectives, is found below. This goal, written by Jamie's parents and teachers, is in the developmental category of movement.

Annual Goal: Jamie will walk upstairs, using one foot per tread, without assistance, at home and at school, by June 1.

Present Level of Performance: Jamie walks steadily on flat ground but goes up the stairs on his hands and knees.

Objective: Jamie will walk upstairs with two feet per tread, holding the handrail and an adult's hand, by October 15.

Objective: Jamie will walk upstairs with two feet per tread, holding only the handrail, by December 1.

Objective: Jamie will walk upstairs one foot per tread, holding the handrail and an adult's hand, by March 15.

The goal and each of the objectives fulfill the requirements for well-written goals and objectives. They describe milestones for Jamie's accomplishment that can be observed within a specific timeframe as he works toward the goal of climbing stairs unassisted. If there were no specific objectives for this measurable goal, the parent would have to make sure that the regular progress reports described in IEP Part 3 of this chapter provided enough information to determine whether Jamie is making sufficient progress on his goals.

- Nina will improve reading level from the 2ⁿᵈ grade reading level to the 4ᵗʰ grade reading level, as measured by the Monitoring Basic Skills Progress tool by May 25.
- Isabel will move from the 1ˢᵗ grade to the 2ⁿᵈ grade level in math as measured by Yearly Progress Pro or similar assessment program by June 1.
- Tom will be able to identify and ask for necessary help (sometimes referred to as accommodations) on his IEP by November 15.

Each of these well-written goals is a positive statement describing an observable skill. They answer the questions of who? will do what? how? where? and when?

You may have many questions as you think about goals and/or objectives for your child. For example:

1. How can I know if a goal is reasonable for my child?

The answer to this question lies in part with the IEP meeting. At the IEP meeting, a group of people, including parents, specialists, and past and present teachers who are knowledgeable of the child and knowledgeable of child development and disabilities, are brought together to discuss reasonable expectations. Goals are set while looking at present levels of performance—what she can do now—at the rate she has been developing thus far, and at the sequence and timing of normal growth and development. In some cases, a more intensive remediation may be necessary so that your child will be better able to keep up with the curriculum or meet a longer term goal. You, or the teacher, do not have to set goals alone. The whole IEP team and other experts work together.

2. How do goals in the IEP relate to the curriculum being used?

There should be a direct relationship between the IEP goals, and the instruction, or curriculum, the child is receiving in the classroom. For example, Jamie's parents asked the physical therapist to describe the sequence of skills Jamie would be working on in therapy sessions so they could support his learning at home. Nina's parents learned more about her reading curriculum so they could see whether she was on a path to meeting her reading goal. The IEP, however, is not intended to be as detailed as an instructional plan. The IEP is to provide the general direction that is to be taken and serves as the basis for the instructional plan (with checkpoints) for each child.

3. Must goals be written on the IEP for the parts of her program in the general education classroom?

Generally, goals are required only for special education services. Goals cover those academic and functional areas in which your child has special problems. If any changes are necessary for your child to participate in the general education classroom, there may be modified goals, based on your child's individualized situation. However, it is more common to specify the modifications, supports, or accommodations that will be provided in your child's general education environments in the *Related Services* section of the IEP. For instance, the sixth grade science curriculum may be modified so that a student who is developmentally at the second grade level can still learn and benefit in that classroom. A child who has a visual impairment may need to use a tape recorder in a lecture class, or sit close to the lecturer. Any specific help that is required in a general education classroom is referred to as an accommodation, and must be noted in her IEP. (See page 102.)

4. Is the general education teacher required to be informed of the contents of a student's IEP?

IDEA requires each general education teacher to have access to the student's IEP and understand her responsibilities for implementing it. She must make sure modifications/accommodations in the IEP are instituted properly in her classroom. General education teachers contribute important information and perspectives in the development of the IEPs for special education students in their classrooms. In addition, the IEP should identify how the special educator or other specialist will consult or give assistance to the general classroom teacher.

In practice, school districts vary as to how much information flows between regular teachers and special education teachers. Talk to each of your child's teachers to make sure they are informed of her educational needs. You may find it necessary to request a joint conference with all of your child's teachers and specialists in order to coordinate the various aspects of her IEP.

5. Is it necessary for parents to learn to write good IEP goals?

Some parents have found that by understanding the essential requirements for writing measurable annual goals with built-in monitoring checkpoints and by applying them to their child, they can write meaningful and measurable goals. Other parents prefer to leave the actual writing of IEPs to the educators who have the training and experience to develop them. They are careful, however, to know in which developmental areas they feel their child needs special attention. By knowing how measurable annual goals are structured, they are able to critique and offer suggestions concerning the goals and/or objectives written by the educators.

In either case, the better you understand the nature of good IEPs and your child's abilities and problems, the more effective you will be as a member of the educational planning team. With your help, goals and/or objectives can be written very specifically for your child's needs and can allow you and her teachers to assess her rate of growth and her developmental progress.

6. What if parents and the committee disagree about whether a child needs short-term objectives included in her IEP? Without objectives included in my child's IEP, how can I keep track of her progress toward her annual goals?

Objectives are only *required* for students who take alternate assessments instead of the standardized statewide assessments taken by students who are not in special education. This is discussed and determined in a different section of the IEP. (See pages 105-106.) Parents can request that objectives be specified, pending a decision about the statewide assessments. However the school does not have to specify objectives in the case of most students. If your child's IEP does not include measurable objectives, the IEP must still specify meaningful and specific ways for you to check your child's progress. (See the next section.)

IEP Part 3: Checking Up-Reviewing Your Child's Progress

To find out whether your child is making progress, you and your child's teachers periodically will assess how your child is progressing in meeting her goals. The critical element in monitoring comes in writing clear, measurable, observable goals. Take, for instance, an annual goal that Eduardo will increase his sign language vocabulary use from 150 to 300 words and ask for help in his classroom and speech therapy by June 30. To evaluate the goal, parents and teachers might ask the following questions:

1. How many words can Eduardo sign right now?
2. What teaching methods will be used to teach Eduardo?
3. What would be a sequence of skill acquisition?
4. How will progress be measured to see if Eduardo's vocabulary is increasing?
5. How often will the teacher let you know about Eduardo's progress?
6. How is Eduardo using his sign language vocabulary in everyday communication?

Specific goals such as those written for Eduardo allow parents and teachers to ask critical questions about his progress. Checking up on his progress allows the team to make adaptations to the instruction, if things don't seem to be working. If Eduardo seems to be learning very quickly, the team may increase the number of words required so that Eduardo can improve his ability to communicate and make up for lost time.

The IEP specifies how progress will be measured and when parents will be notified of progress. In most cases, parents receive progress reports when the school's regular report cards are issued. However, for certain goals, parents may want to be informed of progress on a weekly basis so that they can gauge whether the approach is appropriate and is working. Other goals that are included in the IEP may not need as frequent reporting of progress; or the goals may not be addressed during a particular reporting period. However, parents will want to understand why the goal is not being addressed, and when the teacher will begin work on that goal.

Optimally, progress on goals is measured using what is called criterion-referenced assessment. These are assessments that have been standardized so that different individuals measuring the same child would come up with the same results. These types of assessments can help teachers and parents track progress over the years and have a better understanding of what works or doesn't work for a particular child.

Very often in the space on the IEP for "objective criteria and evaluation procedures" you will see written "teacher-made tests" or "teacher assessment." These assessments may offer useful information for measuring progress, but be sure you understand what is meant by these terms. What will they be? When will they be given? Are there other ways of measuring progress? Tape recordings, examples of schoolwork, classroom observations, completed projects, standardized tests, and many other techniques are useful in evaluating your child's progress.

By using information from a variety of sources, the teaching team comprised of teachers, specialists, and parents can measure progress in a student's growth and learning. At least once a year, and at any other time when a teacher or parent requests it, a meeting is held to review progress toward goals. Regular reviews of your child's IEP help you track progress.

IEP Part 4: What Services Will Help— Special Education and Related Services

To meet measurable annual academic and functional goals, the IEP must identify special education and related services, along with accommodations and modifications, so that your child can

■ advance appropriately toward meeting the annual goals in the IEP;

- be involved in and make progress in the general education curriculum;
- participate in extracurricular and other nonacademic activities; and
- be educated and participate with other children with and without disabilities.

Whenever possible, teachers and other specialists are to provide specialized instruction and accommodations for students with disabilities based upon proven techniques identified by other professionals in the field. This is called peer-reviewed research. See the Resource section for places to find out more about research.

Related Services

Related services supplement the educational services provided in the classroom. They may also help a student improve functional skills in the developmental areas (communication, movement, social skills, etc.). Related services are defined as "transportation and such developmental, corrective and other supportive services that are needed to help a child benefit from special education." Related services include:

- transportation (e.g., a wheelchair accessible bus or a bus with an aide)
- speech-language pathology and audiology services
- interpreting services (for children who are deaf, hard of hearing, or deaf/blind)
- psychological services
- physical and occupational therapy
- recreation, including therapeutic recreation
- early identification and assessment of disabilities
- counseling services (including rehabilitation counseling)
- orientation and mobility services
- medical services for diagnostic and evaluation purposes
- school health services
- social work services
- parent counseling and training
- assistive technology devices or services

See the Glossary for definitions.

Just as overall goals are written for special education services, goals are written to describe what your child will achieve through the provision of related services. If your child needs related services such as speech therapy or a special adaptive physical education program, goals must be written in each specialized area. "Bonnie Jean will receive speech therapy" or "Bonnie Jean will be in adaptive P.E." are not acceptable ways to describe the services. Goals must be written to describe what the child will accomplish in language or physical development. For example, if Bonnie Jean's present level of performance in language describes her use of two-word phrases, an example of a goal for speech-language therapy might be: "Bonnie Jean will speak in three-word sentences using noun, verb, and object construction in the classroom and speech therapy by May 15." This goal, built on her present level of functioning, alerts all teachers and her parents to work consistently toward the next step in her growth in communication skills.

Supplementary Aids and Services, Accommodations, and Modifications

Supplementary Aids and Services

Supplementary Aids and Services are different from related services. They are aids, services, and other supports that are provided in general education classes, other education settings, and in extracurricular and nonacademic settings to enable children with disabilities to be educated with nondisabled children to the maximum extent appropriate. This might mean an instructional assistant who helps a child with autism remain focused on the assignment and to behave appropriately. Or it could mean providing a walker to a high school student with balance problems so she can move from class to class without being knocked over by others in the hectic hallways.

Accommodations

Accommodations are supports that are provided to a child throughout the school day, that do not significantly alter what is being taught or how she participates in school activities. Examples of accommodations are preferential seating (to help the student focus or see the board), extended time for tests, daily communication logs to share information between school and home, use of spell check and/or computer, enlarged print, and books on tape. Children who are using accommodations are learning the same material as children who are not using accommodations; they are just receiving supports that help mitigate the effects of their disabilities on their ability to participate at school.

Modifications

Modification to the curriculum occurs when: a child receives instruction at a different academic level, is tested for different knowledge or skills than other students in the class, or has other fundamental changes to the instruction or testing method that assists her in learning.

Examples of modifications:

■ A child is working on writing single words or sentences, when the rest of the class is perfecting their essay-writing skills.

- A child is tested through a video-taped question and answer session that is reviewed to determine if she has learned the material.
- A child uses an alternate textbook to cover the course material in a grade-level history class.

The School's Legal Duty

Once you and school personnel have determined through the evaluation process that your child needs certain related services (supplementary aids and services, accommodations, or modifications) and have included them in the IEP, the school system has a legal duty to provide them in the least restrictive environment. This duty exists even when the particular related services are not, for any reason, currently available within the school system. For example, if the school system had no employees qualified to provide physical therapy, social work services, or speech-language therapy but your child needed them to benefit from her program, the school system would have to provide these services by contracting with outside professionals. This may be a significant point of potential conflict between parents and schools, especially given restricted school funding and a school's potential reluctance or unwillingness to work to find a solution that provides your child with needed services. However, the school is required, even given funding limitations, to provide all services on your child's IEP.

Decisions about Services, Modifications, and Aids

You may have many questions as you think about possible related services the school might provide your child. What kinds of services does she need? For what length of time each day or week? Who will provide the services? How can I ensure that my child does not have to leave the classroom to receive related services so often that it interrupts her regular school program? How can I make certain that therapists and teachers talk together so there is consistency in my child's program?

To answer these questions, you will need to discuss your child and her needs with teachers, therapists, administrators, and other school personnel. Some parents find it helpful to consult specialists outside the school system, discuss their child's need for related services with physicians, and talk to other parents whose children require similar services. Information and materials on related services available from the organizations listed in the Resources may also assist you in answering these questions.

After you have accumulated information from a variety of sources, you will be able to weigh and balance the needs of your child for related services, the different ways and times for integrating services into your child's program, and the potential benefits your child will receive from those services. In this manner you can determine your priorities for your child's related services as you prepare for and participate in the IEP meeting.

IEP Part 5: Duration of Services—Who, Where, When, How Often, and How Much?

You have moved through four stops along the IEP corridor in the special education maze. The fifth stop is to help make sure you won't get stuck in one place. In this section of the IEP, your child's team determines who will provide the services, where the services will be provided, and the starting times and duration for your child's program. Once the goals are written and the services decided upon, the school system has a duty to begin these services without undue delay. Most states specify the number of days within which a program must begin once parents have signed permission for the program. At no time is a child to wait at home for special education services to begin, unless you and the school system have agreed upon a temporary homebound program. Occasionally, a temporary or interim placement is required, to which parents and the school system must agree.

Under ordinary circumstances, your child's team will determine a starting day for the beginning of each of your child's services. In addition, the expected duration for each service is recorded. The expected duration might be six weeks for a related service of counseling with a social worker, to be followed by an assessment of progress and a recommendation for either continuing this service or ending it. Or the expected duration may be a nine-month school year for such parts of the program as classroom placement.

In general, the long-term duration for services should be projected no further than one year. This is because IDEA requires an annual review of the services provided in the IEP. Once a year at the IEP meeting, your child's special education services are reviewed to determine whether they are still appropriate and are provided in the least restrictive environment. This annual review, discussed more fully in Chapter 10, ensures that no child will be left in special education without a careful examination of her changing needs.

In addition to specifying the long-term duration of your child's services, this part of the IEP should also include short-term, daily hours for each service. For example, "Jessica will attend speech therapy twice a week, for one-half hour each session." Certainly, parents will want to get specific information on the times and timing of all parts of their child's school program. Too often children who receive special services miss some of the most important parts of the instruction in their classroom. For example, when Will went to the learning disabilities resource room for special instruction in math, he missed his reading group in the general education classroom. He was falling behind in reading until his parents talked to his regular class teacher and the resource room teacher. As a result, both teachers adjusted their schedules in order to accommodate Will's instruction in reading and in math.

Extended School Year

Some children with disabilities might require more than the usual number of school days in order to receive an appropriate education. Children eligible for an extended school year include those who show significant regression during breaks in their education and those who regain their losses so slowly that they would be unlikely to attain their potential level of self-sufficiency and independence without a sustained program. In these cases, the decision to provide additional schooling beyond the normal school year must be made on an individual basis and written into the IEP.

IEP Part 6: Everyone Gets Tested—Participation in State and District-wide Assessments

All students must participate in state, district-wide, and local assessments, with appropriate accommodations. If a student cannot participate in the regular assessment, she must take an alternate assessment. This alternate assessment must be aligned with challenging academic standards.

The IEP has a section that specifies how your child will participate in state and district-wide assessments. This section specifies needed accommodations and/or modifications that will be used for the test. The tests that are given to all students in a district usually parallel the general education curriculum. Parents need to become familiar with these tests, how they are administered, allowable accommodations or modifications, test preparation opportunities, and consequences associated with taking the tests.

For example, some states do not allow students to pass to the next grade until they have passed their grade-level assessment. When a student is unlikely to pass the test, even with extensive modifications, it is important to discuss how the student will be able to move on to the next grade and how the student will be able to keep up with peers to the extent feasible. Some states also have certain statewide assessments a student must pass in order to graduate with a regular diploma.

Even if a student is not going to be taking a grade-level assessment, she still will need to take an alternate assessment. There may be implications if this option is selected. Find out whether students taking alternate assessments take classes in the general education classrooms or whether they are educated in separate classes. If so, the student may be limited to taking "basic skills" or "life skills" classes and not be able to take more academically challenging courses. In some cases, students who take alternate assessments are not able to graduate with regular diplomas.

It should be noted that any accommodations and/or modifications used in taking the statewide and district-wide assessments must also be normally used by the child when taking tests. For more information, most states have websites that offer sample tests and curriculum information, along with graduation requirements. Your parent training and information center listed in the Resources at the end of this book can also be a good source of information.

IEP Part 7: After Graduation— Transition Planning

This section identifies the services, support, and plans that help the student transition to life after she completes special education and moves on from schooling. By age 15, or before, as appropriate, your child should take an active role in planning and attending her IEP. Transition planning is described in detail in Chapters 12 and 13.

IEP Part 8: Just for Your Child— Consideration of Special Factors

As previously stated, the IEP contains information about the strengths of your child, your concerns, as parents, and the results of initial or most recent evaluation information about your child, along with her academic, developmental, and functional needs. IDEA also identifies special factors that the IEP team must consider.

Behavior

If your child's behavior sometimes gets in the way of her learning or that of others, the team must consider the use of what are called positive behavioral interventions and supports, as well as other strategies to address that behavior. If you, the teacher, or your child is concerned about behavior (disruptive as well as school phobia), the IEP should include information about a functional behavior assessment (FBA) and what needs to happen for your child to behave appropriately. Positive behavioral supports might include changes to the environment (e.g., changes that make the classroom less overstimulating to your child) or instruction (e.g., rewards or more frequent breaks) that will help your child with her behavior. Positive behavioral supports are usually *not* punishments or consequences for inappropriate behavior.

There is insufficient space to give this topic justice in this book, but if you have concerns about your child's behavior, contact your state's parent training and information center or consult with other sites included in the Resources.

Communication or Language Needs

The team should consider the language needs related to the IEP for students with limited English proficiency.

In the case of a child who is deaf or hard of hearing, the IEP must address the child's language and communication needs, opportunities for direct communication with peers and professional personnel in the child's language, and communication mode (often sign language). If a child uses sign language, she should also receive instruction in sign language.

Braille

In the case of a child who is blind or visually impaired, the team needs to evaluate the child's reading and writing skills and determine whether instruction in Braille or the use of Braille is appropriate to her current or future needs. If so, the school must provide for instruction in Braille and the use of Braille.

Assistive Technology

Whether included in the IEP in the present level of performance, as a goal, related service, modification, or accommodation, assistive technology must be considered for each child. Every child with disabilities may not need assistive technology, but the IEP document must indicate that assistive technology was discussed. If the team decides that your child doesn't need assistive technology, the team must write a statement on the IEP indicating the reasons why.

IDEA defines an assistive technology device as "any item, piece of equipment, or product system, whether acquired commercially off the shelf, modified, or customized, that is used to increase, maintain, or improve functional capabilities of a child with a disability." For example, assistive devices may include language boards, a special chair, a voice output computer, and a head pointer. This category does not include surgically implanted devices, such as cochlear implants.

Assistive technology service is "any service that directly assists an individual with a disability in the selection, acquisition, or use of an assistive technology device." For instance, an assistive technology professional may conduct an assessment to identify available and appropriate technology devices. Another service might include monitoring a student's use of assistive technology, training for the student and/or staff in use of a device, or programming a communication or switch device for a student's particular need.

As assistive devices become more and more available for people with disabilities, schools are faced with decisions to: a) identify and acquire technology devices appropriate to the needs of their students with disabilities; b) train staff in the use of the devices; c) identify appropriate use of computers, communication devices, and other technology in the classroom; and d) finance the cost of the related service.

The IEP Planning Chart

Now that you have learned about the various parts of the IEP, you may wish to copy and complete the chart on pages 110 and 111 to help you prepare for the IEP meeting. Concentrate on the areas of development in which your child has particular problems and needs special services to help in overcoming or compensating for those problems.

In the first column, write a brief description of your child's strengths and accomplishments. Write down what your child has recently learned and accomplished. Consider whether her recent accomplishments have opened doors for learning new skills. This helps you and others think about the assets she currently has and build upon those assets.

In column two, note challenges or needs you would like the IEP team to address. List activities or skills that are not easy or possible for your child to do, including the biggest hurdles and hardest challenges that you and your child want to master.

In column three, write down goals and priorities—what you and your child would most like to accomplish next, that can be addressed in the IEP.

In the fourth column, list the services and supports, and any assistive technology your child may need to address her needs and accomplish her goals. Include any accommodations and modifications that you think she may need.

In the fifth column, write your ideas about when and how you will know that your child is making progress over the next year. Put in key milestones and dates, if you can, to help you see if the IEP is working or if adjustments are needed.

An example of an IEP Planning Chart filled out by Sara's parents is on pages 112-113. A sample of Sara's IEP is found on pages 114-116.

Conclusion

The work you have done in filling out the IEP Planning Chart will lay the foundation for your active, informed participation in the important decisions to be made about your child's IEP and special education services. Once your planning is completed, you will be able to make decisions about WHERE your child will receive special education services. Before you go on to the IEP meeting itself, the next chapter describes important information about placement.

WHAT YOU CAN DO NOW

1. Fill out the IEP Planning Chart.
2. List the most important areas your child needs help in, and list ideas about related services.

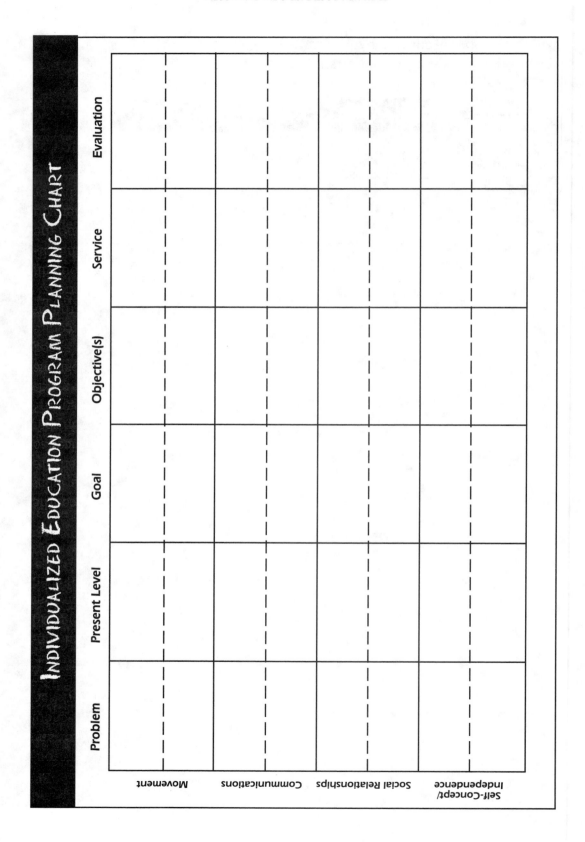

INDIVIDUALIZED EDUCATION PROGRAM PLANNING CHART

	Problem	Present Level	Goal	Objective(s)	Service	Evaluation
Movement						
Communications						
Social Relationships						
Self-Concept/ Independence						

INDIVIDUALIZED EDUCATION PROGRAM PLANNING CHART (CONTINUED)

	Problem	Present Level	Goal	Objective(s)	Service	Evaluation
Senses						
Thinking						
Learning Style						

INDIVIDUALIZED EDUCATION PROGRAM PLANNING CHART

	Problem	Present Level	Goal	Objective(s)	Service	Evaluation
Movement	Uncoordinated	She gives up in the middle of an obstacle course	To find her way across an obstacle course	1. Practice skills for individual sections of course 2. Understand what to do on entire course	Adaptive PE	By June 30 she will complete obstacle course unassisted
Communications	Trouble drawing human figures	Draws simple shapes and people figures	To draw more complex figures in a recognizable way	1. Draw shapes using a stencil 2. Draw shapes without stencil; add on features	Special Ed. Classroom and reg. ed. art class	By June 30 Sara's human figure will include 10 specific parts
	Can't think of common words	Forgets names of common household items—hairbrush, ketchup, radio	To increase her ability to use the right words	1. Work with new vocabulary words 2. Use new words correctly and spontaneously	Special Ed. Classroom	Tape recorded conversations
	Poor sequencing skills	Talks about daily activities with no attention to the proper order	To tell about her day or weekend in sequential order	1. Sara will talk about single experiences 2. She will keep an activity calendar	Speech/Language Therapy	Tape recordings (compare to 9/96 tape)
Social Relationships	Frequently tells peers what to do	Insists her friends play Barbie dolls or she won't play	With a classmate, will plan a project in a "give and take" way	1. Plan with a friend under adult direction and praise 2. Work with classmate independently	Special Ed. Classroom	observation of spec. Ed. teacher
	She feels different from others	Asks why she is in special class and her sister is not	Sara will describe ways she is same/different from a friend	1. Describe same/different clothing 2. Identify some different personality traits	special Ed. and regular classes; home with family and friends	observations; Notes
Self-Concept/ Independence	Makes negative comments about herself when she makes mistakes	She says "I hate myself!" when she does something wrong	Sara will praise herself verbally for a job well-done	1. She will smile when praised 2. Imitate a shoulder shrug when she makes mistakes	All teachers and family	Teacher and parent observations
	Always wants mom to be around	Sits and waits alone on front porch for long periods if mom is not home on time	To make independent decision to go to neighbors when she gets home from bus alone	1. Make a chart describing plan for alone time 2. Explain plan to teacher and neighbor	Spec. Ed. teacher, home and neighbor	Parent observation; Chart completed

INDIVIDUALIZED EDUCATION PROGRAM PLANNING CHART (CONTINUED)

	Problem	Present Level	Goal	Objective(s)	Service	Evaluation
Senses	Doesn't remember details of picture	Remembers vaguely the whole picture but not details	To look at picture and describe more than 2 details	1. Identify missing details in picture by drawing them in 2. She will name missing details	Spec. Ed. classroom	Oral test
	Difficulty following oral directions	Follows one direction at a time	To carry out 3 directions given at one time	1. Follow one command correctly 2. Repeat directions aloud before acting	Spec. Ed. classroom; Speech Therapy; Home	Informal teacher made tests
Thinking	Disorganized way of describing a story she has read	Tells about story in a disorganized way; no attention to proper order	To understand and tell main ideas in short stories	1. Describe main character 2. Describe one event 3. Decide on main ideas	Spec. Ed. classroom; Oral Book report time	By June she will present an oral book report and accurately tell main ideas
	Does not understand value of coins	Confuses nickels, dimes, and quarters, both value and name	To buy something and count the change	1. Learn the name and value of each coin 2. Count money with mixed change	Spec. Ed. classroom	Demonstrate use of money
Learning Style	Haphazard planning	Leaves one homework subject to start another, then leaves both unfinished	To plan alone how to do her school work	1. With adult help, she will learn to break tasks into small steps 2. Make her own charts	Spec. Ed. classroom	Completed planning charts showing accomplishment
	Very concrete—not able to think abstractly	Doesn't understand jokes or puns that are the least bit subtle	To learn to tell a joke	1. Read a riddle— explain meaning to teacher 2. Tell riddle from memory	Speech/Language Therapy	Tell the class a joke or riddle

INDIVIDUALIZED EDUCATION PROGRAM

Student name: Sara Austin

Initial IEP: 9/04

Current IEP: 9/07

School: Queensbury

Grade: 4th

IEP Review: 6/08

In Attendance at IEP Meeting:

School District Representative

Signature: _____ Date: _____

Parents

Signature: _____ Date: _____

Student

Signature: _____ Date: _____

Special Education Teacher(s)

Signature: _____ Date: _____

General Education Teacher(s)

Signature: _____ Date: _____

Evaluator(s)

Signature: _____ Date: _____

Others

Signature: _____ Date: _____

A statement of measurable annual goals, including academic and functional goals:

Sara will be able to correctly count coins and dollars up to $100 and be able to correctly calculate the total of items adding up to $50 and make correct change by December of this year.

Sara will participate in the intensified reading program, increase her reading fluency, and be reading at the 3rd grade level by April of next year.

Sara will continue to receive OT services and practice her handwriting skills, but will learn keyboarding this year and use a computer for most of her writing assignments. She will be able to type 10 words a minute with no more than 4 errors.

For children with disabilities who take alternate assessments aligned to alternate achievement standards (in addition to the annual goals), a description of benchmarks or short-term objectives.

Sara is taking the regular statewide assessment.

A description of:
- **How the child's progress toward meeting the annual goals will be measured.**
- **When periodic reports on the progress the child is making toward meeting the annual goals will be provided such as through the use of quarterly or other periodic reports, concurrent with the issuance of report cards.**

Sara will receive regular progress monitoring reports on a weekly basis for the intensified reading program.

Sara will receive regular reports of progress on IEP goals quarterly as a part of the report card process.

A statement of the <u>special education and related services</u> and <u>supplementary aids</u> and <u>services,</u> based on peer-reviewed research to the extent practicable, to be provided to the child, or on behalf of the child, and <u>a statement of the program modifications or supports</u> for school personnel that will be provided:

Sara will be in an intensified reading program and remedial special education math program. It is intended that she will be able to accelerate her learning and improve her skills 2 grade levels. She will be in the regular social studies program without support and in a team-taught science program. She will learn keyboarding and use a computer for most of her writing assignments. She needs preferential seating due to her distractibility. She will have tests read to her, as appropriate. Homework will be adapted and parents will be able to help Sara at home with the online supplemental assignments that go with the text or that the teacher posts on her class web page.

An explanation of the extent, if any, to which the child will not participate with nondisabled children in the regular classroom and in extracurricular and other nonacademic activities.

Sara will be in special education reading and math classes specially designed to accelerate her learning so that she can get closer to the level of reading and math of her nondisabled peers.

A statement of any individual appropriate accommodations that are necessary to measure the academic achievement and functional performance of the child on State and district-wide assessments.

Sara will take the regular state assessment in a small group setting with the directions and test items read aloud. This accommodation will not be available for test items on the reading test, as that would invalidate the assessment.

If the IEP Team determines that the child must take an alternate assessment instead of a particular regular State or district-wide assessment of student achievement, a statement of why the child cannot participate in the regular assessment.

The particular regular assessment selected is appropriate for the child. Not applicable.

The projected date for the beginning of the services and modifications and the anticipated frequency, location, and duration of special education and related services and supplementary aids and services and modifications and supports.

Service, Aid or Modification	Frequency	Location	Beginning Date	Duration
Speech-language	½ hr a week	Classroom	9/08	6/09
Occupational therapy	½ hr a week	OT room and computer lab	9/08	6/09

Adapted from the U.S. Department of Education Model Form: Individualized Education Program.

(NOTE: Additional components of the IEP as outlined in Chapter 7 and performance or subject area pages would be completed for Sara Austin's IEP)

8. PLACEMENT
Crossroads and Intersections—Which Way to Go?

It is all well and good to have specific goals and services for your child—but goals and services are not enough! Next come decisions concerning placement. Placement refers to the educational setting in which your child's special education and related services may appropriately be met. This chapter looks at the various considerations to make regarding placement in special education for the first time, considerations about least restrictive environment, private school placement, and how decisions are to be made about placement if your child is suspended or expelled from school.

In years past, children with special education needs were placed in classrooms solely on the basis of disability groupings. For example, all children who used wheelchairs were placed in the same classroom. Similarly, students who had learning problems associated with Down syndrome or other intellectual disabilities were automatically grouped with students with the same disabilities. IDEA forbids an IEP team from assuming that children will be grouped according to their disability category. Clearly, the intent of IDEA is to decide on a student's placement only after the IEP goals and services have been determined by the IEP team (including the student, whenever possible). The placement decision is then made on the basis of the strengths and needs of the student, by choosing where the agreed-upon educational goals and services can appropriately be carried out. But, you ask, on what criteria is this placement decision based? Two equally important factors must be weighed and balanced as you participate in making the placement decision:

1. appropriate education, and
2. the least restrictive environment.

IDEA heralds these two provisions which are the heart of the opportunities for our nation's children with disabilities.

> *"It is the purpose of this Act to ensure that all children with disabilities have available to them . . . a free, appropriate public education that emphasizes special education and related services designed to meet their unique needs and to prepare them for further education, employment and independent living."*

> *"To the maximum extent appropriate, children with disabilities, including children in public or private institutions or other care facilities, are educated with children who are not disabled, and special classes, separate schooling, or other removal of children with disabilities from the regular educational environment occurs only when the nature or severity of the disability of a child is such that education in regular classes with the use of supplementary aids and services cannot be achieved satisfactorily."*

What Is Appropriate Education?

What exactly is meant by the words "appropriate education"? How will you know if your child is receiving an *appropriate education?*

For years, parents, educators, and even judges have disagreed as to what is required under the law to meet the standard of an appropriate education. In 1982 the U.S. Supreme Court provided some clarification when it concluded that an "appropriate education" means the provision of personalized instruction with sufficient therapies or specialized services reasonably calculated to permit a child with disabilities to "benefit from special education." While programs and services that provide only *minimal* academic achievement do not meet the requirement of an appropriate education, the Supreme Court stated that an "appropriate education" did not require programs and services designed to *maximize* a child's potential. Some state legislative standards may exceed the federal requirements. It is important to check your own state's requirements for what is considered an "appropriate education."

The Supreme Court's clarification is important because it reinforces the idea that an appropriate education is personalized to the individual needs of your child. Children in special education are not to be given identical programs just because they have the same disabilities. Further, an appropriate program requires that your child receive programming and services that are reasonably calculated to permit him to benefit from them. This means that the proposed program and services must be designed in terms of content, procedures, and duration to lead to the student's continuing development. Finally, a program which would appear to result in only minimal academic achievement would fail to meet the standard of an appropriate program.

The planning activities you have completed for evaluation, eligibility, and the development of IEP goals and objectives will help you to develop a personalized education program to which your child is entitled. Your close work and contact with teachers and other school professionals during this process will allow you to determine whether your child's program and services will reasonably allow him to make more than minimal progress in the coming year. As the year progresses, you will be able to assess the appropriateness of the program by comparing your child's development with anticipated goals and objectives. Should your child's progress appear minimal or nonexistent after a period of months, you may well question the appropriateness of the program. This situation might call for a special meeting of the IEP committee, as is discussed in Chapter 10 (about checking up.)

Least Restrictive Environment and Inclusion

Once you have designed an appropriate program for your child, you must next determine the "least restrictive environment" in which this program can be provided. The least restrictive environment for a child with disabilities is defined by the extent to which the child will be educated with students who do not have disabilities and in the public school building nearest to home.

Rather than being in separate special education classrooms or a separate school with special teachers, more and more children with disabilities are included in general education classrooms in their home schools. The special education teachers and specialists work alongside the general education teachers. In integrated classrooms, all children—both the children with disabilities and those who do not have disabilities—enjoy friendships and the opportunity to learn from one another. Further, following graduation from school, young people with disabilities are more often ready to move into community jobs and independent living if they have had opportunities to work and learn with their nondisabled peers.

IDEA requires opportunities for students with disabilities to participate in all nonacademic and extracurricular activities in the least restrictive environment. These activities include meals, recess, athletics, assemblies, and special interest groups and clubs. You will want to make sure your child is able to take advantage of these activities with children who do not have disabilities. Chapter 15 discusses the equal access and nondiscrimination provisions of Section 504 of the Rehabilitation Act and the Americans with Disabilities Act as they pertain to children's extracurricular activities.

Many school systems, advocacy groups, and families now emphasize that *all* students with disabilities can be successfully placed in a general education learning environment if appropriate modifications and related services are provided. This move to educate children with disabilities in the general education setting is often called "inclusion." IDEA, however, requires school systems to provide a "continuum of alternative placements" to meet the special education and related services needs of individual children. School districts are required to offer a variety of settings in which a child with disabilities may be placed. These settings range along a continuum from general education classes (classrooms attended by both general education students and students with disabilities), to resource room assistance (rooms dedicated to special education services), to separate classrooms (that best accommodate some students with disabilities, who have needs that make the general education classroom unworkable), to private schools, to residential facilities, hospitals, homebound instruction, and correctional or detention facilities.

When determining the least restrictive placement for children eligible for *preschool* programs, the options are somewhat different. As in all placement decisions, the overriding rule is to determine what is appropriate for each individual child. If a school district has any public school programs for preschool-aged children who do not have disabilities, the district is required to consider placing the children with disabilities in these classes. If the district does not have general education preschool, the IEP team first considers placement in other public preschools, such as Head Start or publicly run daycare programs. Sometimes, the least restrictive placement for a child can be in a private preschool, with the school system providing special education services there as identified in the child's IEP.

Placement Decisions

An IEP team, using the concept of a continuum of alternative placements, must go through a series of steps to arrive at a recommended placement. After formulating the IEP goals and objectives, the first question to be answered is, "What are the specific services needed by the student?" The question of *what* services are needed comes before the second question, which is, "Where can these services best be provided?"

The Least Restrictive Environment (LRE) Worksheet (see page 121) outlines what the IEP team needs to consider in making placement decisions. The IEP team must strive to offer your child the greatest opportunity to be educated with students who do not have disabilities. The *burden* lies with the school system to prove why your child, with or without aids and supports, cannot receive appropriate, individualized education in the general education classroom in your neighborhood school.

LEAST RESTRICTIVE ENVIRONMENT (LRE) WORKSHEET *

To the maximum extent appropriate, students with disabilities are to be educated with students who do not have disabilities. The IEP Team should consider the following:

- ❏ The educational needs of the student reflected in the IEP
- ❏ Opportunities for education with nondisabled peers
- ❏ Student attends neighborhood school that would be attended if he/she didn't have a disability
- ❏ Potential harmful effects on quality of services the student needs
- ❏ Student not removed from regular classroom solely because of needed accommodations or modifications to the curriculum
- ❏ Removal from the general education classroom occurs only if the nature and severity of the student's disability is such that education in the general curriculum classes with the use of supplemental aids and services cannot be satisfactorily achieved
- ❏ Supplementary aids and services that are appropriate and necessary for the student to participate in nonacademic settings such as meals, recess, and extracurricular activities

Primary locations where instruction will be provided:

_____ hrs/week
_____ hrs/week
_____ hrs/week

Primary locations where supplementary aids and services will be provided:
Nonacademic settings (recess, meals, art, music, etc.)

_____ hrs/week
_____ hrs/week

Extracurricular activities (sports, clubs, after school activities, etc.)

_____ hrs/week
_____ hrs/week

Explanation of the extent, if any, to which the child will not participate with nondisabled children in the general education classroom and in extracurricular and other academic activities:

_____
_____
_____
_____
_____
_____

For the first three years of school, for example, Juan was placed in a separate classroom for children with intellectual disabilities. Then his parents and teachers decided that this placement was too restrictive. Now Juan is in the general education classroom with children his own age. A resource teacher comes into the classroom to give him special help in reading and math. In all other subjects, he learns with his classmates. The classroom aide, available to all students in the class, is there to help both Juan and all of the other children as well. Juan's program was based on the two requirements of IDEA:

1. **The Appropriate Educational Services.** The IEP goals include academic achievements, developmental milestones, and social/ emotional growth. Juan receives services from a special education teacher thirty minutes every day to assist him in reading and math.

2. **The Least Restrictive Environment.** Juan's goals can be realized in the general education program, which provides the maximum time for Juan in a classroom with children who do not have disabilities. He will not be separated from his classmates who do not have disabilities for any of his academic, social, or extracurricular activities.

In every special education placement decision, the appropriate education and the least restrictive environment must be given equal consideration. Many people believe that the least restrictive environment requirement means that all children with disabilities will be put into the general education classroom. The least restrictive environment concept, however, must always be coupled with what is an appropriate education for each individual child.

Sally is a fourteen-year-old girl who has a disability which causes her to be in constant physical motion and to talk in a loud voice incessantly and inappropriately. The least restrictive environment for her is a special day class. Sally's IEP team decided that behavioral goals should be the primary focus of her IEP. Because she is so easily distracted, the IEP team believed she would most likely achieve her goals in a small, structured class, without the many distractions of the general education classroom. Her involvement with children who are not disabled is with peer tutors from general education classrooms, attendance at assembly programs, regular physical education, and daily lunch in the cafeteria.

Occasionally, public school systems find that they simply do not have the programs or services required to provide a child with an appropriate education. For example, a small rural school system might find it impossible to hire or to contract with professionals needed to provide highly specialized programs. Even in situations like these, IDEA requires school systems to provide the child with a free, appropriate public education. But, how might the school system do this?

When there are no public programs to meet the child's educational needs, school systems place children in private day or residential schools. The law requires that before choosing this placement option, school officials and parents explore every way possible for delivering a free, appropriate education within the public school system. If an appropriate education cannot be provided within the public schools or through other public institutions within the state, then the school system has a duty to provide the child with an appropriate education in a private school at no expense to the parents.

If a parent believes his child needs to be in a private school and the public school disagrees, the parent must notify the school system at least ten days in advance of removing the child from school. This notice must include:

- the reasons the parent is rejecting the school's proposed placement;
- specific concerns and why the child cannot receive an appropriate education in the program offered by the school;
- the parent's intent to enroll the child in a private school; and
- the expectation that the public school will pay for the private placement.

Below are four examples of special education placements planned in IEP meetings for children:

1. Robert will be in the general education classroom throughout the school day. The itinerant teacher for children with visual impairments will provide talking books, consultation with the teacher about classroom adaptations, and individualized instruction on a one-to-one basis for Robert.

2. Martha's homeroom is the third grade classroom. She will participate in social studies, science, music, and art with her classmates. Reading, arithmetic, spelling, and handwriting goals will be met in a learning disabilities resource classroom. Special physical education will be provided by a teacher trained in working with people with physical disabilities.

3. Claudia will attend a special school for children who are deaf. She will participate on the swimming team in a community recreation program and she will be a member of a scout troop.

4. Martin will spend his day in the autism program at the public school where he will receive intensive applied behavioral analysis training. He will spend art, music, and lunch with his peers with and without disabilities.

Although these four special education placements seem very different, they all fulfill two major requirements under IDEA. They are specifically designed to provide each child an appropriate education in the least restrictive environment.

Visiting Placement Options

Special education is not a place. It is services and supports that will help children with disabilities learn and develop as close to their nondisabled classmates as possible. Nevertheless, *where* your child is educated can have a significant effect on the type and quality of educational services and supports he receives. As you consider possible classroom placements for your child's special education program, plan to visit the school.

Occasionally there is more than one classroom within the school system appropriate to meet the goals and objectives and to provide the related services outlined in your child's IEP. In the same way you offered educators unique, valuable knowledge of your child during the evaluation and eligibility phases, you will also be able to give them particular insight into the kind of environment suited to your child's learning style during the IEP phase. By visiting school classrooms, talking to administrators and teachers, eating in the cafeteria, and observing playground activities, you can assess the different options with your child's needs in mind. You will be able to ask questions and perhaps offer suggestions about adjustments or modifications necessary to respond to your child's unique ways of learning.

Many parents feel uncertain when they visit schools. They wonder what to look for as they observe school programs. The outline below serves as a guide for your observations. It provides questions to ask and guidelines to follow in assessing the classroom's activities, materials, methods, and physical layout. This guide can help you decide whether the suggested placement is compatible with your child's educational needs and his learning style. It can also help you decide if the classroom environment will enable your child to build on his strengths, allowing him to learn in ways he does best. You should find this guide useful when you visit a school or classroom before giving permission for your child to be placed there; you should also find it valuable when you have questions and concerns at parent-teacher conferences

Checking Out Placement Possibilities

Find out what kinds of placement options the school is suggesting, and visit them to see if they are appropriate for your child. The evaluation reports will usually list recommendations, though they are to be only suggestions and not a decision about your child's placement and services. You can also speak with the special education coordinator or director to find out what programs and services are available for children with similar needs as your child.

The following is a guide to help you as you observe and learn more about school settings for your child:

I. Classroom Organization

A. PHYSICAL ENVIRONMENT

1. Layout

   a. How is furniture arranged? (Desks lined up in rows? Tables and chairs for small group work?)

   b. Are there large open areas or is the room divided into smaller components?

   c. Is the furniture the right size for the students? Is special equipment available (e.g., chairs with arm supports, individual study carrels, balance stools, bathroom fixtures at appropriate levels, etc.)?

   d. Where is the classroom located in relationship to the cafeteria? The bathroom? Outdoor areas? The special services?

2. General atmosphere

   a. Is the general atmosphere relaxed or formal? Soothing or stimulating?

B. DAILY SCHEDULE

1. Sequence of Activities

   a. What is the daily schedule? Do students seem to understand the schedule?

   b. Are related services scheduled at times that do not interrupt a child's participation in the ongoing school work?

   c. How does the teacher indicate that one activity is over and another beginning?

2. Consistency

   a. Is the schedule generally the same every day?

   b. Are the same teachers there every day?

3. Variety

   a. Does the daily schedule include active times and quiet times?

   b. Is there provision for daily outdoor activity?

   c. How frequently does the teacher change the pace of activities?

C. SOCIAL ENVIRONMENT

1. Peer interactions

   a. Are students allowed to interact spontaneously with one another? When? How often?

   b. Does the teacher encourage students to cooperate with one another? During schoolwork activities? During free time?

   c. Are there student peers with and without disabilities?

2. Teacher-child interactions
   a. How does the teacher relate to the students?
   b. Does the teacher tolerate and adjust to individual students?
   c. Does the teacher enter into conversations or play situations with students?
3. Values
   a. What values do the teacher and the students seem to hold? Success? Creativity? Social manners? Enthusiasm? Docility? Individual vs. group responsibility? Self-advocacy?
4. Behavior
   a. How is disruptive behavior handled?
   b. What is done to promote respect and the types of behavior that work well in school and in life?

II. Curriculum

A. GOALS AND PRIORITIES

1. What developmental areas are included in the curriculum (i.e., movement, communications, social relationships, independence/self-concept, thinking skills, etc.)?
2. What developmental areas receive emphasis in the classroom? What is not a curriculum priority? Where do academics fit in? Are life skills emphasized?

B. MATERIALS

1. Are the teaching materials concrete or abstract?
2. Are the teaching materials appropriate to the developmental level of the students?
3. Do the materials teach through various senses—vision, touch, hearing? Through movement?
4. Are the materials physically accessible to students?
5. Are the materials designed to interest students?

C. METHODS

1. Groupings
   a. Do students work individually, in small groups, or as a total class?
   b. Are the students grouped homogeneously (all at the same skill level) or heterogeneously (different skill levels in the same group)?
   c. Are the groupings different for different curriculum areas?

2. Teaching style
   a. Does the teacher take a highly structured approach, leading all learning activities? Or does he also allow for spontaneous learning situations?
   b. Does the teacher work individually with students or does he focus more on groups?
   c. Performance expectations
      1. Does the teacher expect all students to perform at approximately the same level?
      2. Does the teacher expect students to wait for their turns or to volunteer answers spontaneously?
      3. Does the teacher expect students to listen to and follow group verbal instructions?
      4. Does the teacher expect students to work independently? Without interrupting with questions for the teacher?
      5. How does the teacher work with regular educators, support staff, and service providers?

When Placement is Disrupted

Sometimes students with disabilities are suspended or expelled from school. There are procedures and protections in place for special education students when this arises.

When a child breaks the school's Code of Conduct, school personnel may order a change of placement to an appropriate interim alternative program or may order a suspension for not more than 10 days. In making the decision whether to order the change of placement, the IEP team is to consider any unique circumstances on a case by case basis.

When considering changing a child's placement for more than ten days, the IEP team conducts a special review to determine whether there is a relationship between the child's disability and the behavior that has resulted in disciplinary action. Such a review is called a "manifestation of determination review." In deciding whether the behavior is due to the child's disability, the IEP team, including the child's parent, considers all relevant information. This information includes evaluation and diagnostic results, information supplied by the parents, observations of the child, and the child's IEP and placement. In essence, the IEP team is asking itself, "Did we properly plan for this child?"

The team considers questions such as the following:

- In relationship to the behavior subject to disciplinary action, were the child's IEP and placement appropriate and were the special education services, supplementary aids, and behavioral intervention strategies provided consistent with the child's IEP and placement?
- Did the child's disability impair him or his ability to understand the impact and consequences of his behavior?
- Did the child's disability substantially impair him or his ability to control the behavior in question?

If the IEP team determines that the behavior is a manifestation of the child's disability, the IEP team conducts a functional behavior assessment and implements a behavioral intervention plan; or reviews and modifies the existing assessment and plan. The child is returned to his placement unless the parent and school agree to a new placement.

The school may order a change of placement without consideration for the student's disability—in other words, without going through the manifestation determination, for up to a maximum of 45 days:

- when a student carries a weapon to school or to a school function;
- if a student knowingly possesses, uses, or sells illegal drugs;
- if a student inflicts serious bodily harm on himself or other students;
- or if a student solicits the sale of a controlled substance at school or a school function.

Conclusion

Making the decision about where your child will receive special education and related services can be easy or hard. Sometimes it is very clear from the beginning that your child will go to a particular school or classroom and receive his services there. Other times, parents may have to research, organize information, and prepare extensively to effectively advocate for a particular placement. If you believe this to be the case for your child, be sure to complete the exercises in this book. This will prepare you to present a strong case for your child's placement based on his *individualized* needs and in a manner that will allow him the opportunity to succeed academically and be with his peers. When you and school personnel work hard to understand and agree to what will work best for your child, your child will have the greatest chance of success.

WHAT YOU CAN DO NOW

1. Talk with other parents about the school district's curriculum and programs.
2. Visit placement options.
3. Think about your family's priorities for your child's school experience.
4. Try to list the pros and cons of particular placement options.

9. The Individualized Education Program Meeting

Choosing the Route Forward

Your child's Individualized Education Program (IEP) is the cornerstone of her special education program. The IEP meeting is an opportunity for you and the school system to combine your areas of expertise and jointly plan the appropriate education program for your child. This chapter takes a look at the meeting itself and provides tips to ensure your active participation and involvement.

Who Attends?

Parents and Students

Because your contributions to the IEP meeting are so important, IDEA requires schools to follow specific procedures and timelines to make sure you can participate in the meeting. The school must tell you, in writing and in language you understand:

1. when the meeting will be held;
2. its purpose; and
3. who will attend.

When your child is fifteen, the school must invite her to the IEP meeting so she can be involved in plans for her transition services and life after high school. In this way, by the time she turns sixteen, she will have a transition plan, as IDEA requires. Most parents find that including their child at a much earlier age helps the team to better understand their child as well establish credible expectations for her learning and development. IEP teams find that a student's active involvement leads to more practical and effective IEPs, and children who are included early on learn to plan and make decisions for themselves.

Teachers, Specialists, and School Administrators

The following professionals are required by IDEA to attend the IEP meeting:

- Special education teachers;
- General education teachers;
- Related service provider(s) and other professional(s) who can review the assessments and determine instructional strategies based upon those assessments;
- A school administrator or other school district representative qualified to provide or supervise special education services and be able to commit the school district's resources.

IEP members can serve more than one role. For example, the school administrator may ask the special education teacher to take her place, especially if it is an annual review and no significant changes are anticipated. If a required member of the IEP meeting cannot attend, the meeting can only proceed if parents state in writing that the person can be excused. If that member's area of expertise is being discussed, parents must have written information from the team member in advance of the IEP meeting.

Others

You and the school personnel may invite others who are knowledgeable of your child to attend the IEP meeting. The additional attendees might be other family members or friends, educational or other specialists, and professionals from agencies such as early intervention or adult services. When the school wishes to invite others to the meeting, the school must notify you and obtain your written consent for other professionals to attend.

When?

According to IDEA, the school is required to schedule the IEP meeting at a time that is agreeable both to you and the school personnel involved. This meeting must be held within thirty calendar days of the date the school finds your child eligible for special education services. Some schools include the eligibility determination meeting as the first part of the IEP meeting.

IEP meetings are to be held at least once a year; but they can be held more often if you or your child's teacher requests. With the 2004 amendments to IDEA, states may apply for a waiver allowing them to write multiple-year IEPs— that is, IEPs that are valid for longer than one year. Even if your state has a waiver, however, your child is still entitled to an annual IEP meeting if you request one.

What Is Discussed?

During the IEP meeting, your child's written individualized education program (IEP) is developed, beginning with the Present Level of Performance. The sections of the IEP described in Chapter 7 are discussed in turn, and the decisions that the team makes about each section are written down. You will want to make sure all of the relevant components are covered and included in your child's final written IEP.

Then What?

Once the meeting is finished, you will probably be asked to sign the IEP document. Your signature may have a different meaning in different school systems. Sometimes parents are asked to sign the IEP to indicate their participation in the IEP meeting. When this is the case, you should sign the document as requested. Remember, however, that your signature in this case does not mean you agree with the IEP as written.

In some school systems, your signature on the IEP indicates that you agree with the document and you consent to proceed with the proposed IEP and placement. You may sign it right away; however, you may want to ask for additional time to consider it and make sure you agree. The school cannot proceed with your child's educational services until you have given them consent to do so. If you disagree with any portion of the IEP, you can use the procedures described in Chapter 14 to resolve your disagreement.

This next section offers hints for preparing for your child's IEP meeting and making contributions once you are there. You may not want to follow all of the suggestions; choose the ones that you feel are most valuable for you and your child.

Thoughts on Preparing for and Participating in an IEP Meeting

Parent Statement of Concerns and Priorities

IEP discussions begin with a discussion of your child's Present Level of Performance. Teachers and specialists will talk with you about your child's level of academic achievement and functional performance, and what you think she needs in order to catch up with her classmates. This information helps the team decide what to put in the rest of the IEP. As discussed in Chapter 7, information about parent concerns is included in the Present Level of Performance. This is a genuine opportunity for you to share your own concerns and priorities for your child's IEP that are based on information you have gathered and reflected upon to this point.

You have already collected information necessary to contribute to a description of your child's present level of performance. You have collected data, listened to your child's teachers and other professionals who know her well, and considered your child's strengths and needs. One way to sum up this information and prepare for the IEP is to put all this information together in a form, called here *Parent Statement of Concerns and Priorities*. (See page 140.) This is the parent equivalent of the assessment reports that professionals prepare for the IEP meeting. Since Parent Concerns is a required section of the Present Level of Performance, your statement can be added to your child's IEP; for schools using computerized IEPs, there should be ways to add your statement to the official IEP document.

To prepare your parent statement, gather together:

■ Strengthening Exercise #2; you filled out a column in the Developmental Achievement Chart labeled *Can Do* in each of the developmental areas and identified your child's learning styles;

■ The records you decoded, that show specific strengths and accomplishments in each developmental area, and

■ The IEP Planning Chart outlining your goals and priorities.

With this information, ideas you gather from your child and others who know her, you can use the form on the next page to prepare your statement.

The *Parent Statement of Concerns and Priorities* will help you to communicate to others exactly what sorts of services and goals you have for your child. Information you share can include your perspectives about:

■ How your child should participate and progress in the general education curriculum, in light of her learning style and special education needs;

■ Your child's needs for accommodations, supports, modifications, or related services;

■ What methods, based on current research, might be appropriate for your child (the Resource Section of this book has places to go to find research).

Consider using this Parent Statement of Concerns and Priorities in the preplanning stages of the IEP by sharing it with your child's teachers, special education staff, or others who will be helping to develop the IEP. This will give others an idea of what you are looking for in the IEP so that they can address your concerns in advance of the meeting.

Before the IEP Meeting

Now that you have written your parent statement, prepare yourself, and your child (if she is attending with you) for the IEP meeting. The following are some steps you might consider:

1. Upon notification of the IEP meeting, make sure you know the date, time, length of the meeting, and who is invited. If necessary, call the person who is in charge of the meeting to find out

2. Make sure all these required people have been invited, using the IEP checklist (on page 146). Also, invite anyone you believe should be in attendance.

3. Check with your child to find out more about her perspectives, priorities, worries, and suggestions. Ask her she how she would like to be involved in her IEP meeting.

4. If you feel the time allotted for the IEP meeting may be inadequate to discuss all your concerns, make arrangements to extend the meeting time or to schedule a second meeting.

5. Prepare a *Parent Statement of Concerns and Priorities* to be sure it includes everything you want to discuss at the IEP meeting, including your priorities for your child's goals and objectives, the extent of your child's participation in the general education program, and the special education and related services you believe your child needs. Decide upon the minimum special education program and related services you will accept for your child.

6. Talk to others—teachers, parents, professionals, and so on—about the special education and related services they feel your child needs. Consider sharing your Parent Statement and planning charts.

7. Check out some available placement options and opportunities if you haven't already.

8. Familiarize yourself with your school's IEP format so that you can be prepared to add your suggestions when each section is discussed.

9. If there is a draft IEP, ask for a copy in advance of the meeting so that you can review it and ask for changes, if possible, in advance of the meeting. If there is no draft copy of the IEP, review the current IEP and let others know what changes you may be asking for at the meeting.

10. Decide how to make your child's presence felt at the beginning of the IEP meeting. Telling a short anecdote or bringing photographs of your family, tape recordings, examples of schoolwork, or your child herself can help people unacquainted with her realize that she is far more than a stack of papers!

11. Determine the role you feel most comfortable assuming during the meeting.

- *Very assertive role:* taking a very active part in the meeting very early and remaining very verbally involved throughout. If you choose a very assertive role, a way to ensure that your own agenda is covered is to have it carefully written out and even rehearsed with your spouse or others who support your point of view. To help guide the meeting in the directions you wish, provide a copy of your list of issues for each member of the IEP team.
- *Assertive role:* allowing school officials to lead the meeting but ensuring that all items on your agenda are covered completely to your satisfaction.
- *Less assertive role:* permitting school officials to lead the meeting and pressing only for a few specified items.
- *Supportive role:* helping your child prepare for, and present her own priorities and perspectives and taking the lead on the IEP and encouraging others to listen to, understand, and incorporate your child's information and priorities into the IEP.

12. Ask someone to attend the meeting with you. Often it is very helpful to have someone else to listen, take notes, and support you. Prior to the meeting, discuss with him or her what you hope to do in the meeting and what you want him or her to do.

13. Identify possible areas of disagreement. While you and the school professionals will most often agree about your child's IEP, you might want to think of potential areas of disagreement and develop plans to address those problems.

- Identify the data in the records and elsewhere supporting your position on the potential problem areas.
- Identify the data in the records and elsewhere supporting the school's position.
- Identify information to counter the school's position.
- Develop alternative proposals for achieving your goals/objectives for your child which school officials might accept more readily.

Considerations during the IEP Meeting

1. If school personnel are working with your child for the first time, follow the plans you made earlier to make your child's presence felt.
2. If you are speaking first, begin by reviewing the elements of the IEP you and/or your child have developed and have the school people

comment on each item either as you bring it up or after you have finished your presentation.

3. If the school personnel begin the meeting, make notes about their recommended goals and objectives, anticipated services, and evaluation criteria for your child, identifying how each of these items relate to the IEP you envisioned, or even drafted, before the meeting.

4. Make sure that each item required for an IEP is fully discussed. Your draft IEP comes in handy here, as does the checklist on pages 146-49. Check off every item as it is discussed.

5. When a point comes up that you agree with, express your agreement and check off the item from your list. When a point comes up that you don't agree with, express your opinion, explain your objections, and try to reach an acceptable solution.

   - If disagreements cannot be resolved immediately, make a note of those areas, express your desire to come back to these issues later, and move on to new goals and objectives.

6. As the meeting progresses, keep participants focused on the elements of the IEP and on your child. Do not let the discussion wander off to unrelated matters.

7. As the discussion comes to an end, make sure everything on your agenda has been discussed to your satisfaction. If it hasn't, bring up the issue now. If you disagreed earlier over any aspects of your child's IEP, return to those matters now and seek to resolve them before the meeting concludes.

At the End of the IEP Meeting

1. At the conclusion of the meeting you will probably be asked to sign the IEP document. This calls for the following actions.

   - Ask right away: What does my signature mean? Does it mean that I agree with everything in the IEP document and consent to the proposed placement?
   - Does it mean simply that I attended the meeting?

2. Make sure that you have a written copy of the IEP. If it is a computerized IEP, ask for a printout before signing. Compare the IEP checklist in this chapter with the proposed IEP for your child.

3. Choose one of these options:

   - It is usually a good idea to take a copy home so you can reflect on what is in the IEP. However, if you agree with the IEP and the proposed placement, signify agreement by signing.

- If you are not sure, simply tell the school officials you would like to review the IEP over the next few days. Request a copy and tell them exactly when you will give them your final decision regarding the program and placement described on the IEP.

What If We Can't Agree?

When it is time to give school personnel your decision about the IEP, do so. If you agree with it, simply sign the appropriate documents. If you do not find the IEP totally acceptable, show them the exact portions of the IEP that you want to have changed, and ask them to consider your changes. If they change it to your satisfaction, sign the IEP/permission for placement.

If the school personnel refuse to make your suggested changes, decide which of the following actions you will take:

- Indicate in writing the parts you disagree with, then sign the IEP or permission for placement document. This puts you on record as stating that the IEP does not adequately meet your child's needs.

- Indicate in writing the parts you disagree with and your plan to appeal those portions of the IEP, then sign the IEP or permission for placement. This option should allow your child to receive the special education and related services on her IEP pending appeal of the part to which you object. (See Chapter 14 for information about ways to resolve disagreements with the school.)

- Ask what educational services your child will receive if you choose not to sign the document. If you can accept the services provided in this circumstance, indicate in writing your intention to appeal the IEP and refuse to sign the IEP or permission for placement. If you can't, choose one of the above options.

- If this is the first time your child will be receiving special education services, the school will not provide any special education services without your consent. However, if you do not consent to services, the school is no longer required to provide your child with special education services. Rights and protections for students in special education will not apply to your child, so the school does not have to continue to notify you if they suspect your child needs services in the future. Also, protections for students with disabilities in discipline situations will not apply.

If you cannot agree on the IEP, before school personnel can proceed with services or refuse to take action on services, they must provide you with their reasons, in writing. This document is called Prior Written Notice or Written Prior Notice. The notice must include:

- A description of the action proposed or refused;
- The reason for the proposed change;
- The date of proposed change;
- Evaluations and other information used to make the decision;
- Other options or choices described;
- Other relevant factors;
- What steps to take if you disagree.

Make your request for Prior Written Notice in writing. This allows you to define the area of disagreement and increases the likelihood that their written information will respond to the disagreement as you have defined it. Once you understand the reasons for the school personnel's disagreement, you may change your mind and allow the services to proceed. However, if you still disagree and want to proceed with more formal processes, go to Chapter 14 to learn more about procedural safeguards.

Conclusion

Getting the results you want for your child takes time and energy as you negotiate the special education maze. Your hopes and those of the school system are that your son or daughter will make educational and developmental strides with the program you jointly design at the IEP meeting. If your child is still an infant or toddler, you will need to be aware of other considerations due to your child's young age. Special laws and regulations have been passed for very young children. Chapter 11 has more on Early Intervention and can help you make decisions for your baby and your family that are different from the ones you might make for an older child.

If your older son or daughter is approaching the end of school, you are most likely wondering what lies ahead. It is never too early to begin exploring passageways in the maze that lead to maximum independence in work life, living arrangements, recreation, and community activities. In Chapters 12 and 13 you will find suggestions of ways to work with school professionals to prepare your child for her life as an employee, citizen, and contributing member of society.

WHAT YOU CAN DO NOW

1. Make copies of the IEP checklist or make up your own checklist.
2. Decide how you will take part in the IEP meeting.

PARENT STATEMENT OF CONCERNS AND PRIORITIES

Parent Concerns and Priorities for: _____
(to be included in IEP)

Strengths and Accomplishments: _____

_____

_____

_____

Challenges: _____

_____

_____

_____

Goals and Priorities:

1. _____

2. _____

3. _____

4. _____

Services and Supports:

1. _____

2. _____

3. _____

4. _____

Accommodations, Adaptations, and Modifications:

1. _____

2. _____

3. _____

4. _____

PARENT STATEMENT OF CONCERNS AND PRIORITIES

Parent Concerns and Priorities for: Elena
(to be included in IEP)

Strengths and Accomplishments: COMMUNICATION – Elena smiles to engage people she is close to. She can say a few words like "Ma" for "Marta," "Ba" for "bottle," "Mimi" for "mommy," "wa?" for "walk?"
SELF-CONCEPT/INDEPENDENCE – Elena can drink from a sippy cup and is learning how to eat with a spoon.
MOVEMENT – She is working on crawling, up on all fours. Right now she is scooting.
THINKING – She can look at her picture books

Challenges: COMMUNICATION - Elena cannot communicate well and is often frustrated when she wants something and people don't understand what she wants.
SELF-CONCEPT/INDEPENDENCE – She is very messy when she eats and not very coordinated.
MOVEMENT – She is well behind in being able to walk.

Parent Request for IEP:

1. COMMUNICATION – Learn more words, possibly learn how to talk and sign at the same time. If this is what is to be done, then her sister Marta and I would also like to learn sign.

2. SELF-CONCEPT/INDEPENDENCE – I want Elena to be able to eat with a fork and spoon and drink from a regular cup.

3. MOVEMENT – In six months, I would like Elena to be taking a few steps.

4. I would like for Elena to be able to point to pictures in her picture book and say the words.

PARENT STATEMENT OF CONCERNS AND PRIORITIES

Parent Concerns and Priorities for: Bryan
(to be included in IEP)

Strengths and Accomplishments: COMMUNICATION – Bryan is improving his conversational speech. If he doesn't understand something, he asks for clarification. He is a great creative writer and writes short stories and illustrates cartoons.

SOCIAL RELATIONSHIPS - He has a great sense of humor and is sought out by peers who are younger and older.

SELF CONCEPT/INDEPENDENCE – Bryan works well in a smaller class-room environment and completes work with little or no prompts when he understands the directions or routine.

SENSES/PERCEPTIONS – Bryan can draw intricate and humorous cartoons and has a good sense of color coordination.

THINKING – He can complete difficult 100+ piece puzzles indepen-dently and multiply a 3-digit number by another 3-digit number in his mind. He is advanced in math and reads at grade level.

LEARNING STYLE – He is a concrete thinker and very analytical. He can decode words and puzzles quickly.

Challenges: MOVEMENT – He has difficulty coordinating dribbling and running and cannot ride a bicycle. It takes him longer to write things by hand, so he needs to use a computer so he can get the words out as fast as he can think them.

COMMUNICATION – He is not usually aware of his tone of voice. Sometimes he does not see why he can't be brutally honest with people (e.g., "that shirt is ugly").

SOCIAL RELATIONSHIPS – He has difficulty maintaining friendships with same-age peers. He constantly wants to talk about his favorite subjects, while not wanting to listen to a peer's favorite subject if it is not similar to his own. He has difficulty understanding the social skills associated with team sports.

SELF-CONCEPT/INDEPENDENCE – Bryan perceives himself as an expert at math. So when he comes across a problem that he does not understand, he is reluctant to ask for assistance, since he is an "expert."

ORGANIZATION – Sometimes he spends an inordinate amount of time doing things that others can do quite routinely, like getting dressed in the morning. He often forgets his homework at school, or forgets completed homework at home.

ATTENTION – he has difficulty maintaining his attention on anything that doesn't interest him, and is easily frustrated when he anticipates having difficulties with a particular task or assignment. When he is frustrated, he will either stop trying or try to distract the class by being a comedian.

AUDITORY PROCESSING – He has a very minor delay. When told to take his math book out, he appears noncompliant because he is sitting still, while in actuality he is processing the request.

TRANSITIONS – Although it takes awhile for him to understand routines, he does much better when there is a predictable schedule. When he isn't sure what he should be doing or what is next, Bryan becomes more anxious and it is hard for him to focus on the task at hand. If he is doing something that he loves (like math) and has to go to history next, he will start to worry about what is next and not be able to organize himself to get the homework assignment.

THINKING – He struggles with processing directions that are not given in short concrete sentences. Although he is reading at grade level, he does not like to read. As a result, he dislikes history and science because it involves too much reading.

HOMEWORK – Although he gets help with homework, he frequently has meltdowns when he is frustrated. When this happens, he is unable to complete his work. He becomes even more frustrated when he gets a poor grade on the homework because he did not complete it, or forgot it at home.

Parent Request for IEP:

1. COMMUNICATION - Improve his conversational skills with peers with speech therapy group and an after school opportunity like the drama club where he can practice social skills through role play. Improve his awareness of conversational skills and his voice volume.

2. HOMEWORK – Extended time to do homework, and an assignment book and journal that is checked daily at school and at home, shortened assignments as appropriate, breaking up longer homework assignments into smaller chunks. Parents may need study guide answers so they can help with homework.

3. AUDITORY PROCESSING - Understand and process more complex directions. Instructions given in short, concrete sentences. Visual study guide and written instructions so that he can make more sense of the learning challenge.

4. Opportunity to go to the advanced level math class, including special education support to help him organize assignments and multiple ways to approach a math challenge.

5. Improve his fluency in reading and find reading materials that he can be more engaged in.

6. Help in learning ways to approach difficult situations when he senses that he will not be successful.

7. Use of a computer to take notes.

IEP CHECKLIST

BEFORE THE MEETING

Logistics

☐ Is there enough time to allow parents to make arrangements to attend?

☐ Is the time and place mutually agreeable?

Team Members—Are the people who need to be there invited?

☐ Parent(s)

☐ Student (as appropriate, and invited at age 15 when discussing transition)

☐ Special education teacher(s)

☐ Regular education teacher(s)

☐ Related service provider(s) and other professional(s) who can interpret the instructional implications of assessments

☐ Administrator or school division representative (who is knowledgeable about the general curriculum, qualified to provide/supervise special education services, and able to commit resources)

Optional

☐ Family members/Friends

☐ Peers/Advocates

☐ Specialists

☐ Other Professionals including representatives from Early Intervention or Adult Service Agencies.

DURING THE MEETING AND TO REVIEW THE IEP AFTER THE MEETING

Present Level of Performance

☐ Describes your child in a positive way

☐ Reflects your concerns and priorities

☐ Includes strengths and needs

☐ Includes the results of most recent evaluations and the student's level of academic achievement and functional performance

☐ Reflects the results from a variety of assessment tools including statewide or district-wide assessments

☐ Describes how the disability affects involvement in the general education program

☐ Describes academic, developmental, functional, and behavioral needs

☐ Describes your child's level of academic, developmental, and functional performance in all developmental and functional areas

Annual Goals

❏ Includes academic and functional goals based on Present Level of Performance and evaluations

❏ Are meaningful and attainable within one school year

❏ For students who aren't receiving grade-level instruction, each goal has been broken down into measurable objectives or benchmarks

❏ Each goal specifies how progress will be measured and how/how often parents will be informed of progress

❏ Each goal specifies what the student will do, how, where, and when he/she will do it, including behavior intervention plan and positive behavioral supports, if needed

❏ Each goal promotes high expectations for the student, including how the student will keep up with or catch up to peers without disabilities

❏ Goals are prioritized, especially as related to student's age and time left for schooling

❏ Goals include the development of skills to help the student live as independently as possible

❏ Includes a statement of expected student involvement and progress in the general education curriculum

❏ Extracurricular activities are considered

Related Services, Supplementary Aids, and Supports

❏ Summary statement of services and support is included

❏ For each service/support: start/finish dates; frequency; duration; location; who will deliver; delivery method (individual or group in class)

❏ Services will support the child's progress and participation in the general curriculum program

❏ Support to include the child in nonacademic and extracurricular activities

❏ Specific teacher/staff training necessary to implement program

❏ Assistive Technology devices or services

Special Factors (when needed)

❏ Communication

❏ Assistive Technology

❏ Behavior

❏ Language (English Language Learners)

❏ Braille (for blindness/visual impairment)

❏ Communication needs (for deafness/hearing impairment)

Placement

☐ Decided after goals, objectives, and supports are agreed upon

☐ In the least restrictive environment (first option considered is school child would attend if there was no disability)

☐ Includes interaction with nondisabled peers to the maximum extent appropriate

☐ If student is not participating in all general education activities, a justification is included

☐ Is coordinated with general education classroom, schedules, activities, and programs

Statewide and District-wide Assessments

☐ Lists assessments student will take (same as for all students)

☐ Specifies any needed accommodations and modifications

☐ If participating in an alternate assessment, aligned with challenging standards

Other

☐ Assignment of a case manager or primary contact (if applicable)

☐ Extended school year recommendation (if needed)

☐ Person(s) responsible clearly listed—special education teacher, general education teacher, specialist, aide, parents, students, other

Transition Between Schools/Placements

☐ Plans for a smooth transition to a new setting (preschool to kindergarten or elementary to middle school) are made a year prior to move

Secondary Transition

☐ By age 15, or before as appropriate, student takes active role in planning and attending IEP

☐ Types of classes needed and type of diploma planned for student

☐ Includes postsecondary goals based on student needs, strengths, preferences, and interests

☐ Specific transition services, related services needs, and other agencies to be included

☐ Activities needed to assist student in reaching postsecondary goals

☐ At least one year before age 18, information about what rights will transfer to student at age 18

☐ Summary of Performance for students who are graduating or who will exceed the age of eligibility for special education

For an IEP that is a change in services for the child or change in placement or refusal of parent request (Prior Written Notice)

❏ Description of action proposed or refused

❏ Reason for the proposed change

❏ The date of proposed change

❏ Evaluations and other information used to make the decision

❏ Other options or choices described

❏ Other relevant factors

❏ What steps to take if parent disagrees

Adapted from **PEATC Press** (December 2006), Parent Educational Advocacy Training Center, Falls Church, VA.

10. CHECKING UP

Tracking Milestones

You have traveled a long way since first entering the special education maze. Referral, evaluation, and eligibility determination seem like dim shadows. Even the IEP decisions might feel like they happened a long time ago. But now your child is in the appropriate classroom, with appropriate services scheduled to begin. The maze is completed!

But wait, not so fast! All that you have done so far has been essential for your journey. But your job is not complete. Placing a child in a class, establishing educational goals, and scheduling services on an IEP are not the same as achieving those goals and receiving those services. Your next step involves periodic checking up on your child's progress. For example, you will want to know if your child is moving toward those milestones you set as goals. Is he receiving the related services agreed upon? Is he spending time with other students in the general education classroom and participating in music or art class, going to recess, and eating lunch with friends in the cafeteria?

When your child begins to realize his potential as a result of the education he receives, you'll know you're going in the right direction. When you check up on your child's individualized plan and the educational and developmental milestones spelled out in that document, you can make sure everything's moving forward, or if not, make adjustments.

The principles and techniques described in this chapter will guide you in making sure the program you helped develop is implemented as planned. This chapter gives suggestions for checking up on your child's specialized educational program by using the IEP as your compass.

Why Check Up?

But why must you check up on your child's program and progress? Can't you trust the school systems to live up to what they say will be done? Doesn't there come a time when you have to turn the educational reins over to the "experts"? And isn't now that time?

Yes, most school systems will implement the IEP. Nevertheless, attempts to carry out the IEP may fall short for many reasons: lack of funds to hire occupational therapists, a teacher falling ill for several months, or a sudden increase in enrollment, leaving less time to work with your child. Or, the IEP is being implemented as written, yet your child is still not making progress.

If you know the IEP is not being carried out, you may request a meeting with your child's teachers to get it back on track. Likewise, if the IEP you have agreed to is being carried out to the letter but is ineffective, you may also ask for changes. But if you have not kept tabs on the IEP, you find out too late that your child is not receiving the special education services promised.

The Green Family

The Greens' son, John, had autism and difficulty speaking. The IEP for John, therefore, included individual speech therapy, twice a week, for thirty minutes each period. As the year progressed, the Greens saw little advancement in their son's speech skills. Still, they kept hoping progress would come.

At the end of the school year, the Greens met with John's teacher, Ms. Prizer. During their conference, Ms. Prizer proudly showed off John's language board. The board contained letters of the alphabet, simple signs for frequently used words—I, go, open, close—and other communication symbols. Ms. Prizer explained that John would carry this small board with him throughout the school day. When he wanted to communicate with someone, he would point to the appropriate symbols on his board.

The Greens were impressed with this innovation, although somewhat surprised they had not learned of it before the end of school. When they asked Ms. Prizer how the board was used in John's speech therapy sessions, they learned of yet another innovation in their son's IEP. "Oh," said Ms. Prizer, "John has not had speech therapy for seven months. When he showed no progress after two months of therapy, we decided to use the language board as an alternative to speech therapy to improve his communication skills."

Maybe the language board was more useful than speech therapy, but that is not the point. No change in your child's IEP should be made without school personnel notifying you. Unless you monitor your child's IEP, you won't know whether innovations are being made in his program. Yes, once the IEP is written you can turn the educational reins over to the "experts." But you should continue to check on your child's educational and developmental progress.

Practices and Techniques for Checking Up

Ask Questions

Most parents are unsure of how to approach the topic of checking up on the IEP. They wonder, "Who am I to question what the teachers are doing?" "How will I know whether the IEP is being implemented?" "What do I do if the IEP is not being followed?" Combine this uncertainty with the normal tendency to trust authorities, and no wonder parents are hesitant to second-guess school administrators and teachers.

What can you do to overcome these understandably common fears? Your first concern should be to focus on selected aspects of the IEP to determine:

1. Is the educational plan being carried out?
   a. Is the classroom instruction following the IEP?
   b. Are the required related services being provided?
   c. Are accommodations and modifications consistently implemented?
2. Is the plan working well for my child?
   a. Is the classroom setting truly appropriate for my child's needs?
   b. Is my child making educational and/or developmental progress in school?
   c. Is this progress being documented by objective measures?
   d. Does what my child says or does tell me that school is going well?
   e. Is my child's behavior causing any difficulties?

Opportunities to Check Up

Having identified the questions to ask, your second concern becomes finding the answers to those questions. Parents have found many techniques to be helpful when checking on their child's IEP. The most frequently used methods include the following:

Listening to Your Child. Ask your child how school is going, what activities he enjoys most, and how much time he spends in speech or math. Keep written notes detailing your child's responses. Look over his homework, what he has to do and has done. Help him with homework. Note the length of time spent on homework and how much help you provided.

Volunteering. Find out ways that you can volunteer at your child's school, during school hours or with activities or tasks outside regular school hours. Through informal conversations with parents and school staff you will learn much information that is not traditionally shared during more formal meetings or in reports.

Networking. Join formal groups, like the Parent Teacher Association (PTA), parent support groups, or advisory groups. Interaction with these groups will give you meaningful opportunities to gather information and contribute to efforts that will help your child along with others in your child's school. Develop friendships with other parents at your child's school for mutual support and information sharing.

Holding Conferences. Have individual meetings with your child's teachers, school administrators, tutors, therapists, and other professionals on a regular basis, or whenever there is an issue to be discussed. Keep a written record of the dates of meetings, topics discussed, and outcomes. A schedule of regular meetings can be included in your child's IEP.

Making Classroom Observations. Either visit the classroom with the specific intent of observing some aspect of your child's learning activities, or volunteer in the class and at the school and use those opportunities to observe your child and his program. Keep a written record of when you make each observation and a detailed description of what you observe.

Exchanging a Notebook. Share comments, suggestions, observations, and the like with your child's teacher via a notebook that your child carries to and from school. You can include in the notebook a checklist of important behavioral goals and objectives from the IEP. Note that the requirement for home-school communication can be included as part of your child's IEP.

Communicating via Email and Internet. Increasingly, schools are using email and the Internet to open communication with families. Teachers often share their email addresses for parents with questions or concerns. They may post homework or enrichment activities on the Internet in case your child did not bring this information home. The requirement to provide email or Internet updates may also be part of the IEP.

These are just a few ways that you might assess your child's program and progress during the school year. While the list is not complete, it provides a starting point.

You and Your Child's Teacher

The single most important source of information on your child's progress is his teacher. Your child's teacher is the key communicator about your child: talking with you after school, at the IEP meeting, and at regularly scheduled conferences; completing your child's progress reports and perhaps filling out a notebook you send back and forth; talking with the school psychologist, the physical therapist or other therapists, and administrators about your child's needs and progress, and then talking with you.

The free flow of information between you and your child's teacher depends mainly upon your relationship with one another. If he perceives you as a concerned parent who also understands the needs and problems of teachers, and if you believe he can teach your child effectively, you will probably receive plenty of up-to-date, specific information about your child's progress. But how do you as a parent develop this cooperative relationship with your child's teacher? You may wish to try some of the following suggestions:

1. Try to develop a personal relationship with your child's teacher. Some families feel comfortable inviting their child's teacher to dinner; others find regular telephone conversations helpful.

2. Maintain regular contact through telephone calls, written notes, or email so that you can discuss accomplishments. This regular communication can prevent emerging problems from becoming more serious. A cautionary note: always think twice before you click on the email send button. You do not want to send anything you may regret later.

3. Give the teachers and specialists sufficient time to get to know your child before asking their opinions about his progress, problems, the appropriateness of his program, and so forth.

4. Let the teachers and specialists know you understand the difficulties they frequently face in doing their jobs—be empathetic to their needs, too!

5. Prepare for conferences in advance by developing and bringing with you a list of questions, concerns, and comments. This saves everybody time and ensures that nothing important will be overlooked. If possible, share this list with the teacher in advance of the meeting.

6. Before the meeting, ask the teachers and other specialists about their goals, concerns, and comments, and bring those up in the meeting as appropriate.

7. Let teachers and specialists know what is important to you in the education and development of your child.

8. Tell teachers and specialists, for example, through conversations, notes, or emails—when they have done something that is making a difference for you or your child.

9. Take every opportunity to let others know how you recognize and appreciate their efforts or the efforts of others at the school.

10. Discuss and share your plans for monitoring progress on your child's IEP, and follow through with that plan.

11. Discuss problems you believe have arisen in implementing your child's IEP with the teachers and specialists involved. Don't begin by going right to the school administrators.

12. As mentioned earlier, consider ways you might volunteer time or materials for the classroom.

Each of the preceding activities offers an excellent occasion for you to build bridges of trust and openness with teachers and other specialists working with your child. As these relationships are developed and strengthened, you will experience more and more confidence in your ability to know and understand your child's progress and the extent to which his IEP is actually being implemented.

Observing in the Classroom

Besides communicating with the teacher, another useful way to check your child's educational progress is through classroom observation. Schools vary in their policies of allowing parents to observe classroom activities. How receptive teachers are to parent classroom visits also differs (another good reason for developing an open relationship with your child's teacher). In all cases, however, before you visit your child's classroom, check first with the teacher and then the school principal to determine your school's specific policy.

Once you know the school policy on classroom visits, you are ready to prepare yourself for this activity. Following are several suggestions designed to increase the effectiveness of your classroom visit.

1. Give the teacher sufficient prior notice of your visit—at least a few days.

2. Before visiting the class, obtain general information about the classroom. (When is math taught? When is recess scheduled? What books are being used?)

3. Decide what you want to observe (e.g., reading group, playground time, math class) and then let the teacher know your plans.

4. Talk with your child about your visit, so he isn't surprised by your presence.

5. Tell the teacher how long you plan to spend in the classroom.

6. Respect the teacher's routines and fit your observations within them when visiting the class.

7. Observe only your own child or interactions involving your child and other children or adults.

8. Keep your conversations with professionals or other adults to a minimum during your observation time.

9. After the classroom visit, make some notes describing your observations, impressions, and/or concerns.

10. Follow up your observation with a brief conference, phone call, or note to thank the teacher for the opportunity to observe. Share your findings, thoughts, and questions with the teacher.

11. Tell the teachers and specialists what you like about their teaching style—they'll be pleasantly surprised you noticed.

Whenever you go for a classroom visit, remember that many people, teachers included, can be uncomfortable when they are being observed. The tension created by not knowing why you have come to observe can cause unnecessary anxiety, and even real misunderstanding, between you and the teacher. Notifying the teacher of your plan to observe your child, explaining the purpose of your visit, and following up after the observation can relieve much potential tension. These steps should smooth the way for an informative classroom observation and an open relationship with your child's teacher. You might also want to explain to your child the reasons for your visit in terms that express your interest in his school activities, teachers, and classmates.

Being an Informed Consumer

Besides making classroom visits and communicating with your child's teacher, another helpful strategy is to become an informed consumer. Although you are not expected to be a special education teacher, physical therapist, or other special education professional, you can still learn many basic ideas important to your child's education.

Participate in your local Parent-Teacher Association and in local parent groups such as the Learning Disabilities Association (LDA), The Arc, or the Autism Society. These groups often provide excellent, up-to-date information on programs and school services relevant to your child's IEP.

Learn about current teaching methods and therapeutic techniques as they relate to your child's disabilities. This information can be obtained in many ways:

■ parent groups and associations that conduct workshops, including your state's Parent Information and Training Center (see the Resource section at the end of this book);

■ experts who are willing to share their knowledge with you through seminars, presentations, or individual consultation;

- written information available through books, the Internet, magazines, email bulletins;
- school sources, including the local PTA, professional training for teachers that is often open to parents, and special education advisory committees; and
- professional training opportunities, including continuing education classes at local community colleges and universities.

In these and many other ways, you can become a knowledgeable consumer of the special education services in your local school system. The Resource section identifies many places to begin your research into the current recommended strategies and practices. And as an informed consumer, you will also be able to understand and monitor your child's educational program and progress.

The School Checks Up

Your child's teacher should be using the IEP as a guide for delivering services, supports, and instruction. Your child's school should be regularly informing you about the progress your child is making in his IEP and within the general education curriculum. Most schools do this at the same time other children are receiving report cards and/or progress reports. The IEP specifies how frequently you receive these progress reports. In most cases, you will be receiving samples of work and grades for assignments, quizzes, and tests on an ongoing basis. Make sure you have enough information to gauge your child's progress and ask the teacher for more information if you are not sure. IDEA 2004 no longer requires the school to inform you whether your child is making sufficient progress to meet his annual goals, as was required in the past.

In addition, most students with disabilities will be taking the school-wide assessments that other students in the school are taking, often with testing accommodations based on their special needs. For students for whom the assessments are inappropriate, the schools will have an alternate test, as specified in the IEP. The school will tell you how your child did on the test. Also, your child's school and district will publish their overall test scores. The scores of students within certain groups, including by race, students with disabilities, and students with limited English proficiency, will be reported as part of the overall school-wide and district-wide test scores.

Reviews: Annual and Reevaluation

The results of the annual review are usually reported at the IEP meeting. The review is an opportunity for you, your child's teachers, and other school professionals to look at the past year's IEP goals and evaluate how well your child has met them. The review is a time not only to look at past progress but also to consider next year's IEP.

Sometimes teachers or other school personnel may decide before the review that your child's progress is not satisfactory. If you or the school believes that your child's behavior may be interfering with his ability to learn, a functional behavior assessment should be conducted and a positive behavioral intervention plan developed and implemented. Your child's classroom teacher(s) will be involved in the assessment. All additional evaluations/assessments require the schools to give you notice and involve you in the process. You may want to review the information on evaluation procedures in Chapter 5, as it once again becomes relevant.

The school will conduct a reevaluation of your child a minimum of every three years. As mentioned in Chapter 5, an evaluation every three years is usually the outside limit—you or the school system may choose, for legitimate reasons, to reevaluate your child more frequently than required, especially if your child does not seem to be making progress and the school needs more information to figure out what they need to do to spur that progress. You can request an evaluation before the three years have elapsed, and the school must agree to it if it has been at least one year since the last reevaluation. The school does not have to reevaluate your child every three years if you and the school both agree. However, it is rarely a good idea to go for a long period—even three years may be too long an interval—without a reevaluation to objectively take another complete look at a child.

Keep in mind several practical implications surrounding your active involvement in your child's reevaluation. First, in the three years that elapse between formal evaluations, only the teacher, other professionals working with your child, and you will be checking on your child's progress. Since even conscientious teachers and other school professionals have limited time to provide services, they may not devote much effort to monitoring the results of their work. Therefore, if you don't keep tabs on your child's IEP, three years could go by before you discover that your child has made little or no progress. Your child cannot afford that time.

Don't overlook one other important implication of the requirement for a reevaluation. Every three years, you will be faced with an eligibility determination decision. Pressures on school systems are growing to cut the costs of special education. In the face of these pressures, you must be prepared to present a clear, convincing case for your child, as to what you believe is an appropriate education in the least restrictive environment. By tracking progress on your child's IEP regularly, carefully, and consistently and by following the steps outlined earlier in this book, you should be well on the road to presenting a compelling case for your child each time a reevaluation rolls around.

Making Changes

What happens when information convinces you a change is necessary? Where do you start the change process?

Elements of your child's IEP can be changed at any time through mutual agreement of you and a school representative authorized to approve changes. You can also reconvene all or part of the IEP team. But once you have approved an IEP, you should wait a reasonable time before deciding the program is not working or needs changing.

What is a reasonable time? In part, this depends upon your child's age, rate of development, and the educational skills being taught. If your child naturally develops slowly or the skill requires significant time to acquire, three to five months may be necessary before noticeable progress occurs. If development is rapid or the skill more readily learned, you may feel that changes should begin within one to three months. In either case, a useful approach would be to wait until the time specified in your child's IEP for reporting advancement toward his goal. If the report doesn't show progress, a change in program, services, teachers, or some combination of the three may be in order.

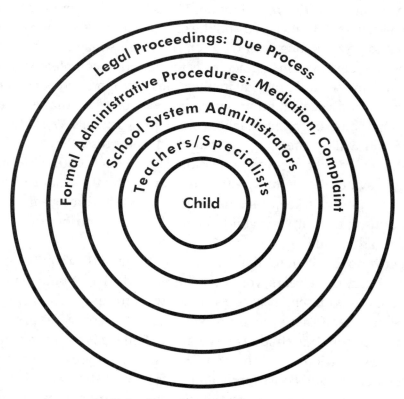

Political and Legal Advocacy

To make changes, work with staff and processes in this order:

Teachers/Specialist. The preceding diagram suggests that the best place to begin your efforts to change your child's IEP is with his teacher or other specialists. If problems are resolved at this level, changes will often be immediate and on target. At this first level of change, the process for correcting problems is the least complicated—although it may not seem so. If your efforts to alter the IEP are unsuccessful at this level, move one level up (out toward the perimeter) and seek change at the administrative level.

School System Administrators. Your first attempts to work with school administrators in changing your child's IEP should be made informally. An informal request for an IEP change sent to the teacher or principal will often be all that is needed. Your request should be accompanied by a written explanation and supporting reasons for your request.

Formal Administrative Procedures. If your less formal approach to the teachers and administrators is unsuccessful, you can then begin the administrative review or conciliatory conference procedures available in most school systems. Formal mediation can help resolve disagreements between families and schools. You might file a written complaint at the local or state level. In cases that involve your child's civil rights, you might file a complaint to the US Office of Civil Rights. Chapter 14 explains the mediation and complaint processes.

Legal Proceedings. If you cannot obtain satisfactory results through the administrative process, including mediation, your next step is to request a due process hearing. As pointed out in Chapter 14, you must consider taking this step very carefully. In some instances, however, you may have no alternative. Therefore, even though several months may pass before a final ruling is made to change your child's IEP, the due process hearing remains a viable method for achieving potential change. Of course, if the due process proceedings all seem futile or their results seem biased and inaccurate, you can also seek changes through court action. Considering the time and cost involved in this action, however, its use should be reserved only for major IEP disagreements.

Political and Legal Advocacy. Where, then, does the last circle on the perimeter—political and legal advocacy—enter the IEP change process? Parents might take this step to force school systems to do something they currently are not doing, such as providing full inclusion opportunities for students with severe disabilities. Political and legal advocacy may also be employed to force school systems to do better and more extensively things they are doing on a limited scale—for example, providing vocational training or reading programs. Parents can work alone or with others to persuade school administrators, school boards, city councils, and state legislators to appropriate additional funds for these activities. Or parents might sue in court to force school jurisdictions, and indirectly, legislative bodies, to abide by the law and to provide appropriate services. Ideally, both political and legal advocacy can produce the same results—children receiving the programs and services in the kinds and amounts appropriate to meet their educational needs.

Although both political and legal advocacy and due process hearings can be highly effective in obtaining educational change, remember: the further you move from the center of the circle, the less the focus is on your child's individual educational needs. Changes made by teachers are usually completed rapidly, with up-to-date information, and in an understanding environment. When IEP changes are generated at points further from your child, the decisions may be slow in coming, out of date, and made out of context. Although political and legal advocacy can help other families down the road, it may not help your situation very much. Again, this underscores the need for close relationships with your child's teachers. Begin and end with a teacher whenever you can. You will be miles ahead.

Conclusion

Checking up on your child's educational program is hard work. Only time, energy, and careful thought can make it pay off. The jargon found in many IEPs is often impossible to decipher. Educators know what they mean by "voice quality"

WHAT YOU CAN DO NOW

1. List your top three priorities for your child over the next three months, and make sure your general observations help you analyze his progress—or a lack of it.
2. Talk to your child, as appropriate, about ways he can ask for help at school and how he feels things are progressing as he works toward his goals.
3. Make notes on your calendar to check in with your child's teacher regularly, to make sure you are staying in touch. In spite of good intentions, everyone is busy and time can slip by.
4. Identify any aspect of your child's progress that makes you uncomfortable or worried, and talk to the teacher or specialist about it. If you can, analyze why you are worried, so you can express your concerns in concrete terms with specific examples. This helps specialists and teachers deal with the issue rather than taking your comments personally.

or "voice intensity," for example, but parents may not. Make certain, therefore, to ask questions at the time of the IEP conference so you do know what the IEP means as well as what it says.

Not knowing whether the goals and objectives are appropriate can cause difficulties also. Your own sense of your child's educational needs helps you here. Completing the Strengthening Exercises described in Chapter 3 will give you added confidence in evaluating the annual goals and short-term objectives suggested for your child's IEP. Checking up on the dates projected for achieving goals can help you further in assessing the continuing appropriateness of your child's goals and objectives. Are the goals being met on schedule? ahead of schedule? or not at all? Answers to these questions will lead you to other questions. For example, if the results are positive or negative, what accounts for those results? Is it the program, the teacher, or the classroom setting? The answers to all these questions may require some changes in your child's IEP.

11. Early Intervention for Babies and Toddlers

A Place to Start

amilies begin the journey through the special education maze at different stages—some begin when their child is school-aged; others discover early that their baby or toddler needs special help. If your son or daughter is an infant or toddler, this chapter is for you.

A Case Study

For his first six months of life, Brian Ellis was a healthy, typically developing baby. Suddenly, he developed seizures and was taken to the pediatrician for observation and treatment. His family felt quite overwhelmed and anxious. A nurse suggested to his mother that she call HUGS, the early intervention program in her community. Before long, the Ellis family was receiving some much needed support both for Brian and for the rest of the family. How did this come about?

In 1986, the U.S. Congress recognized the importance of getting help as early as possible for children with special needs and their families. Legislation was passed to encourage states to set up programs for infants and toddlers with disabilities and for their families. This program is now part of IDEA and is referred to as *Part C—Early Intervention for Infants and Toddlers with Disabilities and their Families*. This chapter discusses some key issues that are specific to "Part C" early intervention services provided by IDEA.

Early intervention provides services that are designed to meet the individual needs of a child and her family, to enhance the development of the young child, and to minimize the need for future special education. They are based on what the parents and a multidisciplinary team of professionals jointly select. They may be provided in the child's home, school, hospital, or other central location. However, to the extent possible, the child and family receive services in places the child would be if she didn't have a disability. You may hear this referred to as the "natural environment." A major focus of early intervention is to help families meet their own child's needs.

The U.S. Department of Education sets policies and procedures that the states must follow. Each state then assigns a public agency, called the lead agency, to administer the early intervention program. In some states, the lead agency for early intervention is the education department. In others, it may be the department of health, mental health, or social services. Regardless of the lead agency, all public agencies providing services to infants and young children should be working together to make sure that services are comprehensive and coordinated. While many states offer their services at no costs to parents, states are allowed to charge parents on a sliding fee scale.

Early intervention can begin at birth and last until a child turns three. At the age of three, if eligible, the child can begin receiving preschool special education from the local public school. The 2004 Amendments to IDEA allow states the option to extend early intervention through kindergarten. If this option is taken, parents of children ages 3 to 5 can choose either early intervention services or special education preschool.

Families can enter the early intervention system in a variety of ways. When a child is identified as having a developmental delay or being at risk of a disability at birth, medical professionals often tell the family about early intervention services in their community. Other families learn about the program from friends, social workers, or pediatricians. Every state has a central directory that parents and professionals may call to find out about resources in their community. Contact the National Dissemination Center for Children with Disabilities (NICHY), which is listed in the Resources section of this book, for the number of your central directory.

Infants or toddlers can qualify for early intervention services in any of the following ways:

- They may be identified as having developmental delays in one or more of the following areas: cognitive development; physical development; communication; social or emotional development; or adaptive skills.
- They may be diagnosed with a physical or mental condition that has a high probability of resulting in developmental delay.
- In some states, babies or toddlers who might develop substantial developmental delays due to one or more risk factors such as prenatal

drug exposure, genetic disorder, or a medically fragile condition are eligible for early intervention.

A Family Service System

When the Part C program was enacted, Congress recognized that in order for early intervention to be successful, services must focus on the whole family and go beyond those which meet the baby's developmental needs. Early intervention can include:

1. making sure the child is identified as soon as possible as needing extra help, and through medical and other diagnostic tests, figuring out exactly what help she needs;
2. arranging for and scheduling the right services that will assist the child and family (to include social services and medical assistance, or benefits such as insurance, food stamps, or Supplemental Security Income);
3. special instruction to families that will encourage their baby to learn and grow;
4. social work, nutrition, nursing, counseling, or psychological services for the child or family;
5. family training, counseling, and home visits;
6. therapies for the child such as occupational, physical, and speech and language, including instruction in sign language;
7. help with vision problems;
8. assistive technology and assistive technology services;
9. health services so the child can receive other early intervention services;
10. transportation and related costs necessary for a child and family to access services;
11. planning and assistance as a child prepares to leave early intervention and move on to new programs or services (such as preschool special education).

Family Centered Early Intervention Services

Families and early intervention professionals have come to recognize the importance of family members as key decision makers for their infant or toddler with disabilities. Families and professionals together have learned that certain principles must guide them as important decisions are made. These family-centered principles are:

- A child with disabilities, like all children, is first a member of a family within a community.

- The family is the child's first and best advocate.
- Families decide what services they need.
- A family's perspectives and values are shaped by life experiences, including their ethnic, racial, and cultural background.
- Family support is an integral part of meeting a child's special needs.
- Effective early intervention services make families feel welcomed and are shaped by the families.
- Families and professionals must work together in a climate of mutual respect and trust to be successful.

The Path to Early Intervention

IDEA prescribes a very specific pathway to early intervention services. Family members and service providers together plan and coordinate the program along each step in the pathway:

1. Identifying and Screening
2. Assigning a Temporary Service Coordinator
3. Evaluating by a Multidisciplinary Team
4. Determining Eligibility
5. Developing the Individualized Family Service Plan

1. Identifying and Screening

If you suspect that your baby or toddler has a disability or developmental delay, or potentially has such problems, you or anyone helping your family can request a screening. A telephone call to your local school system will most likely help you find where to go. You might also check with your child's doctor.

Many communities conduct periodic screening clinics to help identify children who might need early intervention. These screenings, often called Child Find, are advertised in local newspapers, on grocery store bulletin boards, at schools, and at health departments. Screening methods vary from place to place, but can be done in clinics, in your home, by your observation or report, or through a check-up at your pediatrician's office. The purpose is to pick up potential difficulties and to identify children who need further evaluation and diagnosis.

Depending upon the outcome of your child's screening, several things may occur:

- If the screening process indicates your child *does* appear to meet the criteria, you will be assigned a temporary service coordinator
- If your child *does not* appear to meet the eligibility requirements for Part C Early Intervention Services, you may be:
  - ❑ asked to come back at a later date for a follow-up screening,

or
❏ referred to other services your child or family might need.

Even if the screening committee believes your child will not qualify for services, you still can refer your child and request a multidisciplinary assessment and evaluation.

The screening process is not mandatory. If you and professionals agree that your child's diagnosis or condition is likely to qualify her for Part C services, you may decide to bypass the screening process and move directly down the next step in the pathway—the assignment of a temporary service coordinator.

2. Assigning a Temporary Service Coordinator

Once the early intervention agency has received a referral, either directly from a parent or from a screening program, two things happen. First, arrangements begin for evaluation and assessment. Second, a temporary service coordinator is assigned to the family to work with them throughout the evaluation process. Both of these steps must be accomplished within two working days.

The temporary service coordinator is responsible for pulling together the appropriate team to evaluate your child's development and for gathering information from you and from the professionals who have worked with you. The temporary service coordinator is the primary person with whom you will talk during the evaluation process. You must give written permission before the next step—evaluation—can take place.

3. Evaluating by a Multidisciplinary Assessment Team

Within forty-five days of the referral, an evaluation must be completed and a service plan put in place if your child is found eligible for early intervention. Evaluation is the word used to describe all of the procedures used to determine your child's unique strengths and weaknesses. The evaluation includes observations, tests, interviews, and other means of gaining knowledge about your child. Family members may participate in planning the types of tests and evaluation the child might need. You may provide information about your child's growth and development; about your family's concerns, resources, and priorities; and about what types of early intervention services your child and family might need.

Based upon the screening information, your temporary service coordinator will plan with you the procedures used in the evaluation. The evaluation will be multidisciplinary, which means there must be people with various professional backgrounds to evaluate your child. Later in this chapter you will find suggestions for making the evaluation go well for you and your child.

4. Determining Eligibility

After the evaluation is over, you and members of the multidisciplinary team will meet and decide whether your child and family are eligible under Part C criteria to receive early intervention services. Eligibility will be based upon the information you provide and upon whether the tests given indicate that your child meets any *one* of the three criteria below:

1. The child has developmental delays, as measured by appropriate diagnostic instruments and procedures, in one or more of the following areas:
   - cognitive development;
   - physical development, which includes vision and hearing;
   - communication development;
   - social or emotional development;
   - self-help or adaptive skills.

   Example: Brendan was born with a cleft palate. His speech and language development was delayed, so he was found eligible for early intervention services.

2. The child has a record of a diagnosed physical or mental condition which has a high probability of resulting in delay of development.

   Example: Kaia was diagnosed at birth with mild cerebral palsy. Her development measured within normal limits, yet her family and doctor felt that extra help and carefully planned activities would enhance her physical and communications development.

3. The child is regarded as being at risk of having substantial delays in development if early intervention services are not provided. This is an optional criterion which not all states have adopted.

   Example: Tommy's mother was fourteen when he was born two months prematurely. Concern for Tommy's development led to his receiving early intervention services, because in the state in which he lived, children at risk of having substantial delays are eligible.

States have the option of establishing their own definitions of eligibility, as long as they are operating within the federal regulations. Check the specific definition established by your state.

5. Development of an Individualized Family Service Plan (IFSP)

If your child is found to be eligible for early intervention, you and a team will meet to write a plan for addressing the unique needs of your child and your family. The Individualized Family Service Plan (IFSP) has certain requirements. The required parts of an IFSP are:

1. Information about **your child's current development.** Included in this section is information you provide, as well as the evaluation results about her health, vision, hearing, language, speech, social, emotional, self-help, and intellectual (cognitive) development.

2. Information about **your family's resources, priorities, and concerns.** You will be asked about ways in which your family strengths can contribute to your baby or toddler's development. An example of "family strengths" might be an extended family nearby to help with childcare, a strong religious belief, or a network of family and friends who give emotional support. You may choose whether or not to give family information.

3. The **measurable results or outcomes expected** can include your hopes and dreams for your child and your family. If developmentally appropriate for your child, this section should include pre-reading and language skills. This section should also include how and when the program will let you know if your child is progressing as planned. Examples of outcomes are found later in this chapter on a sample IFSP.

4. The **early intervention services** needed to help your child and your family reach the outcomes decided upon by you and the rest of the team. This section also must describe where, when, how, and for what length of time each session of the services will be given. Payment arrangements, if any, are specified in this section.

5. Statement about the **natural environments** in which services will be provided. The natural environment includes home and community settings in which children who do not have disabilities learn, play, and grow. Some babies or toddlers receive early intervention services in daycare centers or at home, while others go to a special center for infant education.

6. If appropriate, **other services** are included, which might address medical or other special needs of your child but which are not required under the IFSP. By including other services, the team can help you plan and secure such services needed by your child and family members.

7. The **dates and duration** of services. This section states when the services will begin and how long they will last.

8. Naming of the **service coordinator.** This person will help you coordinate the various services required by your child and family, includ-

ing helping to obtain the services identified in the IFSP, arranging for evaluations and assessments, and facilitating review meetings for the IFSP. The service coordinator may or may not be the person originally named as your temporary service coordinator.

9. A **transition plan** that includes the steps that will support the transition to whatever preschool services your child will receive, including either public or private preschool. The transition plan should be written at least ninety days before your child's third birthday or when she will be leaving the early intervention program. In addition, this part of the IFSP indicates the procedures you need to follow if your child will require **special education** preschool services. You may be asked to sign permission to have your child's record sent from the early intervention program to help the local school system with the referral process. Further information on transition is found on page 191 in this chapter.

The actual format for a written IFSP differs among various states and localities. The elements described above, as well as your consent for the services, however, are required under the Individuals with Disabilities Education Act (IDEA). IFSPs are reviewed every six months, or more often if needed. A formal evaluation of the IFSP is done each year as your baby or toddler grows and changes.

Provision and Costs for Services

Under Part C of IDEA, several early intervention services must be provided at *no cost* to the family. These include evaluations or assessments, the development of IFSPs, and service coordination for eligible children and their families. Part C, however, does *not* require that all early intervention be provided at no cost to families. Although many early intervention programs do not charge families, early intervention programs *can* charge families for services included in the IFSP according to a sliding fee scale.

Besides being required to pay for services, families sometimes also find that public services included in their child's IFSP are not available. If you encounter problems related to the costs or availability of early intervention, contact your service coordinator.

Your service coordinator is responsible for informing you of options for finding alternative services and for helping you to arrange for the payments. For some families, Medicaid or a private insurance carrier may pay for early intervention services. Other families pay on the sliding fee scale. You cannot, however, be denied early intervention services if you prove you are unable to pay. One thing to remember is that you can say no to any service recommended, including one or more that you don't want to pay for.

Part C was designed to involve many agencies in a coordinated effort to establish a comprehensive early intervention system at the local level. Sometimes problems arise or delays may occur because of misunderstandings or disagreements between several agencies working together. The agencies have a responsibility to work together to provide appropriate and timely services for families and their babies. When waiting lists and other problems arise, the interagency body should address these problems. As parents, you can present your problem to the interagency committee and ask for a solution.

Preparing for Your Participation in the IFSP Process

Do you, like most people, come away from a visit to your doctor thinking, "Why didn't I ask this question?" "I wish I had told my doctor about this when I saw her." All too often, we find anxiety gets in the way of full participation in our own care. This, too, can happen when you are working with professionals who are helping you with your child.

One of the unique aspects of the IFSP process is that parents' wishes and concerns are considered first and foremost. With assistance from a team of experienced professionals, you are in the driver's seat. At each of the five steps along the pathway to develop your child's early intervention program, you will find yourself feeling more in control if you make careful preparations. You will feel better prepared for your role if you get information about your child's condition, prognosis, and effective interventions. Parents and other family members participate more fully by thinking through their perceptions of their infant or toddler's development and writing down information they wish to share with the people helping them.

Before and After the Assessment

Assessment procedures provide useful information about your child's developmental levels from a variety of professional perspectives. Taken together, evaluation results determine if your child is eligible for early intervention and provide a picture of her unique strengths and needs. Tests and observations identify areas on which you and the professionals may want to focus. You also can look objectively at your child's progress and see milestones she has reached and levels mastered. Even so, going through various evaluations and assessments can be trying for you and your child. To get the most accurate results and to reduce your stress, you may find some of the following ideas helpful.

Before evaluations, people have various ways of getting ready. One family asked a professional to guide them through the process by explaining unfamiliar concepts and terminology. Another found it useful to get the advice and support of other parents and to learn about their experiences in early intervention. A third family prepared for the evaluation by writing down what they wanted to say and deciding what they wanted to get out of the meeting. A fourth family did all of the above!

As you decide how to prepare for your child's evaluation and assessment, consider some of the following questions:

- When is your child at her best? For example, after she eats, when you are out of the room, in the early afternoon?
- Who will be conducting the evaluations?
- What are their roles?
- What types of tests will be used? What do these tests measure?
- How are the evaluations and assessments usually conducted? Is there any flexibility if you have suggestions?
- How will the information that you have already received from medical professionals be used?
- Do you need to bring anything? For example, food, toys, immunization records, other reports?
- What role do parents usually play? What role should you play?
- How soon will you know the results of the tests? In what way is this information usually given?
- How do the evaluators use information if your child does something at home that she does not do during the evaluation?

After the evaluations, the professionals will often discuss preliminary results with you. You may be pleasantly surprised about your baby or toddler's progress . . . or disappointed that her progress has been slower than you had hoped. In some cases you may disagree with the people who conducted the assessment or feel as if they have not developed a complete picture of your child. You can bring this up at the eligibility meeting in the next stage.

Before the eligibility meeting, ask for a copy of the evaluation reports. You may have some questions you want to ask before the actual meeting or may want to wait until the whole team is together so that you can get a full picture of your child. Questioning the professionals carefully can help you. For example, parents often hear only the things that are wrong with their child. You will want to ask what they found that is right—the positive things—to provide the rounded picture needed. Many parents find that talking about the evaluation with other family members, trusted professionals, or friends can help them sort through their feelings and their information.

The eligibility decision is based on the results and discussions between you and the team. All may agree that your child does not have enough of a delay to need services right now. If that is the case, ask what you can do to check your child's progress and what to do if you think that your child is falling behind. If you and the team do not agree, ask for the procedures for resolving your disagreement.

A source of help may be the parent-to-parent groups located in many states and local communities. These groups link parents who have had similar experiences in order that they can support one another. There are also parent groups that provide peer support for families of children with common disabilities and rare disabilities. You can find out more about parent linkages by calling your Parent Training and Information Center and by looking through the Resource section at the end of this book.

Organizing Information

Keeping track of the paperwork can feel daunting. Not long after you learn that your child needs special help, you may find yourself buried in a mountain of papers. There are bills, reports, notes, questionnaires, and appointment slips. Take charge of all of these papers before they take charge of you! You also will come in contact with an array of new people—parents, specialists, physicians, insurance claims adjusters—to name only a few. How can you stay on top of all of the information?

Keeping your many reports and forms in a three-ring binder can help you organize your information and have important information at your fingertips. You may feel quite discouraged if you start rummaging through the drawer where you *know* you put a copy of a special report about your baby or toddler, yet be unable to find it! The Key People Chart and Phone Call Record (pages 176-78) are good places to start keeping your information organized.

The IFSP Meeting

Getting Ready for the IFSP meeting

If your child has been found eligible for early intervention services, and you begin to plan for the meeting, remember that you and your family are the primary decision makers on the team. The service coordinator and the other professionals are there to help *you* think through your situation. They can help you to solve

KEY PEOPLE CHART

I. HEALTH

Name	Address	Telephone	E-mail
Primary Care Physician			
Other Specialists			
Hospital			
Nursing Advice Line			
Public Health Nurse			
Pharmacy			

II. EARLY INTERVENTION

Name	Address	Telephone	E-mail
Service Coordinator			
Specialists			

III. FAMILY SUPPORT

Name	Address	Telephone	E-mail
Parent Support Line			
Sitter or Other Helper			

IV. FINANCIAL

Name	Address	Telephone	E-mail
Insurance			
Medicaid			
Supplemental Security Income			
Emergency Services			

V. OTHER CONTACTS: FRIENDS, CHURCH, FAMILY, CONSULTANTS

Name	Address	Telephone	E-mail

PHONE CALL RECORD

Who: _____ Date: _____

_____ Phone: _____

_____ Email: _____

Notes: _____

_____

_____

Follow up? ____ No   Who: _____

____ Yes   When: _____

- - - - - - - - - - - - - - - -

Who: _____ Date: _____

_____ Phone: _____

_____ Email: _____

Notes: _____

_____

_____

Follow up? ____ No   Who: _____

____ Yes   When: _____

- - - - - - - - - - - - - - - -

Who: _____ Date: _____

_____ Phone: _____

_____ Email: _____

Notes: _____

_____

_____

Follow up? ____ No   Who: _____

____ Yes   When: _____

problems and to foster your child's growth and development. You can identify your family resources, priorities, and concerns. You can also identify supports and services that will help your family meet your child's developmental needs. No services will be provided without your written consent. As a member of the IFSP team, you will discover ways that your family can care for your child's special needs, while at the same time preserving a family life that is as normal as possible. The team will work with you to identify the kinds of help and services you require.

To prepare for the IFSP meeting, you can fill out the following *Family Information Form*. The *Family Information Form* helps you plan for the IFSP meeting. Your family's values and routines are an important part of the planning process. Others on the team need to know what you want for your family so they can respond to your family's strengths, areas of concern, and priorities. The plan must respect your family routines and values. All planning will be in your family's primary language so that you and the other team members can understand the plans and outcomes.

Participating in the IFSP Meeting

The temporary service coordinator or the person who has been designated as your service coordinator will arrange for your child's IFSP meeting. Also in attendance will be the other members of your child's team, including you, the parents, and people who provide or can help you gain access to various services.

You may choose to bring a family member or friend with you as a support person to listen with you, to help you explain some of your points of view and wishes, and to take notes that you might need later. Before the meeting, go over your *Family Information Form* with your support person so that both of you have the same agenda in mind. Following the meeting, you might go out for pizza or coffee so that you and your support person can talk about what happened at the meeting.

What is in your child's IFSP is determined at the meeting after considering the points of view of all members of the IFSP Team. You, as the parent, make the final decision about accepting or rejecting the proposals. If you want something different from what is recommended by other team members, you may follow procedures described in Chapter 14 to resolve your disagreements. Without your consent, the IFSP will not be put into effect.

IFSP meetings must be conducted annually and reviewed every six months. Meetings can be held more frequently if necessary, or if the family requests a review or change.

Family-Centered IFSP Meetings

The IFSP is more than simply a written plan. It is a process leading parents and professionals toward a mutual understanding of the child's needs and the

FAMILY INFORMATION FORM

Date _____

My Name _____

My Child's Name _____

Please Call Me _____

Child's Birthday _____

Photograph of your child or family.

1. Description of our family (parent(s), brothers and sisters, grandparents, special

friends and relations): _____

_____

_____

2. What we enjoy doing as a family: _____

_____

_____

   During these family times my child: _____

_____

3. My child's favorite activity is: _____

_____

   Because _____

_____

4. My child's least favorite activity is: _____

_____

   Because _____

_____

5. What I enjoy most about my child is: _____

_____

_____

6. What my child and I enjoy doing the most is: _____

_____

_____

7. I am most frustrated when caring for my child when: _____

_____

_____

8. My child lets me know when he/she needs something by: _____

_____

9. I could do more for my child if I had: _____

_____

(Examples: transportation, someone to talk to and listen to me, time to myself, time for the other children, more information about my baby's condition and about ways to help her, help with medical and other expenses, housing, Supplemental Security Income (SSI), food stamps, etc.)

10. Some changes or progress I've recently noticed in my child: _____

_____

_____

11. What I would like to see my child do in the next six months: _____

_____

_____

12. How my family, friends, or I can help my child do these things: ___

_____

13. Some of my hopes for my child and family are: _____

_____

_____

FAMILY INFORMATION FORM

Date _January 7, 2008_

My Name _Isabel_

My Child's Name _Elena_

Please Call Me _____

Child's Birthday _July 12, 2006_

Photograph of your child or family.

1. Description of our family (parent(s), brothers and sisters, grandparents, special friends and relations): _Mother, older sister, no close relatives. Elena has friends in daycare._

2. What we enjoy doing as a family: _Elena and her sister Marta like to help me go shopping. Marta goes off to find her own list of food (cereal, soup, cookies) and comes back from different directions to surprise Elena. Elena looks for her sister and is delighted when Marta comes back to the shopping cart._

3. My child's favorite activity is: _going for walks._

Because _she is in the stroller and holds onto the dog's leash. She likes to point to things and say "dat?"_

4. My child's least favorite activity is: _bedtime_

Because _she wants to keep playing with her toys. She always gets fussy and has a hard time calming down and going to sleep._

5. What I enjoy most about my child is: **how she smiles and laughs.**

6. What my child and I enjoy doing the most is: **going for our walks.**

7. I am most frustrated when caring for my child when: **I see how much more delayed she is than her sister was.**

8. My child lets me know when he/she needs something by: **pointing. Sometimes she just fusses while I guess what she wants. When I do give her what she wants, she gives me that beautiful smile.**

9. I could do more for my child if I had: **some way of know what she wants. She is delayed in speaking so I don't often know why she is fussing.**

(Examples: transportation, someone to talk to and listen to me, time to myself, time for the other children, more information about my baby's condition and about ways to help her, help with medical and other expenses, housing, Supplemental Security Income (SSI), food stamps, etc.)

10. Some changes or progress I've recently noticed in my child: **She says a few words like "Ma" for "Marta"; "Ba" for "bottle"; "Mimi" for "mommy"; "wa?" for "walk?"**

11. What I would like to see my child do in the next six months: **I want her to be able to tell me what she wants.**

12. How my family, friends, or I can help my child do these things: **I heard somewhere that they are teaching children with Down syndrome to talk and sign. Maybe that might help.**

13. Some of my hopes for my child and family are: **I want Elena to live as normal a life as possible and have friends.**

family's wishes. The written IFSP is a guide leading to the future. Families and service providers suggest that the following steps be taken to ensure productive and constructive IFSP meetings:

1. Families and service providers agree to a convenient time and place for the meeting so that parents and other important family members or friends may attend. The meeting is scheduled at least one week in advance to allow everyone time to prepare.

2. Families receive copies of all written reports before the meeting so they can understand the information and are prepared to discuss it. If this is not possible, it may be necessary to schedule a second meeting soon after the first.

3. Parents and the service coordinator meet before the IFSP meeting to prepare information and plan ways for the family to be active participants in the meeting.

4. Enough time is allowed for the meeting so that no one feels rushed and participants have time to discuss what they consider the most important outcomes for the child and the family.

5. The meeting determines what the family believes is important for their child to do or to accomplish. The IFSP outcomes (goals) are the result of what the family identifies.

6. The outcomes for the child and family are developed at the meeting, giving parents and other members of the family a full opportunity to participate. Parents may not know what aids or therapies will help their child reach these outcomes. Professionals contribute knowledge about specific ways to accomplish an outcome identified by the family.

On pages 185-87 is an example of an IFSP prepared by the Jackson family and their IFSP team. The format may be different in your locality, but the required parts will be the same.

When Services Begin

You might think that once you have written the IFSP you can sit back, relax, and let things happen. Now, however, is the time for the important work outlined in your baby or toddler's IFSP to begin. You and other family members will be involved in helping your child and family move forward on the pathway toward growth and change.

Early intervention services take many forms. Families whose babies have specialized health care needs often feel that services should be in their homes, in part

INDIVIDUALIZED FAMILY SERVICE PLAN

Identifying Information

Child: **Martha Dee Jackson**

Parent/Guardian: **Bernice Jackson**

Address: **4421 Main Street**

Home Phone: **(218) 467-9999**

Foster Home: [ ] yes [X] no

Date: **8/23/07**

Birth Date: **8/20/05**   [ ] M [X] F

Work Phone(s):

Language Spoken in Home: **English**

Dates

Present Meeting: **8/23/07**

Anticipated Six Month Review: **2/08**

Anticipated Annual Review: **8/08**

IFSP Meeting Information

Type of Meeting: [X] Initial

[ ] Six Month Review

[ ] Annual Review

[ ] Interim

Amendment of IFSP   Dated: [ ] To add or [ ] delete

Information Update

[X] Identifying Information

[X] Family Concerns, Priorities, & Strengths

[X] Child's Strengths and Needs

[X] Outcomes

[X] Other Services

[ ] Transition Plan

[ ] No longer eligible

[ ] Moved out of county

[ ] Parent withdrawal

[ ] Whereabouts unknown

[ ] Transition to: _____

[ ] Other

Eligibility

1. [X] Child is eligible for Part H services based on **"at risk" status**

Functional Description of Disability: **Spina Bifida**

2. [ ] Specific eligibility undetermined; recommend: _____

3. [ ] Child does not meet eligibility for Part H services _____

INDIVIDUALIZED FAMILY SERVICE PLAN (CONTINUED)

IFSP Participants

The following individuals participated in the development of the IFSP. Each person understands and agrees to carry out the plan as it applies to their role in the provision of services.

Service Coordinator: _Mary E. Morgan_   Representing: _Early Intervention_   Date: _8/23/07_

Name: _Bernice Jackson_   Representing: _Mother_   Date: _8/23/07_

Name: _Ann Adams_   Representing: _Easter Seals_   Date: _8/23/07_

Name: _____   Representing: _____   Date: _____

Name: _____   Representing: _____   Date: _____

The IFSP was developed with telephone consultation from the following people:

Name: _Nina Baxter_   Representing: _Parent Center_   Date: _8/24/07_

Name: _____   Representing: _____   Date: _____

Name: _____   Representing: _____   Date: _____

Family Approval

[x] I had the opportunity to participate in the development of this IFSP. I agree with and support the outcomes and services in the IFSP for my child.

[ ] I have had the opportunity to review the proposal of the IFSP Team and I do not agree with the outcomes or services selected. I do not give my permission for it to be implemented.

Parent/Legal Guardian _Bernice Jackson_   Date _8/23/07_

Parent/Legal Guardian _____   Date _____

Family's Concerns, Priorities, & Resources (as described by parents)

Martha Dee's gross motor and language development are the primary concerns of the Jackson family. Martha Dee speaks 4-5 words and responds well when her brother plays and talks with her. They believe that consulation by a language therapist will increase Martha Dee's speech.

Child's Strengths and Needs (as described by parents)

Martha Dee has made significant progress in her gross motor development. She sits, crawls, and now uses a "stander" at home 2 times per day, half hour each time. Her mother plays with her with a large "therapy ball" 15 minutes, 3 times a day. Martha Dee and her brother sing and play together. Her language development is her major area of need.

INDIVIDUALIZED FAMILY SERVICE PLAN (CONTINUED)

Outcome #1—Part H Services

Martha Dee will identify pictures in familiar picture books and will increase her vocabulary to 15 words by 2/08. She will receive broad-based infant development programming to address her special developmental needs, particularly in motor and language skills.

1.1 Home-based infant development services—3 hrs./month
1.2 Center-based services—16 hrs. per month at Easter Seals
1.3 Speech language teacher to consult with both home and center teacher

Services/Actions (How will outcomes be reached and success determined?)
Teachers at the center and in the home and Martha Dee's mother will reinforce new words and keep a vocabulary list as she learns new words

Providers: Easter Seal Society
Location: 1:1 teaching at home; 1:3 Easter Seal Society
Frequency: home-based: 3 hrs/month; center-based: 16 hrs/month
Duration: 9/6/07—8/20/08
Responsible Agency: Travis County Early Intervention Services (TCEIS)
Signature of Responsible Agency Person: *Marye Morgan*   **Date:** *8/23/07*

Outcome #2—Not Funded by Part H

Martha Dee has a VP shunt and requires catheterization for urine every 3 hours. These needs will be medically monitored, along with her regular pediatric needs.

2.1 Spina Bifida and Urology Clinics will monitor the neurological and urological development
2.2 Ongoing medical monitoring and treatment to be given at Greenway
2.3 Martha Dee's mother will administer catheterization every 3 hours as directed by a physician

Services/Actions (How will outcomes be reached and success determined?)
Physician and Martha Dee's mother will discuss the ongoing catheterization needs.

Providers: Spina Bifida and Urology Clinic and Greenway Children's Clinic
Location: San Jacinto
Frequency: semi-annually and as needed
Duration: 9/6/07—8/20/08
Responsible Agency: Medicare
Signature of Responsible Agency Person: *Marye Morgan*   **Date:** *8/23/07*

(Martha Dee's IFSP would have three additional outcomes developed in the areas of motor development, parent support group, and case management.)

to avoid exposing their child to colds or other infections. Generally, service providers also recommend home-based early intervention for fragile children. Yet other families want their child to face the rough and tumble of everyday life and request center-based infant education for their child. They want the exposure to other children and their families both for themselves and for their child. While you may or may not have a choice as to whether your child receives services at home or at a center, Part C requires that services be provided in the child's natural environment, which may mean for your child that she be with other children without disabilities. If choices are available, you can express your preferences at the IFSP meeting.

The different services on your child's IFSP may be provided for an hour a week, twice a month, or at other intervals. Between times, parents practice activities such as language games, physical exercises, or eating skills with their child. Each session, either at a center or at home, offers opportunities for discussion between the service provider and the family.

Families in which the single parent or both parents work can find themselves in a bind at their workplace if participation with their child in early intervention services cuts into their workday. Some families arrange for another caregiver or childcare provider to be the primary person who works with the baby as the teachers or therapists suggest. Others may ask a relative to go with the baby to the center-based services. Some families try to arrange for sessions at times that minimize time lost from work; for example, before work or during their lunch hour. Remember, parents should be the primary decision makers as these types of issues are discussed and resolved with the multidisciplinary team.

Depending on the services described in the IFSP, your active involvement will help to ensure positive results. Working as a partner with service providers helps you build a support group. Your service coordinator or a parent-to-parent program can also link you to other families who are living and dealing with a family situation similar to yours. This can help, too, in expanding your network of support.

Different families find different ways to become partners with people who are there to assist them. The most important way to build a partnership with people who will be helping you and your family is by practicing good communication techniques. Often infant intervention services are given at home. You may find that having a friend there at the end of the therapy session to play with your child will give you time to have a discussion with the therapist. Or you might set up a separate time when your child can be cared for by someone else, so that your full attention can be on the conversation about your child's progress and development.

Good communication requires you to build relationships. There are many ways to strengthen relationships with professional people—most take little time. A "thank you" in person, on the telephone, by email, or in a short note shows your appreciation. Professional people, like all people, like to know you care.

When Disagreements Arise

Even in the best of relationships, disagreements can arise. When you have made the effort to build positive partnerships with professionals, however, disagreements have a good chance of being resolved quickly and satisfactorily.

You and your child have certain rights under IDEA. You have assurance that:

- Parents and families are served by programs that are conducted in a voluntary and nondiscriminatory way;
- Parents and family members have access to the information they need to know in order to participate in early intervention programs and to make clear decisions;
- Family members' preferences and choices are respected regarding the services for their child and their family.

As a parent, you have the right to:

- give written consent when your child is to be assessed or evaluated;
- be given written notice in your native language of actions proposed or refused by the service providers;
- see copies of and correct records about your child and family;
- protection of the confidentiality of any private information about your child or your family;
- have a service coordinator who will assist you in pulling together the information and the people needed to develop an IFSP;
- decide whether to accept or decline any early intervention services without jeopardizing others;
- go through a mediation or formal hearing process if there are disagreements or complaints that can't be resolved informally with the service provider.

Families are involved in all steps of the early intervention process. Although the process is designed to minimize conflict, disagreements may occur. Examples areas of possible disagreement between parents and professionals are:

- Professionals believe an initial assessment and evaluation are not necessary.
- Parents believe an initial evaluation is not necessary.
- The family and service providers do not agree on the type, frequency, or duration of services.
- The family and service providers have difficulty getting the help needed for the child and the family.

What happens when the process does not go smoothly? What should parents and professionals do when differences of opinion persist?

Informal Problem Solving

You may reach a point where you can't think your way through a difficult situation, either in relationship to another person or as you make choices for your child and family. If so, a problem-solving approach can be very helpful. First, clarify the situation, identifying what you believe to be unsatisfactory. Second, make a plan of action by exploring various alternatives and deciding which of these to pursue. If you can find a partner to go through these steps with you, and/or write them down, you may find the situation under control.

Problem Solving: A Case Study

Brendan Lindsay's speech and language are delayed. He was born with a cleft palate that was corrected by surgery when he was six months old. The rest of the IFSP team recommended that a home educator come to his family's home once every two weeks to help Brendan's mother learn how to help Brendan learn to eat better. Brendan's mother agreed reluctantly, although she felt that speech services and occupational therapy should be added because of Brendan's sensitivity to certain food textures and touch.

After six weeks, Ms. Lindsay decided a change was necessary, as she felt that Brendan's progress was much too slow. She believed he needed more intensive therapy services. She talked to her service coordinator, sharing her thoughts and observations. Together they decided to reconvene the IFSP Team. After discussing Brendan's slow progress, the speech therapist thought that more intensive speech therapy services were needed. The occupational therapist offered to consult with the home educator on ways that Ms. Lindsay could help Brendan improve his ability to interact with and touch different textures and stimuli. They all agreed that the speech therapist and home educator would coordinate services with the occupational therapists and go alternating weeks so that Brendan would receive weekly services. They agreed to try this for a few more weeks and reevaluate whether the increased level of services was helping. Ms. Lindsay and the professionals felt good about their informal way of solving the problem.

Other Options for Resolving Disagreements

If informal problem solving does not resolve a disagreement, IDEA provides other procedures. When a family believes that services are inappropriate, there are formal administrative processes at the local and state levels. At the state level, the parent can ask the lead agency to investigate whether the child and/or family's assessment, services, or service coordination have been appropriate. Additionally, most states have both mediation and due process hearings. Parents may file a due process complaint asking for a hearing by an impartial hearing officer or bring civil action in state or district court. Most families find, however, that a formal due process hearing or court proceeding takes such an enormous amount of time, money, and energy, that these actions are not practical for an infant or toddler. Before taking that step, more informal problem solving or mediation may help clarify understanding of each other's perspective and find mutually agreeable solutions. Chapter 14 contains more discussion of ways to resolve differences.

Transition into Preschool Services

Just as you feel life is settling down into some kind of pattern, things change. When your toddler nears age three (or six, depending on the state where you live), a new program is on the horizon.[1] How do you prepare yourself and your family for the next step in your child's life? Each IFSP must spell out the steps in the transition from the early intervention services to the preschool services appropriate for your child. Ideally, you should begin to prepare at least six months before your child moves to the next program. IDEA requires the transition process to begin no later than three months before the change.

Now is your time to ask others about future options, placements, and services so that you can make informed decisions about these and other matters related to your child's transition. The transition plan should describe the help your child will receive to prepare for changes in service delivery, including steps to help her adjust to the new setting. Once the early intervention program receives your permission, it will forward information about your child to the local school system. A well-developed transition plan will lead to a smooth transition to preschool special education or another appropriate educational program when your child turns three.

The local school system may require new evaluations and assessments to establish your child's eligibility for preschool special education. In some states the early intervention system will do evaluations, while in other states the school system wants to do their own. No matter who does the evaluation, the school system depends upon up-to-date information to make its eligibil-

---

1. *States have the option to extend early intervention services through age six. If your state offers this option, it is up to you, the parent, to decide whether to take it or to choose to move on to preschool special education services when your child reaches age three. If you decide to remain in Part C, services must include education that promotes school readiness, including pre-reading, language, and numeric skills.*

ity decision. An Individualized Education Program (IEP) will be written for your child if she is eligible (see Chapters 7-9). A representative from the early intervention program is invited to the first IEP team meeting by the education agency. If you have a preference about who this person should be, let the school representative know.

There are steps you can take to ease the change both for you and your child. Families may choose from among the following steps:

- Gather as much information as possible about available options.
- Explore possible alternatives in order to select one or two of the best choices.
- Find another family whose child has been in the proposed program and learn about their experiences.
- Talk to the person who is in charge of the proposed program.
- Visit the proposed program in advance.
- Talk to teachers and administrators of the program, describing your family's experiences in early intervention and your expectations for the new situation.
- Ask for written materials and learn the procedures for entering and participating in the new service or system.
- Evaluate the proposed program carefully and realize that you are in charge and can say either "yes" or "no" to the services recommended for your child and family.

Major Differences between Early Intervention and Special Education

Part C—Early Intervention	Part B—Special Education
Eligibility based on developmental delay or condition likely to result in developmental delay	Eligibility based on categories of disabilities
Child and family focused	Child focused
Individualized Family Service Plan (IFSP)	Individualized Educational Program (IEP)
Services provided in the natural environment	Services provided in the least restrictive environment (LRE)—primarily in school settings
Families may be charged for services	Services are at no cost to families

When the time comes for the actual change, you may want to prepare yourself, your child, and your family for the new routines. For example, you can visit the new program or service in order for your child to become acquainted with the new people and the new environment. Perhaps sending a favorite toy with your child might make her more comfortable in the new situation. And maybe other family members may need to be alerted to the new routines brought on by the change.

Conclusion

As time goes on, you will find that changes or transitions present many of the same problems you have previously worked through with success. The past certainly can help prepare you for new experiences. What you have learned in the early intervention program can be applied if your child enters a preschool special education program. As in all of the decisions you have made and will be making, the more information you gather and the stronger the relationships you develop, the easier the transition will be for you and your family.

WHAT YOU CAN DO NOW

1. Find out the purpose of all evaluations and make sure you understand the results.
2. Review the sample IFSP and think about what you would like included on the IFSP for you and your child.
3. When it's time to select or change programs, visit the proposed program or programs, and take notes about what you find.

12. Transitions

Opportunities to Explore

Can my child really learn to live away from home? Will he have a job? What are his chances for further education after he leaves high school? No matter how young your child is, you may have thought about these and many other questions. As your child grows older, your family will be faced with many perplexing concerns about his future. With your hands full just coping with day-to-day life, planning to address the future is often difficult. Without a crystal ball to provide a vision of what lies ahead, you may wonder if it is worth the time and effort required for such planning.

Whatever a child's disability, steps you take now can help create a more positive future for both you and your child. You have an important role to play to make sure that your child with disabilities—as with all of your children—will have as independent and self-sufficient a life as possible. This chapter will help you understand the nuts and bolts of transition. The next chapter takes a look at the process of transition planning and how to use transition plans to help your child move toward a future of maximum independence.

Hopes and Facts

Families understand that their children with disabilities are entitled to a *free and appropriate public education* in the *least restrictive environment* through high school. There is no similar educational entitlement when your child leaves school. Once a young adult with disabilities leaves the public school system, there is no guaranteed program that takes up where IDEA leaves off. No current federal or state laws provide all young adults with disabilities with rights to continuing education, or to the housing, jobs, or support services needed to help them live independently.

While life after high school comes with no guarantees for services, increasing numbers of young people with a range of disabilities are graduating from high school, going to college, working in the community, and even starting their own businesses. They are piecing together what they need for success through family, friends, publicly funded programs, community support, and creative solutions.

School personnel, parents, people with disabilities, and advocates have been working hard in recent years to address the problems faced by young people who leave school between the ages of eighteen and twenty-one with nowhere to go. IDEA now requires that at fifteen, students take a much more active role in their education and planning for life after high school. As a result, all students in special education—beginning with the IEP in place when they turn sixteen—need to have plans and services to help them achieve or continue working toward their lifelong goals. The following example shows how one family began planning for transition from school.

One Family's Transition Plans

Early in life, Maria Moran showed strong interest in caring for pets, young children, and her elderly grandfather. She often pretended to be a nurse or doctor with her dolls and pets. Her family made sure she had many opportunities to be with other children and adults and to help with household chores, especially when company was coming. As the years went by, they thought about how Maria's interests and strengths might lead to a possible career for her.

When Maria was fourteen, she began to explore career options. Mrs. Moran arranged for her to work with a teenage family friend as a baby sitter's helper. When her friend, Carla, had a childcare job, Maria would accompany her and help put the young children to bed. At school, Maria's IEP included a goal for her to visit four different jobs to observe people at work and learn about the various occupations. She was also taking a cooking course to learn to plan and prepare simple meals.

In high school, Maria spent a part of her day in a special nursing assistant program. Students in this program worked in a variety of community settings, providing care to others each day. First, Maria worked with the nurse in an elementary school, keeping the equipment clean, putting fresh sheets on the cots, and staying with young children as they waited for the nurse. Six weeks later, she worked in a nursing home alongside a skilled nurse's aide. Her final experience during that school year was at the pediatric unit in the local hospital, learning to make beds, to sterilize toys and equipment, and to be a companion for young sick children.

With help from her high school counselor, Maria and her family located a junior college with a two-year nursing assistant program. The program provides Maria with instruction and support in living on her own, as well as training for her chosen career.

Maria and her family were able to plan for her life after high school and get services in place with the help of the transition requirements of IDEA.

Transition and IDEA

Transition services are meant to prepare children with disabilities for their next steps after high school. The definition of transition and the process schools are to follow are outlined in IDEA: transition services are a coordinated set of activities for a child with a disability that

- help your child to prepare for a successful life after high school;
- are results-oriented and focused on improving your child's academic and functional achievement;
- are based on your child's specific needs and talents, taking into account your child's strengths, preferences, and interests;
- include instruction, related services, community experiences, the development of employment and other post-school adult living objectives, and, when appropriate, vocational evaluation and daily living skills.

Your child is to be directly involved in deciding between options and opportunities in a transition plan that will lead to successful results when special education ends. Planning for this success means the student, family, and rest of team consider various options after high school including: *post-secondary education, employment, adult services programs, independent living, and community life.* What are the options and opportunities? What can your child do after his special education services and support ends?

Post-secondary Education

Colleges

Colleges, whether they are two-year community colleges or four-year colleges and universities, offer an opportunity for students with disabilities to continue their education and earn a certificate or a degree. A few colleges are specifically geared for students with disabilities. For example, instruction may be based on a model that looks much like special education did in high school, providing individualized instruction and support for a student with learning disabilities, sensory impairments, or physical disabilities. Almost all colleges have a disabilities service center that can help students who are requesting accommodations such as note-takers, tutors, audio-recording, interpreters, and mobility aids.

Continuing and Adult Education

Continuing education courses offer opportunities for personal enrichment in areas such as photography, arts, and recreation, as well as courses for enhancing career goals, such as business management, childcare, culinary arts, and computers. The programs may include vocational and technical education courses, coursework to prepare for the General Education Development (GED) high school equivalency exam, and English language instruction. You can find information about continuing and adult education through your local school district, recreation department, or community college.

Trade and Technical Schools

Preparation for employment in recognized occupations such as office assistant, air conditioning technician, computer programmer, culinary arts, electrician, and carpenter is provided through these schools. Course work can take anywhere from two weeks to two years, and the schools generally require a high school diploma or high school equivalency degree to enter.

Apprenticeships

People can enter some trades such as mechanics, draftsmen, metallurgists, cosmetologists, and pastry chefs by working for some period of time under the expertise of a skilled tradesman. Apprenticeship programs can be formal or informal. In some programs, an apprentice may earn a stipend for work performed while learning a job. In other programs, the apprentice must pay to learn the trade.

Under the Americans with Disabilities Act (ADA) and Section 504 of the Rehabilitation Act post-secondary education institutions and apprenticeship programs cannot discriminate and must provide needed modifications, accommodations, or auxiliary aids that will help a person with a disability participate in and benefit from all educational programs and activities. For example, a young man with limited reading skills can learn the written materials through tape recordings of the manuals and participate fully in auto mechanics certification program. Chapter 15 provides more information about the requirements and protections provided by Section 504 and the ADA.

Employment

Transition services should prepare students for employment during and after high school. There are many different employment options for people with disabilities, depending on their skills and the level of support they need.

Competitive Employment

Competitive employment includes everyday jobs in the open labor market, such as healthcare worker, data entry clerk, legal assistant, waiter/waitress, retail clerk, secretary, and mechanic. These jobs pay wages at the going rate, and can be either part-time or full-time. Training, job search skills, and work experience can boost a student's opportunities for competitive employment.

On the Job Training

On the job training is short-term training that enables a person to work on a job site while learning the job duties. Many vocational rehabilitation agencies, disability organizations, and large corporations provide this type of training and job placement.

Supported Employment

Supported employment is paid employment, with support from a job coach or through supports and accommodations built into the work environment, called "natural supports." A job coach helps the employee to improve his job skills, interpersonal relations, or work through other job-related needs. Job coaches generally reduce their involvement as the worker becomes more skilled in his job. Salaries for supported jobs are generally at or above the minimum wage. Examples of supported jobs include grounds keeping, assisting at a veterinarian's office, working in medical laboratories to keep equipment ready for the scientists, or assembling electronic circuit boards.

Self-employment and Entrepreneurship

Some adults with disabilities may earn income through a service or skill they have. Examples of self-employment and entrepreneurships can include pet sitting, catering, lawn mowing, photography, vending and sales, web design, and painting.

Volunteer Jobs

In addition to, or concurrent with, some of the employment options above, volunteering can keep people with disabilities engaged and connected to their communities, especially if no paid jobs or training programs are available. Volunteer jobs let workers find out what types of jobs they like while building a resume and showing future employers that they are capable. Some volunteer jobs that have led to paid work include teaching assistant, park maintenance, museum assistant, hospital volunteer, website design, and office worker.

Adult Services

Adult service programs, which include adult day programs, work activity centers, and sheltered workshops, provide a work environment in a supervised setting without integration with workers who are not disabled. In adult day programs, participants usually receive training in daily living skills, social skills, and recreational skills. Work activity centers and sheltered workshops provide structure, supervision, and training for workers with disabilities. Workers may do contract work such as preparing bulk mailings, refinishing furniture, or assembling bicycle brake parts, and often earn money based on their productivity. In some cases, a group of workers may do supervised work in the community including recycling, laundry services, or other activities.

Independent Living

To live independently, young adults must learn the skills they need or obtain the support they require to live on their own. This usually means managing several parts of daily life, such as obtaining food and clothing, learning to manage time and money, and knowing ways to have fun.

Depending on their financial independence and independent living skills, young people with disabilities may continue living with their parents, other relatives, roommates, or paid companions, or they may live on their own. Increasingly, family members, adult service providers, and people with disabilities are developing creative programs that enable individuals with disabilities to live in their own homes or share homes with nondisabled housemates.

For young people who need significant support in independent living, family care, supervised living arrangements, and facilities that provide intensive care may be available. Family care is provided by individuals who are licensed by the state to provide family-like settings for elderly people and adults with disabilities. Supervised living arrangements, such as group homes, are managed by public or private agencies that own or rent homes or apartments. Paid staff supervise the residents and assist them with daily living such as budgeting, food preparation, and transportation. In some cases, a person might live in a supervised apartment with roommates of his choosing. Paid staff will check up on the residents, as needed, to address needs and help make sure things are running smoothly. Specialized Nursing Homes and Intermediate Care Facilities are state-licensed facilities operating under strict regulations and providing intensive support for people in the areas of personal care, communication, and behavior management.

Transition services can assist the student in applying for public benefits that are available to help people with disabilities live as independently as possible. Public assistance may include Section 8 housing, Supplemental Security Income (SSI), Medicaid, Social Security, and Medicare. Provisions within each of the public programs are complex, applying to some and not to others. You and your son or daughter may want to consult with adult services specialists to learn how these programs, alone or together, can maximize independent living choices. You can include goals for applying for benefits as part of your child's transition plan and ask the staff member of the adult service agency serving on the team to guide you.

Community Life

Being a part of the community can take many forms—volunteering at the local hospital, planting trees in the neighborhood park, attending church, serving on the board of a nonprofit agency, and walking the neighbor's dog. Young people with disabilities who take part in the community make new friends, possible work contacts, and contribute to the life and well-being of the community. Social clubs and recreational activities for people with and without disabilities are other ways to be involved in the community.

Young people may need help in arranging for transportation, through special services, public transportation, or friends, so they can be comfortable getting around in their communities. Online communities, web postings, and email can be a way for people to make connections and establish relationships. Transition plans that include such activities help ensure that young people with disabilities can be a part of their community and participate to the fullest extent possible.

The Importance of Self-Advocacy

In the past, the predictable transition for students with disabilities was from segregated school settings to segregated specialized adult day programs or workshops restricted to people with disabilities. Thanks to resolute people with disabilities, parents and professionals, innovative programs, and laws such as IDEA, the ADA, and the Rehabilitation Act, this is no longer true. Today's young people are more fully included in all aspects of school life and, therefore, are learning to make choices about their adult lives. They expect that they will have opportunities to be workers, students, family members, friends, and community participants.

Legislation, research, and best educational practices emphasize that a young person's transition to adult life must be based upon his unique interests, capacities, career goals, and needs for support. As you and your child's teachers encourage your child to make decisions about his future and to express his own views about his interests and preferences, he will become a more articulate and competent self-advocate.

Self-advocacy is important to people with disabilities: they must speak up for themselves out of an understanding of their basic human rights; take responsibility for their decisions and life; and ask for help when they need or want it. Self-advocacy skills are needed in all areas of life—on the job, in school, at home, in the community, with family and friends, when using medical services, in meeting transportation needs, and during recreation and fun times. This is why self-advocacy skills are important throughout your child's years in school—and why you may want to consider including specific self-advocacy goals in every one of your child's IEPs.

When you think about your child, you may worry that he will not be able to learn to make responsible decisions and speak up for himself. Certainly, the amount of independent self-advocacy a young person is able to demonstrate varies depending upon his abilities and the degree of disability. While some young people are not able to speak verbally for themselves, they communicate their preferences in many other ways. All young people need the involvement and support of their family members, friends, teachers, and others as they learn to solve problems, be assertive, and make their own plans for transitions from high school. IDEA recognizes the importance of self-advocacy skills by requiring that decisions about transition activities be based upon the student's preferences and interests.

Transfer of Parental Rights at Age of Majority

When a student reaches the age of majority (age eighteen, in most states), the rights of parents as spelled out in IDEA automatically transfer from the parent to the student. The student will be notified of meetings and will sign his own IEP. Schools must inform parents at least a year before this occurs. In most instances, parents still may continue to be invited to IEP or transition team meetings and they will continue to play an active role in planning and advocating for the student. When parents and their children realize this change is coming, they understand how important it is for students to develop self-advocacy and decision-making skills at an early age.

Sometimes a court deems a student incapable of making personal decisions. In these cases, a parent or other guardian is appointed to make decisions on the student's behalf. In some cases, a student may want his parents to continue to have decision-making authority. The student and his parents can take formal steps for the parents to retain this right. This can often be easily done (and undone). Procedures may be different in each state, so be sure to check your state's special education regulations and speak to advocacy organizations in your state or community to find out the options where you live.

Conclusion

Opportunities for further schooling, work, independent living, and community participation differ from community to community. Many families find that the best avenues into the world for their child with disabilities are the same as for their children who do not have disabilities. What has been called the "self, family, friends network" is often an effective way of developing resources and programs for young people with disabilities. Calling upon family connections and contacts is one of the surest ways to explore education, living, and work options for young people. For example, Mrs. Moran asked her friend's daughter to let Maria accompany her when Maria first expressed an interest in baby sitting. A second example comes from Maria's uncle, who owns a paint and hardware company. He has created jobs for several young men and women with disabilities.

Another way to explore opportunities for work, training, or further education is to seek out community service agencies and organizations serving people with disabilities. Many states have developed model programs throughout the state which improve services for students with disabilities. Your state's Department of Rehabilitative Services or Vocational Rehabilitation, the Department of Mental Health and Developmental Disabilities, and, of course, the Department of Education can provide you with information about such programs and further direct you to programs which might be of assistance. Support, advocacy, or educational groups such as The Arc, United Cerebral Palsy, Autism Society of America, and the Learning Disabilities Association may also provide important information on post-school programs and services. Check with the Parent Training and Information Center in your state for organizations that might be appropriate in your child's situation.

Remember that communities may not offer their citizens with disabilities every type of option described in this book or every opportunity you may have learned about from other sources. Once again, parents often find themselves on the cutting edge of developing programs and services for their young adult children. Planning effectively for your child's life after high school, however, requires you to explore options that are available well in advance of your child's graduation or twenty-first birthday. Transition planning meetings can provide a source of information about eligibility criteria and the availability of programs and services. You and your child can visit the programs, assess their suitability, and understand the requirements for gaining entrance. By advance planning, you can use the school years, the IEP and formal transition planning process, your child's network of family and friends, and the assistance of public and private agencies to help prepare the way for a smooth transition from school to citizenship in the community.

WHAT YOU CAN DO NOW

1. Make a list of classes or vocational support your child needs to meet her transition goals.
2. Identify the type of secondary and postsecondary (if appropriate) diploma your child may want to pursue, and make sure she is on track with coursework and planning to get the diploma.
3. Write down a possible plan for your child for the time immediately after she reaches the age of majority—such as, she will attend another year of high school, she will go to junior college, she will complete vocational training, etc.
4. List a few opportunities that your child can volunteer for.
5. Write a list of five things your child needs to understand about sexual development and relationships as she enters adulthood.
6. Write a list of five things your child needs to understand about health, risk, and safety issues related to substance abuse, victimization, and the law.

WHAT YOUR CHILD CAN DO NOW

What your child can do now to prepare for transition, with help, if appropriate:

1. Make a list of possible jobs or plans to pursue after leaving high school.
2. Describe her disability, abilities, and aspirations.
3. List some of the support and services she may need to reach her goal.

13. Transition Plans

Pathways to the Future

Now that you've had a chance to contemplate the various opportunities for your child after secondary school, it is time to take a look at how to plan with your son or daughter for the future. Some people believe that transition planning is only for students with significant disabilities. However, IDEA requires transition planning for all students eligible for, and receiving special education services. Whether your son is headed for college and requires accommodations because he uses a wheelchair, or your daughter needs to learn independent living skills to thrive in her group home, transition planning is for you and your family. This chapter takes a look at the transition planning process itself.

Planning Transition with the Schools

As you consider ways to plan for your child's transition to the adult world, the logical place to begin is with the school. By using the school system's resources wisely, you can go far in preparing her for success and opportunities in adult life. You, your child, school professionals, and people from adult service agencies all possess important knowledge and perspectives. If everyone works together as a team, your child will be able to develop the skills, find the opportunities, and obtain the support services that will be necessary for her to participate successfully in continual learning opportunities, work, and community life.

Transition planning is meant to be a part of the special education process—not a side trip or detour on the road map of the special education cycle. Most of the same people who develop your child's IEP are involved in the meetings to plan for her transition. In fact, in many school systems, IEPs and transition plans are discussed and written at the same time. Additional people may attend the meeting, depending upon the types of transition services your son or daughter may need.

Who Attends the Transition Meeting?

IDEA requires that schools invite students to any meeting when transition plans are discussed. For example, Maria Moran began attending her IEP meetings when she was twelve and made sure her ideas were a part of the plan. As she entered high school, she shared her thoughts about the future, her interest in childcare, and her hopes for working with children or elderly people. Mr. and Mrs. Moran worked with Maria to write down Maria's answers to questions on relevant sections of the Transition Planning Chart at the end of this chapter. Maria handed out this document at her transition meeting when she gave her oral presentation and the team included this summary of her strengths, desires, and needs in her transition plan.

Parents are also crucial members of the transition planning team. The team needs to hear your perspective of your child's strengths, interests, and need for support. You can help your child explain her ideas and questions to the other team members. You can also model and support a respectful interchange among the team and check to make sure that each member of the team understands and supports informed decision-making by your child.

School staff are, of course, part of the transition team. Your child's teacher(s), guidance counselor, vocational coordinator, and school administrator may attend the transition meeting. Many school districts appoint at least one transition coordinator who manages transition services for students with disabilities and would probably attend transition meetings. Any other school staff that you or the school thinks would be helpful can be included as a part of the team as well. The transition coordinator was an integral part of Maria Moran's transition teams, managing the work experience program for her and ensuring the activities were consistent with her career goals.

Adult service agency staff, such as vocational rehabilitation counselors or staff of an independent living center, may attend if your child may require services from such an agency. Because Maria needed some assistance with using public transportation, the "On-The-Move" program coordinator from the Independent Living Center attended several of Maria's transition planning meetings. As mentioned earlier, adult services experts can help students find out about public assistance programs.

Other individuals, at the request of you, your child, or school staff, may also take part in the transition meeting. For example, Carla, the friend Maria helped with baby sitting, attended all of her transition meetings. As Maria was preparing to graduate and apply for a two-year college program, her employer from the daycare center also attended to offer her thoughts and insight.

Considerations for Transition Planning

Educational Assessments and Course of Study Planning

Early on, the IEP team, including the student, will begin to plot out the course of study necessary to graduate, prepare for postsecondary education, and/or vocational education programs. In some cases, this planning needs to start in middle school when course choices might affect what options are available in high school. Parents and students need to understand their school system's graduation requirements and any exit exams needed for a high school diploma.

The transition team then can map out the course of study of classes, services, programs, and supports that will be required to meet a successful and realistic outcome. Students planning to attend college need to be aware of college entrance requirements that may be in addition to requirements for a regular diploma. Many school systems have fairly rigorous requirements for graduation. IDEA promotes high expectations for students with disabilities and presumes that most high school students, given the right educational support, accommodations, modifications and services, will be able to graduate from high school.

Transition planning offers a structured opportunity to discuss goals for graduation and postsecondary education. As students take more responsibility for making decisions, they can better understand and appreciate what is needed to reach academic goals and take a greater responsibility for putting in the effort and getting the needed support to succeed academically. If the team believes that a regular high school diploma is not a realistic option for your child, even with accommodations, the team can work on other courses of study that will lead to successful employment and self-sufficiency.

Special Considerations for College

Students with disabilities are attending college and other postsecondary educational programs in greater numbers before heading into the workforce and independent living situations. Preparation for college involves:

- Doing research to find out about different postsecondary educational options and opportunities;
- Finding and visiting schools or programs that might be right for your child;
- Taking preparatory classes and sometimes passing college entrance tests such as the ACT or SAT test;
- Filling out applications and attending college interviews;
- Planning ways to pay tuition and expenses;

- Developing self-advocacy skills so that your child can explain her disability when she is in college and obtain needed modifications and accommodations;
- Involving the school counseling services to plan how your child will meet deadlines and complete necessary coursework to become eligible for college entrance;
- Obtaining any needed documentation of your child's disability and required accommodations, modifications, supports, and services that will be needed to gain access to the college.

Students are finding scholarship programs, rehabilitation services funding, Supplemental Security Insurance options, and other ways to support their continued education. Parents can also plan early to use opportunities such as pre-paid college plans, Individual Retirement Account plans, student grants and loans, work study, and other options available for students with and without disabilities. Your child's high school guidance counselor will be able to direct you to resources for more specific information about financing.

Evaluation and Transition Planning

An important part of transition planning is to ensure that the plans and services are based upon your child's interests, aptitudes, and preferences. Evaluations can provide helpful information in these areas, although not all assessments will be appropriate for all students. You will want to choose which type of testing will provide you and your child with the information that is most useful. And, like Maria Moran in the example in the previous chapter, your child will have some ideas of her own about transition activities and plans for the future. Evaluation information for your child comes from a variety of sources, some of which are described below.

As a part of the high school curriculum, all students are offered testing, usually in the ninth grade, which gives them a better understanding of their unique interests and career strengths. Your child's school guidance counselor can provide information regarding these tests.

Through your child's high school career/vocational technical centers, she can participate in vocational assessments and other opportunities to explore possible career paths. Maria Moran participated in community-based instruction that was both an assessment opportunity and a job-training program. She learned skills while she tried out a variety of jobs to assess her preference and suitability for each.

Vocational assessment is a required transition service, for students who need it. Vocational assessments might include paper and pencil activities, interest assessments, technology assessments, and actual samples of work activities to determine physical abilities, current skills, and areas for skill development. Formal testing and informal observations need to be included to get a full picture of your child's abilities, interests, and preferences.

In most states, the local rehabilitation services agencies can provide vocational assessments before your child leaves school. Some have special programs where they work with students who have disabilities, providing them with opportunities to undergo intensive assessments in a setting away from home.

Your child's participation in vocational assessments and programs can be spelled out in the transition plan. Ask your school transition specialist or special education director to provide you with more information about the vocational assessments and programs in your community.

Individualized Education Program and Transition

IDEA requires that the secondary transition plans in IEPs include statements describing the necessary courses of study for graduation and/or career and tech education as well as transition services, including any interagency responsibilities or interconnections. The school is to make sure that the services are provided, even if another agency is the one identified as the service provider. If an agency other than the school system has not provided services they agreed to in the plan, the school must call an IEP meeting to identify other ways to meet the transition goals.

When developing plans for transition, the team discusses appropriate transition assessments that have been given to your child and services that your child might need to meet postsecondary goals in the area of employment (including integrated employment, supported employment, and adult services), education/ training (including continuing and adult education, and vocational education), independent living, and community involvement.

If the team—which includes you and your child—decides that the student does not need services in any of those areas, a statement must be included as to why and how that decision was made.

Placement and Transition

For some students, transition services are incorporated into their current high school classes. Others attend specific programs to prepare for their lives after high school. For example, Maria Moran's transition plan included both "regular" high school classes and a specialized program. Examples of specific programs include:

Work-Study Programs in the Community

Here, your child would receive training leading to employment and also receive credit toward graduation for the work experience. Work-study programs sometimes involve paid employment, and the students are supervised on the job by their work supervisor, not school employees. For example, Maria Moran's friend Katy was employed as a physical therapy assistant four hours per day, and attended English and history classes two hours per day in her senior year of high school. She received credit toward graduation for her entire day of work and classes.

Regular Vocational Education Courses/Programs

These high school courses help to prepare students with and without disabilities for jobs in areas such as construction, cosmetology, auto mechanics, food service, or electronics. Some school districts have separate vocational centers or high schools; others incorporate the vocational programs within their high schools.

Special Education Vocational Programs

These programs are designed specifically for students with disabilities and include vocational training, training in appropriate work behaviors, and social skills development. They often include training in such areas as food service, office support, gardening, assembly, and maintenance services.

Community-based Instruction

Students participating in community-based instruction receive supervision and instruction from school staff while they work at jobs in the community. Part of Maria's school program included community-based instruction in various locations and settings as she was gaining skills and knowledge to be a nursing assistant.

Work Support from State, Local, and Nonprofit Agencies

During a student's transition phase, schools will also coordinate their services with appropriate agencies and adult services providers. State and local agencies may provide transitional and adult services through a variety of funding sources. The following are some you may encounter. Check with your school to find out what is available for your child:

- **Centers for Independent Living (CILs).** If your child needs to develop skills in the areas of self-help, self-advocacy, and independence, she may be able to attend a CIL program as a part of her school day or in addition to her school activities. Check with your child's special education teachers for information about local CILs.

Maria Moran supplemented her school home economics class with a nine-month independent living skills program at her CIL. She learned to balance her checkbook, plan and cook healthy meals, and do her own laundry.

- **State Rehabilitation Service Agencies.** These agencies provide services and supports to help people with disabilities prepare for finding and keeping jobs. Eligibility for state rehabilitation services is somewhat different than special education because they are looking at whether a person is able to succeed in competitive work and the severity of any functional limitations. While there is no cost for evaluation, there may be sliding scale costs for services. If there is a possibility that your child might be eligible, ask for a referral to determine eligibility as soon as your child meets your state's age criteria. If appropriate, a representative from the State Rehabilitation Agency may be invited to the transition IEP meeting to coordinate services.
- **State Employment Agencies.** The Workforce Investment Act funds state programs that increase employment, retention, earnings, and occupational skill by participants and explicitly covers individuals with disabilities. Young people with disabilities aged fourteen to twenty-one are considered a family of one when determining eligibility based on income criteria for the youth program. This program provides incentives for employers to hire clients and offers job training and summer work opportunities to students.

Before Special Education Ends

Some students receiving special education graduate from high school with a diploma like other students. Others may "age out," meaning they are no longer eligible for special education because they have passed the age when they can legally receive services—in most states, age twenty-one. In either case, the school is required by IDEA to prepare a Summary of Performance.

This summary includes:

- Academic Achievement—what your child knows related to subjects such as reading, math, learning skills, communication;
- Functional Performance—behavior, self-care, work skills, social skills, self-advocacy, independence;
- Accommodations, modifications, assistive technology, and other support necessary for your child to be successful in postsecondary environments;
- Recommendations for supporting and attaining postsecondary goals.

This summary provides important documentation of abilities and disabilities that can help your child get needed accommodations or modifications in work or educational environments. However, the school is *not* required to conduct an evaluation within a year before your child graduates with a regular diploma or ages out of special education. Some parents are finding it useful to request needed evaluations that document disabling conditions and needed accommodations through the transition assessment or evaluation provisions. Request this evaluation two to three years before your child's graduation or planned exit from special education, as the alternative may well be for you to pay for a private evaluation out of your own pocket.

Person-Centered Planning

How do you begin to plan for the future? If your child is a teenager and has been enrolled in special education for a number of years, you are used to the IEP process. Transition planning, however, is different. Rather than emphasizing a person's shortcomings and working toward remediation, transition planning focuses on the future. It is centered on your child's interests and preferences for her future. It requires exploring what is involved in learning a job and living on one's own.

One technique that is helpful in preparing for the development of transition plans is a process called person-centered planning. In person-centered planning, the person with disabilities helps choose members of her planning team and often runs her own meeting. Her hopes and dreams for the future and other important information such as strengths, talents, goals, and needs for support are identified during the person-centered planning process. The results of the planning process provide the basis for the more formalized transition plan.

Maria Moran's first person-centered planning meeting took place when she was fourteen years old. She invited her mom, dad, and Uncle Fred. Her friends Carla and Katy, her mom and dad's friend Jane, and her favorite teacher from middle school also were invited. One of her high school teachers, also a family friend, ran the meeting.

During the meeting, the group answered questions together, including:
- *Who is Maria?*
- *What is her dream for the future?*
- *What are her interests, strengths, and talents?*
- *What are her needs? What do we do to meet these needs?*
- *What is her nightmare?*
- *What can we do to make the dreams come true?*
- *What can we do to prevent the nightmare from happening?*

During the course of the meeting, Maria spoke for the first time of her strong desire to learn more in school—specifically, to be able to take more challenging courses such as algebra and biology. She and her parents talked about Maria going to college, of living on her own someday. Everyone agreed that the strong ties to family and friends Maria enjoyed were an important part of her life and needed to be a central part of her future. Maria talked about her desire for work that involved helping people, possibly older people, or maybe young children.

In subsequent meetings, Maria and her transition planning team refined their thoughts and developed a formal transition plan. They used a planning chart, like the one that follows, to write down their ideas. Maria and her team meet frequently to review her progress and solve any problems that may arise. At a minimum they know her transition plan needs to be reviewed and updated annually. The practical insight and information provided by Maria, her parents, and other family members and friends are vital when planning successful transitions from school to the workplace.

Transition Planning Chart

To help you and your child plan for transition beyond high school, the Transition Planning Chart is included at the back of this chapter for you to fill out and guide your thinking about transition.

Part I: Student Information. In this section, you and your child can write down information summarizing the information you and her team gathered during the person-centered planning process about her needs, strengths, talents, and gifts. There is also space to write down your child's long-range career goal. This can be as broad as "going to college" and "getting a job" or as specific as "becoming a car mechanic" or "learning to be a childcare worker."

Part II: Summary of Transition Activities to Date. Based upon information summarized in Part I and upon other observations made in the home, community, and at school, you can write your family's initial thoughts and suggestions for a transition program. In addition, transition activities in which your son or daughter has participated can be described briefly in this section.

Part III: Priorities. Rank the areas of transition planning you believe need attention at this time. If you and your child decide that two areas are of equal importance—for example, independent living skills and employment—goals and objectives will need to be developed in both areas.

Part IV: Goals for Transition. The process for writing goals and objectives is the same as for the IEP. Teachers, transition specialists, vocational educators, or others familiar with transition can assist you in formulating appropriate goals and objectives. The Transition Planning Chart prepared by Maria Moran and her parents is found on pages 218-19. On this chart you can see examples of transition goals and objectives.

Part V: Services Needed to Meet Goals. In this section you write the name of the agency that will provide the services, the contact person at the agency, the specific services, and the responsible funding party. For example, if your child needs to learn to use public transportation, the local vocational rehabilitation agency may provide and pay for that training. Any individuals who will be providing services need to be a part of the transition planning meeting.

You can use the Transition Planning Chart to plan services for and with your child and to monitor services once they are in place. Remember, no plan is permanent. Make sure your child's transition plan is reviewed and updated by the team at least annually and changed as your child's needs change. By taking the time and effort to write your ideas and plans on the Transition Planning Chart, you will find that the planning meetings with school officials and adult service providers will be more focused on your child's and family's needs, and, hopefully, will lead toward greater opportunities for your child.

Just as IEPs are different for each child, transition plans are going to vary according to the preferences, interests, and life goals of each young person with a disability. According to IDEA, transition plans are to be developed for all students enrolled in special education. Therefore, students with disabilities have the opportunity to think about the future, what they would like to do once they leave high school, and obtain the supports and services they need to assist them in reaching their goals.

Conclusion

Transition planning provides a systematic introduction to the world for young people with disabilities. Through participation in planning for transition, students learn the importance of work, continuing education, self-advocacy, and independent living. You, as a parent of a young person with a disability, have an important role to play in your child's transition. It is essentially the same role enacted by parents of any other young person. You are preparing your child to be as independent and self-supporting as possible. Because of the obstacles most young people with disabilities face, however, your role in planning the transition from school to adulthood becomes more critical. By planning with your child for transition, you can assist her in gaining the skills, confidence, and positive attitudes needed to participate as fully as possible as a citizen in the community.

WHAT YOU CAN DO NOW

1. List extracuricular activities your child enjoys; find out how she can continue to participate after she reaches the age of majority.
2. List some places your child can volunteer.
3. Help your child organize person-centered planning meetings.
4. Visit adult service agencies to find out about their programs and services.
5. Find out if your area has an interagency transition council that helps coordinate transition services.

WHAT YOUR CHILD CAN DO NOW

1. Participate in person-centered planning.
2. Work with you to fill out the Transition Planning Chart.

TRANSITION PLANNING CHART

Date: _____

Student's Name: _____

I. Student Information

Interests _____

_____

_____

Strengths/Capabilities_____

_____

_____

Career Goal_____

_____

_____

II. Summary of Transition Activities to Date

_____

_____

_____

_____

III. Transition Priority Areas

Rank areas as High (1) Moderate (2) or Low (3) priority.

      a. Employment _____

      b. Community participation _____

      c. Independent Living\Self-advocacy _____

      d. College or Vocational Training _____

TRANSITION PLANNING CHART (CONTINUED)

IV. Transition Goals

a. Employment _____

_____

_____

b. Community participation _____

_____

_____

c. Independent living\self-advocacy _____

_____

_____

d. College or Vocational Training _____

_____

_____

V. Services Needed to Meet Goals

(Representatives should be included in Transition Planning meeting)

Agency	Contact Person Telephone No.	Services	Agency Responsible for Funding

TRANSITION PLANNING CHART

Date: _____ August 10_____

Student's Name: ____Maria_____

I. Student Information

Interests __She loves school, movies, animals, and marching bands__

_____

_____

Strengths/Capabilities __She is friendly, has a good sense of humor,__
__likes to be around others, will try new things_____

_____

Career Goal __Work in an environment where she can be with other__
__people, that is highly structured, closely supervised, and provides__
__several different types of activities she can do (to avoid__
__boredom). She might like to do something with animals.__

II. Summary of Transition Activities to Date

__She has done community-based training through the school__
__system in a variety of settings (grocery store, department store,__
__restaurant, nursing facility, childcare center)_____

_____

III. Transition Priority Areas

Rank areas as High (1) Moderate (2) or Low (3) priority.

        a. Employment ___2___

        b. Community participation ___1___

        c. Independent Living\Self-advocacy ___1___

        d. College or Vocational Training ___1 (vocational training)__

TRANSITION PLANNING CHART (CONTINUED)

IV. Transition Goals

a. Employment ___Train in a setting in the community where she can decrease dependence on others for redirection while working___

b. Community participation ___Make friends, community activities like the youth group she has been in, perhaps dancing..___

c. Independent living\self-advocacy ___Find placement in a 24 hr 7 day per week group home that can provide additional help with learning daily living skills___

d. College or Vocational Training ___Continue to get vocational training after high school graduation___

V. Services Needed to Meet Goals

(Representatives should be included in Transition Planning meeting)

Agency	Contact Person Telephone No.	Services	Agency Responsible for Funding
Community Services Board	Transition Specialist	Group home, transportation, MR Waiver	Community Services Board

14. Resolving Disagreements

Detours

When Disagreements Arise

As you and your child participate in the special education process, you may sometimes find yourself disagreeing with observations, conclusions, and recommendations school people have made concerning your child and his educational program. Disputes usually stem from dissatisfaction with the services, support, and progress of the child. And school people may not always agree with ideas you have about your child, either. Fortunately, IDEA provides several avenues for parents and schools to follow to resolve differences that develop as they negotiate the special education maze.

This chapter describes informal and formal routes to take to resolve disagreements. It also begins with important information about making sure that your child's records are complete and accurate. As you move on to the more formal dispute resolution processes, your documentation of information and what is in your child's written records can make all the difference in a successful case.

The procedures described in this chapter may also be used to resolve disagreements that might arise as families seek early intervention services for babies and toddlers under IDEA, as described in Chapter 11. In most instances, the due hearing process hearing and appeal to the court, the most formal and legalistic procedures, should be the parents' last resort for obtaining a free, appropriate public education for their school-aged child. The experiences of parents and educators demonstrate that problems are usually resolved much more quickly and satisfactorily in an informal setting, beginning with the teacher, and, if necessary, moving on to include principals and other administrators.

School Records: The Legal Requirements

As a parent of a child with disabilities, you have a special interest in knowing what is contained in your child's school records. This is true because of the significant information these records offer you about your child and also because of the emphasis schools place on these records when making educational decisions. If any information in your child's records is inaccurate, biased, incomplete, inconsistent, or just plain wrong, this material may well result in inaccurate decisions regarding your child's right to special education services. You must know how to obtain, interpret, and correct these records and how to use them effectively in school meetings. To find your way through the corridor in the special education maze pertaining to school records, read on.

Schools are required by federal and state laws to maintain certain records and to make these records available to you upon request. The federal Family Educational Rights and Privacy Act (FERPA) and IDEA establish the minimum requirements school systems must meet in maintaining, protecting, and providing access to students' school records. State laws will sometimes go beyond these minimum requirements and provide parents with additional rights to review, modify, or seek other changes in these records. For this reason, you should obtain a copy of your own state's school records law by contacting your local director of special education.

FERPA requires schools to show parents all records, files, documents, and other materials that are maintained by the school system and contain information relating to their children. This includes all records referring to your child in any personally identifiable manner—that is, records containing your child's name, social security number, student ID number, or other data making them traceable to him. You are also entitled to review the results of any tests administered to your child by school psychologists, although you are not allowed to have copies of them, to protect the tests' future validity. These rights transfer to your child when he reaches the age of 18 or attends a school beyond high school level.

Excluded from the records schools must show you, however, are the following: (1) notes of teachers, counselors, and/or school administrators made for their personal use and shown to nobody else (except a substitute teacher); and (2) personnel records of school employees. Personnel records are exempt from review under FERPA and are not open to parental examination.

These exclusions may concern you. However, note that, if the personnel-file-related qualifications of your child's teachers or the raw scores from your child's evaluations become issues in due process hearings, you may obtain this information either from the files or from direct examination of witnesses. There is more about this later in the chapter.

Types of Records and Data Available to Parents

Your child's records include a cumulative file, a confidential file, and, sometimes, a compliance file and results of tests administered to your child by a school psychologist. You also have a right to information about your child's teacher licensure/certification.

Cumulative File

The principal will have the local school's *cumulative file* on your child, which you will want to see and copy. Often the cumulative file contains little more than a profile card with personal identification data and perhaps your child's academic achievement levels, some teacher reports, and report cards.

Confidential File

The *confidential file* may be kept at your child's school or in a central administrative office where the special education program offices are located. The file is called confidential because access to the information is limited to certain individuals—including you. Your child's confidential record includes all of the reports written as a result of the school's evaluation; reports of independent evaluators, if any; medical records that you have had released; summary reports of evaluation team and eligibility committee meetings; your child's Individualized Education Program (IEP); and, often, correspondence between you and school officials.

Compliance and Discipline Files (If Any)

Some school systems keep the report of referral meetings, correspondence between the parents and school officials, and other similar documents in a separate *compliance file.* The contents of the compliance file demonstrate that the school system has complied with timelines, notification, and consent regulations under IDEA. In addition, schools may maintain a separate file regarding discipline issues involving long-term suspension or expulsion. A good bit of detective work is sometimes required to understand your school system's individual filing system!

Psychological Evaluation Results

According to the Office of the General Counsel, U.S. Department of Education, test papers (protocols) completed in psychological evaluations and maintained in personally identifiable form are educational records under FERPA.

If the school psychologist refuses to show you tests administered to your child, challenge him or her. Claims that the tests fall within the personal-notes exemption or that the tests are copyrighted and cannot be disclosed to nonprofessionals are not valid. On your request, psychologists must show you the test papers and other materials completed by your child during his evaluation.

To protect the future validity of the tests, however, psychologists cannot give you copies of these materials.

Teacher Qualifications

You have a right to know whether your child's teacher has obtained full state certification or licensure as a regular or special education teacher, and a right to know the teacher's competencies in teaching core academic subjects.

Requesting Copies of Records

Getting copies of your child's school records (except for psychological tests) should be very straightforward. While federal law does not specifically require school systems to provide parents with copies of these records, in practice most school systems do so upon request. Begin by asking the school principal about the location of your child's various files or records. Work with the school administration or special education director to get copies of these files.

Release of Information Form

To get a copy of your child's records through the mail, you will probably be required to sign a release-of-information form. Call or write your school principal or special education director. Often school systems will send records upon receiving a written request for release of information from parents. For this service, a school system can charge you only for the cost of reproducing and mailing the records, not for personnel time or other costs incurred by the school system.

Appointment

Another way to obtain a copy of your child's records is by appointment. A telephone call to the appropriate office requesting a mutually convenient time for you to review and to make copies of the records often results in a school professional being on hand to guide you through them and to answer any questions. Again, your only expense will be the reproduction costs.

You might ask, "Wouldn't it be better if I go into the office unannounced to see the records?" In fact, there are several reasons why a surprise visit may not be the best strategy:

1. Even if you do visit the office unannounced, school personnel are not required to produce records on demand. Often, however, they will accommodate you in an emergency. School systems are required by FERPA to make records available within forty-five days. Most systems respond to a parent's request within two to five days.

2. Perhaps you are concerned that if you give the school system prior notice, someone might remove parts of the record and then replace

them following the appointment. Although isolated cases of schools removing material from files have indeed been reported, the good faith of both parents and school systems is needed in this area. Should problems develop, several procedures let you challenge and request removal of records of questionable value to your child. These procedures are described later in this chapter.

3. A school office, like any office, is run most efficiently when the needs of the people working there are taken into consideration. If you arrive unannounced and ask for services that involve the time of office staff, you can interrupt important routines and schedules. By asking for an appointment you continue to build the bridge of mutual respect and consideration needed in effective educational advocacy.

Who Sees your Child's School Records

FERPA prohibits schools from disclosing your child's records to anyone without your written consent. The only exceptions are:

1. school officials, including teachers, in the same district with a legitimate educational interest as defined in the school procedures;
2. school officials in the school district to which your child intends to transfer. Before the records are sent, however, you will want to review them and challenge their content, if necessary;
3. certain state and national education agencies, if necessary, for enforcing federal laws;
4. anyone to whom a state statute requires the school to report information;
5. accrediting and research organizations helping the school, provided they guarantee confidentiality;
6. student financial aid officials;
7. people who have court orders, provided the school makes reasonable efforts to notify the parent or student before releasing the records;
8. appropriate people in health and safety emergencies such as doctors, nurses, and fire marshals;
9. state and local authorities within the juvenile justice system, as specified in state law.

It is important to note that FERPA permits school officials to disclose any and all education records to another school or postsecondary institution to which the student is transferring or seeking admission without the parent's or student's permission. Records include IEPs and reports that were generated as a part of the special education process, and include disciplinary actions. Parents can request a copy of the information that was disclosed and have the right to a hearing as described later in this section.

In addition, FERPA allows information that school personnel may overhear or obtain from their personal knowledge and not obtained from education records to be revealed without permission. For example, if a principal overhears a student making a threatening remark, he may disclose what he heard to the proper authority.

With the preceding exceptions, schools must have your permission to release material from your child's records to anyone other than yourself. When requesting release of the records, the school must tell you which records are involved, why they have been requested, and who will receive them. Likewise, if you want someone outside the school system to see your child's records, you will be asked to sign a release granting such permission. All these precautions have been instituted to protect your privacy and that of your child.

Amending Your Child's School Records

As you review your child's school records, you may find information about your child or family that conflicts with your own assessments. If left unchallenged, this material could lead to decisions about your child's educational program that are not in his best interest. To prevent this from happening, you can follow two paths. First, you can informally ask the principal or the director of special education to delete the material, giving your reasons for the request. Often school officials will honor the request and no problem arises.

If difficulties do develop and they refuse to remove the requested material, your second approach to correcting the records is the formal hearing.

When you ask for a formal hearing, you should do so in writing, with a letter addressed to the school principal or the school official designated in your school's written procedures. Be certain to keep a copy of the letter for your files in the same way you will want to keep track of all correspondence with the school. The hearing you request will involve a meeting between you and school professionals, presided over by a hearing officer. The hearing officer in this case is usually an official of the school system who does not have a direct interest in the outcome of the hearing. The purpose of the hearing is to allow you and the school system to present evidence about the school record in dispute and to let the hearing officer determine who is right.

Under FERPA, the school must schedule a hearing on any disputed records within a reasonable time, and you must be notified of the time and place of the hearing reasonably in advance. What is reasonable in your school system will be

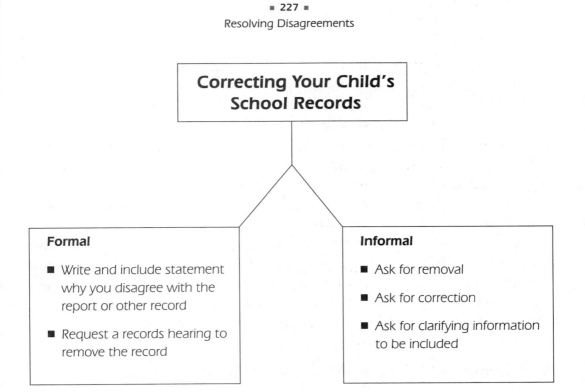

Correcting Your Child's School Records

Formal

- Write and include statement why you disagree with the report or other record

- Request a records hearing to remove the record

Informal

- Ask for removal

- Ask for correction

- Ask for clarifying information to be included

spelled out in your local school or state board of education regulations. These same regulations will also explain: (1) your right to have someone, even an attorney, assist or represent you at the hearing; (2) the length of time the school system has to make its decision after the hearing; and (3) the requirement that the hearing officer include in the decision a discussion of the evidence and the justification and rationale for the decision reached.

Since the hearing officer at a records hearing can be a school official, parents might feel that the proceedings are not fair. Although unfair decisions have been rendered, more often than not the hearing officer will act impartially in deciding the issue. Even if parents are denied their request to have a record removed, further actions may be taken to reduce the negative impact of the disputed report.

The most effective way to handle this problem is to amend the record by attaching a signed, written explanation of your objections, detailing why you believe the material is inaccurate, biased, incomplete, or otherwise inappropriate. Because the school must, by law, keep your statement with the record, everyone who sees the record will be informed of your objection to its contents. The parent dispute needs to be noted each place in the record that is in dispute.

Besides amending the disputed record, you can take several other steps when you believe your requests to correct the records have been improperly refused. First, you can file a complaint with your state education agency following the procedures described in your state's school records law. Second, as soon as possible after the incident you could also send a letter of complaint to:

Family Educational Rights and Privacy Act (FERPA) Office,
Family Policy Compliance Office
U.S. Department of Education
400 Maryland Avenue, SW,
Washington, DC 20202-5920
Phone: (202) 260-3887
www.ed.gov/policy/gen/guid/fpco/index.html

This office is responsible for enforcing FERPA and will look into your complaint.

A final action you can take in some areas is to sue in court. Since most recent court decisions deny individuals the right to private suit under FERPA, you should consult an attorney to see if such action is possible where you live. All three of these options require significant time before action occurs. Therefore, if you use them, you should also amend the record in anticipation of having it removed later.

Change Comes with Warning

IDEA requires that parents receive prior written notice before the school initiates certain actions. This term is a bit confusing but once understood, can be a powerful tool for resolving disagreements. You must be informed, in writing whenever the school district: 1) proposes to begin or change the identification, evaluation, or educational placement of your child; or (2) refuses to begin or change the identification, evaluation, or educational placement of your child. The school district must provide the notice in understandable language. This notice must include:

1. A description of the action that the school district proposes or refuses to take;
2. An explanation of why the school district is proposing or refusing to take that action;
3. Each evaluation procedure, assessment, record, or report the school district used in deciding to propose or refuse the action;
4. Any other choices the IEP Team considered and why those choices were rejected;
5. Other reasons the school district proposed or refused the action;
6. Resources for you to contact for help in understanding Part B of IDEA.

If you disagree with an action the school is proposing, read the notice carefully to see if there is information that is inaccurate or incomplete. Using the information you have accumulated through the various activities in this book, write down your requests, with evidence from your child's school records, IEPs, and evaluation reports as a back-up to your position. Review the school's actions from a procedural perspective to ensure they have complied with all required components of the special education process. Then follow up with a letter stating clearly your remaining areas of disagreement and how you would like these addressed. These steps can go a long way in clearing up any problems at an early stage. Your perspective and the school's perspective will be clearer and you can pursue the appropriate alternatives for resolving your disagreements. In the case of a complaint to your state department of education or request for a due process, the prior written notice serves as documented evidence of attempts by you and the school to resolve the disagreement.

Resolving Disagreements

Special education disputes are resolved through these methods, listed in the order that most effectively and quickly resolves the issue at hand:

1. Informal Problem Solving;
2. Formal Complaint;
3. Mandatory Mediation;
4. Due Process Hearing;
5. Appeal to Court.

Informal Problem-Solving

The first approach you should always use is simply talking to your child's teacher, or the staff member most closely involved with the issue. This informal problem-solving is often the simplest and most effective approach.

As you are making your way through IEP meetings and other interactions with the schools, you may reach a point where you can't think your way through a difficult situation, either in relationship to another person or as you make choices for your child and family. If so, a problem-solving approach can be very helpful. By addressing potential conflicts early on with a creative approach, you can often keep your child as the focus and move forward while keeping your relationships with school people positive and productive.

Problem-solving: A Case Study

Cynthia Johnson's son, Jamal, is about to begin middle school. He continues to struggle with basic reading skills and Mrs. Johnson is concerned he won't be able to graduate from high school with a diploma. The school has offered to continue to place him in a remedial reading class, but Ms. Johnson believes he needs more specialized help. She has asked the school to pay for Jamal to attend a private reading clinic, but the school has refused.

1. Define the problem in a way that focuses on the student and frames the issue in a way that encourages alternative solutions:

>Jamal Johnson is not learning to read, despite his placement in a remedial reading class.

2. Describe options you have considered and suggest an alternative plan:

>Ms. Johnson has learned about a private reading program where many students with reading problems similar to Jamal's have been very successful. She would like Jamal to be able to be tutored there, and wants the public school to pay the tuition.

3. Listen to the response:

>After discussing the situation with Ms. Johnson, the teacher understood Ms. Johnson's concerns about Jamal's lack of basic reading skills, but she was not convinced that the private reading program was the solution. Ms. Johnson and the teacher both realized they didn't have enough information about why Jamal was not learning basic reading skills.

4. Determine the course of action:

>Ms. Johnson and Jamal's teacher agreed to request a thorough evaluation by a reading specialist skilled in both diagnosing specific causes of reading disorders and developing reading intervention strategies. Once the testing was complete, the teacher and Ms. Johnson would meet and determine the next steps.

5. Revise the plan:

>In the follow-up meeting, the teacher and Ms. Johnson met and changed the old plan to incorporate new methods.

6. Plan to reevaluate:

>Both parties agreed to monitor Jamal's reading progress each month once the new plan was put into place.

>*Several important factors helped make this a relatively simple problem to solve. First, Ms. Johnson communicated her concern to the teacher in a way that did not blame her but focused on Jamal. Second, Ms. Johnson based her concern on observed behavior, or what she saw. The family knew the most about Jamal and his needs and suggested a reasonable alternative. Finally, the teacher listened*

and responded by explaining her reasons for not immediately recommending the private tutoring program and offered a compromise.

Other Options for Resolving Disagreements

Not all problems are defined and resolved as easily as the one above. Often a combination of factors comes together to create an unhappy situation. Many school districts are now using a variety of strategies to avoid or resolve conflicts between families and the schools. These strategies, sometimes referred to as alternative dispute resolution, include such things as:

- facilitated IEP meetings, where an unbiased person—that is, one who is not directly involved in either the school or with the family—leads an IEP meeting;
- parent to parent assistance, where specially trained parents assist other parents before, during, and after IEP meetings;
- administrative review, which may also be called a resolution session, where the school reviews records and reports or may also hold a meeting to resolve the disagreement;
- ombudsperson, who responds to parents immediately when they call with a complaint to the school and tries to help resolve problems before they escalate into larger complaints or a due process hearing

It is sometimes difficult to know which processes are available in your own area. And, it is nearly impossible to know if the solutions offered will lead to the desired results for your child.

The U.S. Department of Education funds parent training and information centers, where state-wide and community-based centers offer information and assistance about special education rights, advocacy, and dispute resolution. The staff of the centers are knowledgeable about informal dispute resolution techniques and can inform you of the options available in your area.

Increasingly, a number of national information centers provide parents and teachers with information about what the research says helps children learn. When parents and schools have a shared understanding of possible solutions, the team is able to try a solution that has had proven results in similar situations.

The Resource section at the back of this book has information on locating The National Dissemination Center for Children with Disabilities and a parent or community parent training and information center that serves your area.

It is usually a good idea to take advantage of the opportunities to resolve your disagreements through informal channels. These informal methods, however, should never interfere with your rights for the more formal procedures.

Formal Complaints

IDEA requires each state to provide parents and school personnel with an opportunity to present complaints with respect to any matter relating to the identification, evaluation, or educational placement of the child or the provision of a free, appropriate education. Usually this involves writing a letter to the state department of education, detailing your concerns about your dispute with the school, explaining what you have tried to resolve the dispute, and offering an alternative action you would like the school to take. Each state department of education is required to have a system in place to ensure complaints are investigated and the results of the investigation are provided in writing to the person filing the complaint.

Complaints can only be filed concerning violations that occurred not more than one year prior to the date the complaint was received. This one-year limitation does *not* apply if:

1. Your state law has an explicit time limitation for filing a complaint;
2. You were prevented from filing a complaint because of misrepresentations by the school district that it had solved the problem; or
3. The school district withheld information from parents that it was required to provide.

Your state regulations and procedural safeguards will tell you about the process in your state. You can also call your Parent Training and Information Center (see Resources section). Because filing a complaint does not involve the complicated steps of a due process hearing, it can be a very effective way to achieve the changes you think necessary for your child's education.

Mediation

When the people involved in a disagreement are unable to reach a solution through informal problem-solving or do not wish to file a formal complaint, they may decide to try mediation. IDEA requires each state to offer mediation at no cost to parents.

Mediation offers many benefits and is increasingly used to solve disagreements arising under IDEA between parents and public school officials, including those involving young children in early intervention programs. Mediation generally has the following characteristics:

- It is a voluntary process; therefore the participants in the mediation are likely to be interested in coming to a mutually agreeable solution.
- It begins with the present and focuses on the future, encouraging the parties to concentrate on how to resolve the current dispute and

move forward. The mediator facilitates a discussion among the participants about the problem, rather than past actions, allowing the group to come to a solution they might not have been able to reach on their own.

- While it is structured, it is a less formal process that is unrestricted by legal rules of evidence or other rules of procedure. Mediation is not dependent on the presentation of facts by attorneys or others not directly involved in the situation.

- It is scheduled and completed in a short period of time, permitting the parties to concentrate on a resolution rather than preparation of a case for a hearing.

- It is much less expensive than more formal proceedings, since lawyers aren't required attendees.

- Once a plan of action is agreed upon by all parties, the mediator puts the agreement in writing, and each party signs it. The written agreement contains a statement that all discussions that took place during the mediation are confidential and may not be used as evidence in any subsequent due process or court proceeding. The agreement is legally binding and is enforceable by the courts.

Request mediation whenever you feel that communication has broken down. Your school district's special education office will be able to provide you with information about mediation in your district and state.

Remember, mediation does not mean that you give up the right to a due process hearing at a later time if attempted mediation fails. Mediation *does not* eliminate any rights a child or family has under IDEA; it is an available alternative.

Mediation: A Case Study

Mr. and Mrs. Singh were very concerned about their daughter, Tara. She seemed depressed and unhappy at home. She often refused to go to school; when she did go, the special education coordinator of the school often called the Singh home, demanding that someone pick Tara up from school because she was misbehaving in class. Tara attended special education classes for students with emotional problems, but participated in general education classes for math, government, and English. She was constantly missing class, and her parents were worried she was not going to be able to graduate from high school.

The principal and counselors at Tara's high school were also concerned. Tara was disrupting her classes and fighting with other students in the hallways. The special education coordinator called an IEP meet-

ing. During the meeting he recommended that Tara attend the alternative school where she could receive more structured support.

Mr. and Mrs. Singh were very upset and angry. They didn't understand why Tara couldn't stay at her high school. They believed the alternative school would not be a healthy environment for their daughter and they refused to grant permission for her placement to be changed. Tara agreed that she didn't want to go to the alternative campus because she was having a hard enough time getting along with her peers at her own high school.

After several unhappy meetings, the staff and family decided that they were at a standstill and could no longer have constructive meetings. They agreed to meet again, with a mediator present.

The mediator telephoned both the school staff and Tara's parents to set a convenient time for the meeting and explained the mediation procedure. At the meeting, the mediator opened the session by explaining its purpose, emphasizing its confidentiality and the necessity to focus on the future, rather than on past events.

The mediator listened as the Singh family explained their reasons for keeping Tara at her high school rather than attend the alternative school. They discussed their frustrations that the school was "just trying to get rid of Tara" and not provide her with the proper help. The special education coordinator pointed out that they had tried to help Tara, but she was disrespectful of the teachers and caused trouble with other students. He felt that the family was not providing enough support for Tara at home.

By guiding the discussion toward outcomes and the future, the mediator was able to focus the Singh family and the school on Tara and what was best for her. They all agreed Tara was making progress in her classes but her behavior was problematic. Tara, as a participant in the mediation process, revealed that she felt she was unfairly singled out and disciplined by her teachers. She was refusing to go to school because she was harassed in the hallways by older male students. Her English teacher made remarks about the way she pronounced certain words and rarely gave her positive feedback for her accomplishments. She wanted to graduate from high school, but she felt unsafe and harassed at school.

With the mediator's help, they came to an agreement. The principal and the special education coordinator would investigate Tara's experiences of being harassed by the students and develop a plan for dealing with the harassment. They would place her in a different English class where the teacher would be more supportive. Tara agreed to meet with

*the school counselor once a week to get help with managing her anger.
The Singh family and the school agreed to try this approach for three
months, then revisit their options.*

*The mediator wrote up the agreement, obtained the signatures of
the school personnel and Mr. and Mrs. Singh, and sent them a copy of the
agreement.*

Due Process Hearing

If you have tried the preceding methods of resolving a disagreement with
the schools, and are unable to achieve the results you believe are necessary for
your child, you have a few more options. The due process hearing offers another
opportunity for you to secure the educational rights to which your child is entitled. IDEA establishes broad guidelines for local schools to follow in providing
special education and in protecting the rights of parents and children entitled to
those services. While state and local laws and regulations may be more detailed
in their provisions than IDEA and related federal statutes, their provisions cannot conflict with the federal law. If you find yourself headed for a due process
hearing, you should be sure to obtain your state and local laws and regulations
so you understand how the process works in your community.

IDEA describes the due process hearing procedure for resolving conflicts in
obtaining special education for your child, and it identifies the specific conflicts
that may be resolved by this process. It is important to note that a due process
complaint must be filed within two years from the date the parent knew, or should
have known about the action resulting in the complaint. IDEA requires parents
to notify the special education director in the school system of their intent to
file for a due process hearing. The notice must contain the name and address
of the child, where the child attends school, a description of the problem, and a
proposed solution. Schools must inform you of this notification requirement and
provide you with the forms as well as assistance in filling out the forms.

You may initiate a due process hearing only when you believe the school
system has not fulfilled a duty it is required to perform under the law itself. Just
what are these duties IDEA requires of school systems?

1. School systems must provide a free, appropriate public education for
   all children with disabilities aged three through twenty-one. Because
   IDEA specifies only the minimum requirements that states must sat-
   isfy, some states provide a free, appropriate education for children
   with disabilities younger than three and older than twenty-one.

   Students who are suspended and expelled from school must
   also receive special education services. Check your state laws and

regulations to determine the policy in your state. This education is to be provided completely at public expense.

2. School systems must ensure that children with and without disabilities are educated together to the maximum extent appropriate. Children with disabilities are to be placed in special classes or separate schools only when the nature and severity of their disability are such that education in general education classes, even if supported with supplementary aids or services, cannot be achieved satisfactorily. This is the legal provision mandating the education of children with disabilities in the least restrictive environment.

3. School systems must set forth in writing in the Individualized Education Program the specially designed instruction and related services your child will receive to meet his unique educational needs.

From the school's perspective, the preceding three items are duties the law requires them to perform. From the child's and parents' perspectives, these are rights IDEA gives to the child. To guarantee that these rights are exercised, the law outlines further duties for school systems and further rights for children and parents.

4. School systems must give reasonable written notice to parents before they evaluate or place a child, change his special education placement, or refuse to take such actions. The notice must contain a full explanation for the school system's decision and be communicated to the parents in their native language and in a manner they can understand.

5. School systems must obtain parent consent before any evaluation is conducted and before the child is first placed in special education on the basis of the IEP. After the initial services or placement, parents must be notified in advance of any changes. Parents can initiate a due process hearing to challenge changes with which they disagree. Should parents refuse to allow initial special education services for their child, school officials may not request a due process hearing or initiate court action to override the parents' objections.

6. School systems must evaluate a child using multiple tests, along with information from the child's parents. A child's eligibility for services cannot be determined solely on the grounds of one test or the observations of one professional.

7. School systems must ensure that evaluation tests are nondiscriminatory. Tests and other evaluation material must be free of cultural

bias. They must reflect accurately the child's aptitude or achievement level and not be biased by the child's impaired sensory or
speaking skills or by other disabling conditions. A brief explanation
of the tests to be used and the information they provide must be
made available to the parent.

8. School systems must make available to parents for inspection and
review all records used in the evaluation, placement, and IEP processes as well as those records that are a part of the child's official
school file. These records must be maintained in strict confidentiality, as discussed beginning on page 222.

9. School systems must provide for the child to have an independent
evaluation at public expense if the parents disagree with evaluation results obtained by the school system. The only exception is if
school officials believe their evaluation data are accurate and sufficient. In these cases, school personnel may request a due process
hearing to prove their claim. If the hearing officer does not agree
with the school system, an independent evaluation at public expense will be ordered for your child. Should the hearing officer up-
hold the school's position, however, you will be unable to secure a
free, independent evaluation. But remember, unless school officials
request and hold a due process hearing to validate their evaluation
data, they cannot deny your request for an independent evaluation.
They have a duty to honor your request.

10. Upon request, school systems must provide an impartial due process hearing to parents who believe any of the preceding rights have
been violated. Conflicts concerning school records, however, do not
require an impartial due process hearing. The hearing must follow
procedures described by state statute or regulation, or the written
policy of the state education agency. Hearings conducted at the local school system level allow both the parents and the school system
a right of appeal to the state education agency.

If you believe the school system has violated any of the preceding rights
and you have been unable to resolve your differences informally, you can request a formal due process hearing by writing the local superintendent of
schools. Parents whose children are in early intervention programs can make
their request to the administrator of the local lead agency. Remember, this process cannot be used to settle all disputes—only those arising from rights and
duties provided in the federal law as outlined above or as set forth in your own
state and local laws.

The Hearing: Factors to Consider and Weigh

The decision to request a due process hearing is a serious matter. For this reason, you should consider each of the following matters carefully and thoroughly.

1. The School's Position

Do you understand clearly the position of the school system regarding the education of your child, and do you know what evidence—facts, reports, professional testimony—the school will present to support its position? At least five days prior to the hearing, you can obtain from the hearing officer a list of the witnesses and the documents the school system will present. Without this knowledge, you will be unable to determine what issue you are questioning at the hearing, your chance of winning the hearing, and, ultimately, whether or not you should request a hearing.

2. Why You Disagree with the School

Are you absolutely clear as to what you believe is wrong with the school system's actions or decisions? Do you possess or can you obtain evidence demonstrating that the school's actions or decisions are incorrect? Unless you can articulate precisely where and why the school system is in error, you will be unable to gather evidence to support your case. Furthermore, unless you can submit evidence at the hearing to prove the school's error, the hearing officer cannot rule in your favor.

3. What You Want for Your Child

Do you know exactly what services, placement, or other actions you believe the school system should take to provide your child with a free, appropriate public education in the least restrictive environment? Can you obtain evidence to support these educational recommendations for your child? Hearing officers are often not educators. Therefore, it is not enough for you merely to show that what the school system is proposing is inappropriate. You will also need to convince the hearing officer of the correctness of your own educational recommendations. This requires additional research and evidence gathering.

4. Evidence

When you look at the evidence supporting your position and weigh it against the evidence supporting the school's position, which is more convincing? If the evidence for both positions is equally persuasive, the hearing officer will usually give the educational professionals the benefit of the doubt. Documentation from experts and between you and the school can be used to support your position. Lack of documentation about your attempts to communicate and find agreement can be problematic. Unless the evidence is well over 50 percent in your favor, you will have a very, very difficult case to win.

5. *Your Child's Placement and Services*

Where will your child be placed during the time required to conclude the hearing? Normally, your child will remain in the existing placement pending the outcome of the hearing. If you like your child's placement and the school is recommending a placement you do not like, you may want to request a hearing merely to keep your child where she is until your disagreement is resolved. But what if you do not like your child's current placement but still want to continue with the hearing?

If you believe your child should be placed in a private school and expect the school district to eventually pay for it, you must notify the school at least ten days in advance of removing your child from school. This notice must include the reasons you are rejecting the school's proposed placement, your specific concerns, and why you believe your child cannot receive an appropriate education in the program offered by the school; your intent to enroll your child in a private school; and your expectation that the public school will pay for the private placement.

If the private placement is upheld by the hearing officer, the school system will be directed to reimburse you. Similarly, if you move your child without the school's permission, you may still receive reimbursement if the hearing officer or court concurs that the placement you have selected is the appropriate placement for your child. If, however, you move your child to a private school, with or without the school's agreement, and your position is not upheld, you will have to pay the private school expenses yourself.

Sometimes even if you do not like your child's current placement, there is no alternative to leaving him in that placement until the hearing is complete. Once the hearing officer announces a decision, your child will be placed in the education program required by that decision—either the program you proposed, the program the school proposed, or yet a third alternative specified by the hearing officer. Should either you or the school system appeal the hearing officer's decision, your child will remain in his current placement.

6. *Who Will Represent You?*

Do you want a professional to represent your interests in the due process hearing? While you may be well informed regarding educational advocacy for your child, most parents find they are too emotionally involved to represent themselves effectively. Schools almost always have attorneys on retainer whose full- or part-time business is representing them in hearings. Parents report that they usually obtain the services of an attorney to prepare and present their case.

If you select a lawyer, you should first make certain that anyone you are considering is experienced in the practice and procedures of special education due process proceedings. Otherwise, you will tend to increase your expenses as your attorney learns on the job and to reduce your chances of receiving competent representation. You can often find the names of experienced attorneys by contacting your state and local bar associations, organizations for persons with disabilities, such as your state's Protection and Advocacy organization, members of the local special education advisory committee, or Parent Training and Information Centers in your community or state. (See Resources section.)

The costs of representation in due process hearings are usually significant. Therefore, before hiring any representative, you should ask for an informal estimate of the costs likely to be incurred. While this informal estimate is not binding, you will at least have a general idea of the amount of money involved.

7. Costs of Representation

IDEA states that courts may award reasonable attorney's fees to parents or guardians of children with disabilities who have been the prevailing party in a due process hearing or civil action. When costs are awarded, parents are reimbursed by the school system for most expenses involved in preparing and presenting their case. Costs may include travel expenses, transcripts, and the like. Should you lose your case, however, you remain solely liable for all the costs you have incurred. To understand fully your rights to reimbursement under this statute, consult an attorney familiar with your state and federal courts and laws.

IDEA also allows for school districts to recover their attorney's fees from parents when the school district wins the case because the complaint is frivolous, unreasonable, or without foundation. Attorney's fees may also be awarded to schools when the parent or parent's attorney submits issues that the court determines have been submitted simply to harass, cause unnecessary delay, or needlessly increase the cost of litigation. In these instances, parents would be in the position of being required to pay the costs for the school district's attorney.

Obviously, a decision to go to a hearing is a commitment of substantial time, money, and emotional energy. When two adults share responsibility for a child, they should not go to a hearing unless both agree that such action should be taken. Preparing for and participating in a hearing requires the cooperation and support of all adults responsible for the child. If both do not agree that a hearing is the only route to go, neither will probably weather the hearing process very well.

8. Benefits

The final factor to consider in deciding whether to request a due process hearing is the benefits of winning your case. The most important benefit, of course, is that your child will receive an appropriate educational program designed to meet his specific educational needs. You could even put a dollar value on the benefit by determining how much a similar program would cost—if you could get it—from a private school. A second benefit is that you will have spared your child the harm that might have accompanied an inappropriate educational program. For example, the school system might have diagnosed your child as having an emotional disturbance rather than a learning disability. If the school is wrong and is proven so, the benefit you receive is saving your child from the inaccurate label, seriously emotionally disturbed, as well as potentially denying him the proper educational program.

Once you have examined the potential costs and benefits of a hearing and have weighed the chances of winning your case, you are ready to make a final decision. If the potential benefits are greater than the potential costs, you may well want to go to a hearing. If the potential benefits and costs are about equal, you may want to consider alternative ways to provide your child with what you believe is an appropriate educational program. For example, you may want to obtain private placement or services at your own expense. If the costs are much greater than the potential benefits, you will have to decide if you can afford those costs should the hearing officer rule against you.

The decision to request a due process hearing is not an easy one to make. By examining each of the preceding matters, you can understand more completely the implications of your choices and have greater confidence in the correctness of your final decision. One last suggestion—once you have considered all of the pros and cons you can think of, discuss them with friends, professionals, and others familiar with your situation. You will be amazed at how often someone with a fresh perspective will see potential costs and benefits that you have overlooked.

Examples of Conflicts Resolved in Due Process Hearings

1. Whether a child should receive related services such as assistive technology, occupational therapy, or counseling.
2. Whether a child should receive special education services in a general education classroom with support services.
3. Whether a child should be placed at public expense in a private school.
4. Whether a specific test discriminates against a young, nonverbal child.
5. Whether a child is eligible to receive special education services due to his chronic health condition.

6. Whether a child is receiving the program outlined in his Individual-ized Education Program (IEP) or Individualized Family Service Plan (IFSP).

7. Whether a child's appropriate education requires more than the normal 180 school days a year—an extended school year.

8. Whether the school is providing meaningful access to a challenging curriculum similar to that of other students

9. Whether a child receives services at home or at a school.

10. Whether a child receives a vocational or academic education.

11. Whether a school can move a child to an interim alternative setting without parent consent.

As you can readily see, the preceding conflicts center upon some aspect of the child's right to a free, appropriate public education, outlined by an IEP or IFSP, and provided in the least restrictive environment. Disputes like these represent the vast majority of conflicts brought to due process hearings. These are the areas most crucial in determining the educational progress your child will make. At the same time, decisions regarding these matters are ones where professionals may well disagree and where school systems may be forced to spend additional money if their opinions are not upheld. If you go to a hearing, the chances are quite good that it will concern issues of this nature.

Due process hearings are generally not permitted to address school systems' performance of their procedural duties to provide notice of proposed actions, obtain parental consent for testing, offer appropriate evaluations, or allow parents to review their child's records. However, there are times when the procedural violations are so substantive that they have interfered with a child's and family's major rights under IDEA. Therefore, parents can file for a due process hearing over procedural violations when the procedural violations have:

■ prevented the child from receiving a free, appropriate education;

■ significantly obstructed parents from participating in the decision-making process; or

■ prevented the child from benefiting from his education.

Conflicts Not Resolvable through Due Process Hearings

What about disagreements with the school system involving issues other than those outlined above? For example, what about other situations in which you believe your position is reasonable and that the school's position is unreasonable or just plain wrong? A due process hearing cannot be used to settle all conflicts. The process is only available for resolving disputes directly related to the rights and duties of parents and school systems under IDEA.

Examples of Conflicts Not Resolved through Due Process
1. You find school personnel condescending and sometimes abrasive to work with. Although you have mentioned this to them, their behavior has not improved.
2. You want your child moved to another class because he has a personality conflict with the teacher, but the school will not approve the change.
3. You feel that school officials could move faster in placing your child, but they always use the maximum number of days legally allowed in making their decisions.
4. You dislike the school psychologist who will do your child's evaluation and would like another psychologist to do the testing. The school says no change can be made without violating the time guidelines set by the state education agency for completing your child's evaluation and eligibility determination. In this situation, you can later request an independent educational evaluation at public expense or challenge the results of the testing in a due process hearing.

In each of these examples, the school system has discretion in making decisions or is not required by law to perform a specific duty. To make changes in these situations, parents must informally negotiate with school personnel or lobby for help from the local school board, PTA, or other relevant groups. Due process hearings cannot be used to resolve issues of this nature.

Due Process Complaint Notice

To initiate a due process hearing, you must first file a due process complaint notice with the school system, or for a child in early intervention, with the local lead agency. You then forward a copy to the State Education Agency or the state lead agency for infants and toddlers. The due process complaint notice can be filed only about a violation that occurred not more than two years from the date the parents or school knew about the violation. The two-year limit does not apply if the parents were prevented from knowing about their rights or if the school withheld required information from the family. If the State has a specific timeline for due process filings, their timeline must be followed.

This notice must include the following information:
1. Name, address, school or program the child attends;
2. Nature of the problem;
3. A proposed solution or alternative.

Both school districts and parents have the right to file for a due process hearing, and therefore are required to file the due process complaint notice. A due process hearing cannot occur until the notice is filed. And, it is very important that the notice is complete and covers all areas that are to be addressed through the due process hearing, otherwise those matters cannot be raised in the resolution session or the hearing.

There are additional requirements once the notice is filed:

1. If either parents or the schools believe the notice is incomplete, they must notify the hearing officer and the other party within fifteen days of receiving the due process complaint notice. Within five days, the hearing officer must make a determination as to the completeness of the notice and immediately notify both parties in writing.

2. A complaint notice can only be changed if the other party agrees in writing and has the opportunity to resolve the amended disagreement through the resolution session, described below. The hearing officer can grant permission for an amended complaint no later than 5 days before the hearing.

Mandatory Step in Due Process: Resolution Session

Within fifteen days of receiving the complaint and before proceeding to a due process hearing, schools are required to convene a meeting, called a resolution session. The meeting includes the parents, relevant members of the IEP team, and a person within the school district who has authority to make decisions and commit the resources of the school district. Prior to the reauthorization of IDEA in 2004, many school districts had a similar requirement called an administrative review, conciliatory conference, or the like. Now schools are *required* to go to mediation or convene a resolution session to give the school officials one last opportunity to resolve the problem before proceeding to a due process hearing. The parents and schools have 30 days from referral to resolve the disagreement before a hearing must be held.

Important details to know about the resolution session:

■ The parent and the school decide which relevant IEP team members will attend.

■ The school district cannot bring their attorney if parents do not bring an attorney. Attorney's fees cannot be paid for services during the resolution session.

■ The resolution session is not necessary if the school system and the parents agree in writing to waive the meeting; or if they agree to use the mediation process.

■ If an agreement is reached at the resolution session, the agreement must be in writing and signed by both parties.

■ The agreement is legally binding and enforceable in court.

■ Either party has the option to void the agreement within three business days.

Because you will be asked to sign the legally binding agreement, be sure you fully understand what you are signing. If you are at all uncomfortable with the agreement, have a trusted friend or school professional review it with you. Should you decide you are unhappy with the agreement, you can cancel it within three business days from the day it was signed.

What Happens at the Due Process Hearing

The purpose of the due process hearing is to allow an impartial third party, the hearing officer, to examine the issues upon which you and the school system disagree and to settle the dispute by making an unbiased decision. Hearing officers are usually appointed by the state education agencies and often are lawyers, educators, or other professionals familiar with special education. The hearing officer cannot be an employee of a public agency involved in the education or care of the child and cannot have a professional or personal interest that could adversely affect the officer's objectivity in the hearing. The hearing officer also must be knowledgeable of IDEA statute and regulations as well as federal and state case law, know how to conduct hearings, and make and write decisions in accordance with appropriate, standard, legal practice. Each state maintains a list of persons who may serve as hearing officers. Refer to your state and local regulations to determine how hearing officers are selected in your state.

IDEA does not describe in great detail the procedures to be followed in due process hearings. Most states, therefore, have developed procedures more fully in their own laws, regulations, and policies. States' laws differ over matters such as the degree of formality followed in the hearing; whether the hearing officer is a lawyer, educator, or other professional; whether the hearing is conducted by one hearing officer or a panel of hearing officers; and whether or not witnesses are allowed to hear the testimony of one another. Regardless of these differences, IDEA gives you certain rights that you may exercise during the hearing.

Timelines for Hearing Decisions

In general, once a complaint has been filed, the parents and school system have fifteen days to convene a resolution session and thirty days to resolve the disagreement before a hearing must occur. This period is called the thirty-day resolution period.

The hearing officer must convene a due process hearing by the end of the thirty-day resolution session. This also begins a forty-five-day timeframe within which the hearing officer must issue a final decision and mail the parent a copy of that decision.

The federal regulations include a number of exceptions that may shorten or lengthen these time periods. If the parent and school waive the resolution session, the hearing officer must convene the hearing and issue a decision within forty-five days. If the child has been placed in an interim alternative setting for discipline reasons, the hearing must occur within twenty school days from the date the complaint was filed, and the hearing officer must render a decision within ten school days from the date of the hearing.

In practice, school systems may fail to meet the time limits. When parents complain of these time violations at due process hearings, most hearing officers will criticize the school officials and direct them to comply with time requirements in the future. Seldom, however, will a hearing officer render a decision in favor of a parent merely because the school system has failed to observe legally imposed time guidelines. You can, however, file a formal complaint with the state education agency. Your complaint may lead to the state education agency reviewing the matter and instructing the school system not to violate these time lines in future cases. Failure to follow these instructions may ultimately result in federal and state funds being withheld from the local school system. Therefore, local school systems usually will bring their procedures into compliance and will not violate parents' rights in future cases.

Think Twice (Or More) before Requesting a Hearing

The decision to resolve your differences with the school system through a due process hearing should not be taken lightly. This step will ultimately involve significant time, money, thought, and physical and emotional energy from both you and school people. Consequently, it is seldom advisable to seek a due process hearing unless you have reached the point where you feel any further discussions with school officials are futile and the only way around the impasse is a hearing. Before you reach this point, use every possible means to resolve disagreements. Attend meetings. Request conferences with the teacher, principal, or special education director. Make sure you fully understand the school's perspective. Listen to and seriously consider all proposed solutions. Ask questions. And provide all the information you have to prove that your view or recommendation is correct. Take advantage of mediation or the resolution session to present your evidence as clearly as possible and be open to offers from school officials.

Final Steps before Requesting a Hearing

As the previous sections have discussed, there are many options to pursue before a due process hearing, both formal and informal. Among these are complaints, mediation, and alternative dispute resolution. The resolution session offers you and the school a final opportunity before proceeding to a full-blown due process hearing for you and the schools to resolve your disagreements. Numerous opportunities are available to help you achieve what your child needs.

Parents are sometimes skeptical about the less formal processes for resolving disagreements. They may feel that the school is using these procedures to delay the ultimate decisions and not be required to provide required services to their child. Experience shows that acceptable solutions frequently *are* developed when parents and school professionals work in good faith. If you find the outcome of these conferences unsatisfactory, though, you may still go forward with a due process hearing.

Due Process Decision

The hearing officer's duty is to make an independent judgment either affirming what the school system has done or proposes to do, or directing school officials to take a specific action to correct a mistake they have made. This judgment clarifies the rights and duties of children, parents, and school officials as to exactly what must be done in order to meet the requirements of the law. The written decision must include both the hearing officer's findings of the relevant facts of the case determined at the hearing and recommendations for resolving the conflict. The decision of the hearing officer is final unless one of the parties appeals to the state education agency or brings civil action in court within ninety days of the decision (or within timelines established by the State education agency).

Appeal to the Court

In some states, if you or the school system do not agree with the hearing officer's decision, you may appeal for another hearing with the state education agency, often called the State Board of Education. Refer to your school's parent handbook or procedural safeguards information sheet for specific information about your district's procedures.

Should you or the school system believe that the decision of the hearing officer is incorrect, IDEA gives either party the right to file suit in the appropriate state court or in a federal district court of the United States. IDEA 2004 requires that suits be filed within ninety days of the hearing officer's decision. If a suit is filed, the court will receive and examine the records of the prior hearings; will sometimes hear additional evidence at your request or that of the school system; will base its decision on a preponderance of the evidence (meaning the side having more than 50 percent of the evidence in its favor); and will direct the losing party to do whatever is believed appropriate to remedy the existing problem. Since courts are heavily burdened already, legal action of this nature may take far too long to serve as a practical remedy for problems you may face with your child's school.

Conclusion

Opportunities for disagreement over the education of a child with disabilities can arise at every step of the special education process. Opportunities for agreement also present themselves. Resolving disagreements in a way that benefits your child and family should be the focus of your efforts. This chapter has sought to inform you of how and when to use the variety of dispute resolution avenues offered by IDEA.

Informal approaches—discussions with teachers, administrators—as well as mediation, alternative dispute resolution, and complaints can often get you the results you want for your child. The informal approaches have distinct advantages over the formal due process hearing and can be very effective in most situations.

The due process hearing is a highly legalistic process to use when all else has failed and you have no other options. Even so, it has promoted the objectives of the Individuals with Disabilities Education Act in two important respects. First, the existence of this process has put school officials on notice that their actions may be reviewed by impartial third parties if parents feel that mistakes have been made. Consequently, school officials have become more careful and open in their work with special children and their parents.

The second way due process hearings have advanced the goals of IDEA is by actually correcting mistakes made by school systems. Considering the thousands of children with disabilities which school systems serve each year, it is little wonder that mistakes are made. These mistakes, however, need not go uncorrected.

As parents learn more about their children's and their own due process rights, as well as understand how to use alternative dispute resolution and mediation, they become more knowledgeable, influential educational advocates. In the final analysis, the due process hearing should be a last resort for correcting mistakes made by school systems. But because the due process hearing exists for parents to use, its use is needed less often. That is as it should be.

WHAT YOU CAN DO NOW

1. Keep good records of your correspondence with the schools. This includes written correspondence, emails, and a written log of telephone conversations.
2. Make sure you have a copy of your procedural safeguards.
3. Find out about available dispute resolution options, including mediation, in your area.
4. Check the Resources section in the back of this book. The U.S. Department of Education funds a national dissemination center on dispute resolution. (Click on "TA&D Network" at the IDEA.ed.gov site listed in the Resources.)

15. PROTECTION AGAINST DISCRIMINATION

Alternative Routes through the Maze

Some children don't qualify for services under IDEA, but still struggle in school and socially because they have a learning or other disability. The options for these students are more limited and rest on laws involving anti-discrimination and civil rights, rather than creating new rights as the IDEA does.

Two key laws are Section 504 of the Federal Rehabilitation Act of 1973 and the Americans with Disabilities Act (ADA) of 1990. This chapter spells out how both laws have been frequently used to obtain equal access to educational services for students who are eligible for special education under IDEA. These laws have also been used to gain equal access to educational services for students with disabilities who have been declared ineligible for services under IDEA. This chapter discusses some important features of these laws.

Section 504 of the Rehabilitation Act

Section 504 serves a much different purpose from IDEA. Section 504 neither creates new rights for students with disabilities nor supports those rights with federal money. Rather, Section 504 prohibits agencies and organizations that receive federal funding from discriminating against qualified individuals with disabilities. They may not exclude students with disabilities from participating in, or obtaining the benefits of, any preschool, elementary, or secondary education program, or *any* activity or program, educational or otherwise, receiving federal financial assistance.

If your child is found to have a disability under Section 504, she is to be given the aids, equipment, and accommodations that will allow her to benefit from her school program. For example, she might receive special seating in the classroom or simplified instructions about class assignments. One limitation to this requirement is that the accommodations must be reasonable and they must not impose an undue financial or administrative burden upon the education system. This law also prohibits daycare facilities, technical schools, colleges, and universities from discriminating against students with disabilities when those institutions receive federal funds.

The Americans with Disabilities Act

The Americans with Disabilities Act (ADA), likewise, prohibits discrimination by schools through Title II of that act. Section 504 and Title II of the ADA are both nondiscriminating statutes rather than entitlement statutes like IDEA. They provide procedures to ensure that people with disabilities enjoy the same rights as those without disabilities. And when those rights are thought to be violated, the laws provide a procedure for addressing the alleged violations, as described later in this chapter.

Examples of Nondiscrimination

The following examples illustrate how Section 504 and the ADA can be used to prevent unlawful discrimination against students with disabilities:

> *Judy is a general education student. She is very limited in her ability to walk and most often uses a wheelchair. When her class took a field trip, they traveled on a yellow school bus. The teacher would not let Judy ride with her classmates, even though the bus driver said it would be OK and that she could store the wheelchair in the back of the bus. As a result, Judy's mother drove her on the field trip.*
>
> *After the field trip, Judy's mother filed a complaint with the Office of Civil Rights (OCR) of the U.S. Department of Education. OCR investigated the situation. They ruled that the school district had violated Section 504 and the ADA regulations when it failed to arrange transportation that would give Judy an equal opportunity to participate in the field trip. Subsequently, the district developed a two-part plan to accommodate Judy's needs to travel with her schoolmates and to counsel her teacher concerning Judy's rights of equality with other students. In this way they addressed the violation of Section 504.*

*Reggie was receiving special education with adaptive physical educa-
tion (PE) services. Reggie's parents believed he was being denied an equal
education because he had to miss the end of his math class in order to
attend his special PE class. After Reggie's parents contacted the Office of
Civil Rights, an investigation was conducted. OCR found that the school
district violated Section 504 by requiring him to miss his math class in
order to receive adaptive physical education services. The school district
was required to rearrange Reggie's schedule so he could attend his adaptive physical education class and also attend his entire math class.*

These cases demonstrate how Section 504 and Title II of the ADA may be
used to benefit children, both those in special education and those who have a
disability not requiring special education. Due to the similarity and overlap of
these two laws, the U.S. Department of Education generally uses Section 504
regulations to interpret Title II of the ADA. For this reason, the following pages
primarily address the educational rights and procedural protections provided
for children with disabilities under Section 504 of the Rehabilitation Act.

Students Whose Rights Are Protected under Section 504

To qualify for protection against discrimination under Section 504 and to be
provided the reasonable accommodations she may need to benefit from school
programs, your child must meet three criteria:

1. She must have a demonstrated physical or mental impairment, or
   have a history of such an impairment. Also, people who are regarded as having an impairment, such as testing positive for HIV, would
   be protected even if they had no symptoms.
2. The impairment must limit major life activities, such as caring for
   oneself, walking, seeing, hearing, speaking, breathing, learning,
   and working.
3. The services or other accommodations needed to enable your child
   to benefit from the school program must be identified.

When these criteria are met, the school then is responsible for accommodations or services that let your child participate in the general education curriculum, but only those that are available to all students in the general education
curriculum and that do *not* incur undue financial burden on the school.

1. Disabilities Protected under Section 504, But Not under IDEA

All children who qualify for special education and related services under IDEA also qualify for the nondiscrimination protections of Section 504. This factor often becomes important when access to nonacademic services and programs—such as bus transportation, after school daycare, and participation in extracurricular activities—becomes an issue.

In addition, there are many children who do not qualify for services under IDEA but are eligible for protection under 504. Although all eligibility determinations must be made on an individual basis, the following list illustrates situations in which students often qualify for reasonable accommodations under Section 504 in the provision of their educational services:

- Students with Attention Deficit Hyperactive Disorder (ADHD) who are not found to be eligible under IDEA within the categories of specific learning disabilities, emotional disturbance, or other health impairment (although the condition has been diagnosed, the school has determined that it doesn't have an adverse effect on the student's ability to learn);
- Students who have health needs, including insulin dependent diabetes, chronic asthma, severe allergies, or temporary disabilities after an accident;
- Students with learning disabilities who do not meet the more exacting criteria of IDEA but do meet the broader criteria for a disability under 504;
- Students who have contracted communicable diseases, including those testing HIV positive;
- Students with depression or anxiety disorders who do not need special education services, but require medication management;
- Students dropped from the special education rolls because they no longer meet the IDEA requirements for eligibility;
- Students with drug and alcohol dependencies, as long as the students are not currently engaging in the use of illegal drugs or alcohol;
- Students with physical disabilities that do not affect their ability to keep up with the general education curriculum.

The examples above illustrate how Section 504 and the ADA increase the number of children with disabilities eligible for protection under these laws. While your child may not be eligible for educational services under IDEA, educational rights and protections may well be available to your child under Section 504 and the ADA.

Remember, the presence of any of the preceding conditions alone will not make your child eligible for Section 504 protections. You must also: 1) show that your child's impairment substantially limits a major life activity, and 2) identify the needed aids, equipment, or accommodations that will enable your child to enjoy the benefits of the school program.

2. Establishing That Disabilities "Substantially Limit" Major Life Activities

To qualify for protections under Section 504, your child must also show that her disabling condition "substantially limits" a major life activity. Regulations describe major life activities as: walking, seeing, hearing, speaking, learning, working, taking care of oneself, breathing, and performing manual tasks.

Regulations under the ADA define the term "substantially limits major life activities" in the following manner:

> *"A person is considered an individual with a disability (for purposes of the definition) when the individual's important life activities are restricted as to the conditions, manner or duration under which they can be performed in comparison to most people . . . taking into consideration both the duration (or expected duration) of the impairment and the extent to which it actually limits a major life activity of the affected individual.*

> *"The question of whether a person has a disability should be assessed without regard to the availability of mitigating measures such as reasonable modifications or auxiliary aids and services. For example, a person with hearing loss is substantially limited in the major life activity of hearing, even though the loss may be improved through the use of a hearing aid. Likewise, persons with impairments, such as epilepsy or diabetes, that substantially limit a major activity are covered under the first prong of the definition of disability, even if the effects of the impairment are controlled by medication."*

The definition from the ADA is not binding under Section 504, but it does illustrate the wide range of disabilities encompassed by the term "substantially limits a major life activity." For example, a child with cystic fibrosis might qualify for 504 protections because she is unable to breathe adequately in a particular classroom contaminated with mold. In practice, decisions must be made on an individual basis as to whether a student's impairment "substantially limits" learning in either academic or nonacademic activities. State and/or local education agencies are required to publish written criteria for determining the definition of "substantially limits academic or nonacademic activities," and parents should obtain these written definitions from the special education director early in their educational advocacy efforts.

3. Reasonable Accommodations—Aids, Equipment, Accommodations, and Services

If your child is found to have a disability under Section 504, you then must identify the kind of aids, equipment, or other accommodations that will be needed to enable her to benefit from the school program. More specifically, Section 504 regulations define an appropriate education for an eligible child as, "regular or special education and related aids or services that are . . . designed to meet individual educational needs of the person with disabilities as adequately as the needs of nondisabled persons are met." Types of aids, equipment, and accommodations which may be required under Section 504 include, but are not limited to:

- Use of a word processor for classwork and/or homework;
- Extra time for all writing assignments;
- Occupational therapist observation and recommendations ;
- Seating at the front of the class away from distractions;
- Repeating and simplifying instructions about in-class and homework assignments;
- Using tape recorders;
- Extended time to complete homework for a child who is often unable to complete it due to migraines;
- Modifying how tests are given—e.g., orally rather than in writing.

Parents and school people alike need to recognize the importance of Section 504 and how it differs from the educational rights and protections under IDEA. First, Section 504 covers a broader and more inclusive range of disabilities than IDEA. Its protections apply both to students receiving special education services and to students whose disabilities fall within its more encompassing criteria. Second, the effectiveness of services provided under Section 504 is not held to as high a standard as those under IDEA. Under IDEA, services must be sufficient to allow the student to *benefit* from his schooling. Under Section 504, the services must merely be *comparable* to those received by students without disabilities, with no requirement that the student benefit from the services. Finally, Section 504 gives school systems the duty of ensuring that students with disabilities are not discriminated against if the school or any program operated by the school receives federal funds.

Limitations on the Provision of Reasonable Accommodations

The following factors will be weighed and balanced when deciding whether proposed accommodations are required to be made by the state or local education agency.

1. Is the equipment, aid, or service provided to general education students?
2. Is the equipment, aid, or service necessary for the student to receive the benefit of a specific activity within the instructional program?
3. Will the student, with reasonable accommodations, be able to meet all the program's or activity's requirements in spite of existing disabilities?
4. Can the proposed accommodations be made without imposing an "undue financial and administrative burden" upon the education agency?

If school officials answer "yes" to the first and second questions, they will usually provide the requested aid, equipment, or service. If the answer to question one is "no," but the answers to questions two, three, and four are all "yes," again, schools will usually provide the requested accommodations. If school officials answer "no" to either question 3 or 4, however, they will often refuse to provide the requested accommodations. Parents' options for responding to a refusal for reasonable accommodations will be discussed later in this chapter.

Prohibitions of Discriminatory Practices

Section 504 and the ADA prohibit school agencies from discriminating against students with disabilities in the provision of general education services. The following are examples of practices that have been found to be discriminatory by the U.S. Department of Education, and in each case the school system was required to correct the practice.

1. The parent of a student who used a wheelchair complained that the bus ride for his child was longer than for children without disabilities who rode the bus. Further, the bus ride often resulted in his child getting to school after classes had started. This practice was found in violation of Section 504.
2. A school district placed a student with disabilities on homebound instruction. A violation of Section 504 was found when the school

district limited the number of hours of instruction and the availability of related services without a full assessment of the child's individual needs. A further violation was found because there was no plan to provide the homebound student with opportunities to participate in nonacademic and extracurricular activities with nondisabled peers.

3. A school district scheduled graduation ceremonies for students with severe disabilities at a different time and location from all other students. A violation under Section 504 was found because there was no educational necessity for separate graduation ceremonies.

4. A school district limited its extended school year program to students with severe disabilities. Parents of other children were not notified of the availability of such services and some who obtained them were charged fees. Violations found included: services were limited to students with severe disabilities rather than considering each student's individual needs; the school system had no written policy, criteria, or procedures for determining when extended school year services were necessary; and the school system had provided no in-service training for its teachers on extended school year services.

5. A school district refused to provide program modifications to a student with attention deficit hyperactivity disorder (ADHD). A violation under Section 504 was found because the student was considered "handicapped" within the definition of Section 504.

Harassment

In 2000, the Office of Civil Rights issued a policy letter alerting the education community that the protections afforded by Section 504 and Title II of the ADA apply to students with disabilities who may be subjected to disability harassment. Disability harassment is defined as "intimidation or abusive behavior toward a student based on disability that creates a hostile environment by interfering with or denying a student's participation in or receipt of benefits, services, or opportunities in the institution's program." Harassing conduct can include "verbal comments, name calling, graphic or written statements, or conduct that is physically threatening, harmful, or humiliating. Disability harassment, when severe, persistent, or pervasive, can create a "hostile environment," thereby affecting the student's ability to participate and benefit from the programs and services.

The Office of Civil Rights provided the following examples of harassment that could create a hostile environment:

- Students frequently call a student with learning disabilities deaf and dumb; as a result the harassed student has difficulty doing work in class and her grades decline;
- A student repeatedly places classroom furniture in the path of students using wheelchairs, preventing the students from entering the classroom;
- A school administrator frequently denies a student with a disability access to lunch, field trips, assemblies, and extracurricular activities as punishment for taking time off from school for required services related to the student's disability;
- A teacher repeatedly belittles and criticizes a student with a disability for using accommodations in class, resulting in the student's poor class performance.

Schools are required to develop policies that expressly prohibit harassment based upon disability and they must also provide grievance procedures for addressing disability harassment. When schools are made aware of disability harassment, they must investigate quickly and respond appropriately, including taking steps to end the harassment, preventing it from reoccurring, and remedying the effects on the student who was harassed.

Procedural Requirements of Section 504

1. Self-Evaluation and Signed Assurances

Under both Section 504 and the ADA, school systems must have a self-evaluation that determines whether their policies, practices, and procedures discriminate on the basis of disability. Where discrimination is found to occur, steps must be taken to make the necessary modifications. The final evaluation should include: a list of the interested persons consulted; a description of areas examined and any problems identified; and a description of any modifications made.

For school systems employing fifty or more employees, the ADA requires that the self-evaluation be retained and made available for public inspection for at least three years following its completion. In addition, school systems must sign annual assurances that they have read the Section 504 regulations and that they promise to comply fully with them.

2. Required Notices

Schools must provide *general notice* of the availability of special education and related services to students who are eligible for services under Section 504. The notice will usually be in newspapers, in general mailings that are sent to all students, in student handbooks, or in parent newsletters. A school must not wait until eligibility for special services is established before notifying parents or guardians of the availability of these Section 504 services.

Under the requirements of IDEA, every school system must plan and implement procedures for identifying, locating, and evaluating children within the district who may have disabilities and may need special education. When schools carry out their annual "child find" activities, they are also required to provide an explanation of the specific procedural safeguards they have developed to meet their Section 504 responsibilities. Since the rights and procedures under Section 504 are somewhat different from those provided under IDEA, parents should ask school officials for information pertaining specifically to Section 504 rights, responsibilities, and procedural safeguards.

School systems must identify one or more individuals responsible for receiving complaints and coordinating the grievance processes required by Section 504 and the ADA. In addition, school systems must adopt and publish written procedures that govern the grievance process under both Section 504 and the ADA and that explain parental rights in the grievance process. These procedures must be published along with the name, office address, and telephone number of the grievance coordinator.

3. Evaluations, Eligibility Decisions, and the Individualized Plan

As discussed earlier, the definition of a child with a disability under Section 504 and the ADA is broader and covers more children and circumstances than IDEA's definition. Therefore, school systems may often find they must evaluate students under Section 504 even though these same children would appear ineligible for special education under IDEA.

Unfortunately, many school systems in the past have not provided for Section 504 evaluations and have restricted evaluations only to students they believed possibly eligible for services under IDEA. Likewise, when students were evaluated but found not to fully meet the requirements for services under IDEA, school officials often told parents they could not legally provide additional educational services to their children.

Section 504 *specifically* requires school systems to evaluate children who are believed to have a disability significantly limiting their ability to learn. And when these students are found to be disabled under the definition of Section 504 and the ADA, school systems are required to provide an appropriate education for these students even if they are not eligible for special education services under IDEA.

School systems implementing Section 504 must have written procedures which provide for:

a. determining students' eligibility under Section 504;
b. ensuring that the evaluation procedures employ nonbiased tests and materials which accurately reflect the students' abilities; that the evaluations are administered by trained personnel; that the evaluations assess specific areas of educational need; and that the tests are selected and administered to reflect accurately the factors the test is supposed to measure;
c. identifying the persons who must attend the evaluation meeting to discuss the evaluation and determine students' eligibility for services and/or accommodations; and
d. describing the elements of the individualized plan (sometimes called the 504 Plan or the Individualized Determination Plan) designed to implement an appropriate education as required under Section 504.

Section 504 does not require school systems to allow parents to participate actively in either the evaluation or eligibility processes. If your school system does provide opportunities for participation, you can follow the steps described earlier in this book for contributing your unique knowledge to evaluation and eligibility decision making. If your school system does not allow substantial participation, you should contribute as much information as possible to the decision processes, review the procedures and data used to reach final decisions, and use the appeals process if you believe inappropriate decisions have been reached.

When interpreting evaluation data and making eligibility decisions under Section 504, school systems must draw upon information from a variety of sources. In addition, school systems must establish procedures to document that the evaluation information has been considered in reaching its decisions. The documentation should include such things as meeting notes or evaluation reports or summaries. Regulations further require that school systems inform parents as to the outcome of the Section 504 evaluations of their children. While notification is not required to be in writing, parents can request such written confirmation. Likewise, parents have the right to examine all documents, records, and information relevant to decisions regarding their children's evaluations and service eligibility. Finally, while regulations do not specify timelines for the completion of Section 504 evaluations, the Office of Civil Rights has directed school systems to follow the timelines applicable under state special education rules unless other local procedures have been established.

4. Placement Decisions

Section 504 does not specify the membership of the team that will make the final decision on your child's school and classroom placement. In practice, the placement team and the evaluation/eligibility team are often one and the same. Still, at a minimum the placement team is required to be comprised of people who are knowledgeable about the student, the meaning of the evaluation data, and the placement options available for the student. Placement decisions under Section 504 must meet the same least restrictive environment required as under IDEA.

5. Suspension and Expulsion

Students protected under Section 504 are entitled to the same procedural safeguards as IDEA-eligible students before they can be suspended from school beyond ten days or expelled. Please note that the school system may employ its regular disciplinary procedures for students suspended for ten days or fewer. In addition, IDEA protects students who are not yet eligible for special education if the school had knowledge that they were students with disabilities before the behavior occurred. For example, if a student had been referred for special education and was in the process of being evaluated when she was disciplined, she would be protected.

6. Parental Notice and Consent

Similar to IDEA, Section 504 requires school systems to notify parents about the identification, evaluation, and placement of their children. In contrast to IDEA, however, Section 504 does not require that parents provide written consent prior to their children's initial evaluation or their initial placement.

7. Impartial Hearings

To resolve disputes arising under Section 504, state education agencies must provide for impartial hearings and reviews with the participation of parents and their attorney or advocate. Many states have authorized state IDEA hearing officers to hear and to rule upon Section 504 complaints. In other states, alternative impartial hearing procedures have been established to comply with this requirement.

Parents may use the impartial hearing process to raise any questions they have about whether the school system is appropriately observing their child's protections and procedural rights under Section 504. For example, you may request a review of your child's evaluation process, the eligibility decision, the adequacy of educational accommodations, the placement decision, or the implementation of the individualized plan. In addition, you may use the impartial hearing process to question whether your child is being unfairly discriminated against in the provision of general education programs and/or extracurricular activities.

As is true under IDEA, requesting a hearing should be one of the last actions you take to secure your child's educational rights under Section 504. If necessary, however, read the information in Chapter 14 about dispute resolution, mediation, and due process hearings. Some changes in these steps may be necessary to adjust for the legal requirements of Section 504 and specific 504 procedures developed by the school system. Nevertheless, this information should provide you with a sound basis for addressing the legal, factual, and procedural issues that will arise in resolving disagreements with the school.

Enforcing Students' Rights under Section 504 and ADA

Students and parents may follow numerous paths to correct errors they believe have occurred in meeting their rights under Section 504 and the ADA. First, parents may contact the Section 504 grievance coordinator within the local school system. The coordinator will then follow existing local procedures designed to resolve informally any conflicts or misunderstandings arising under the implementation of these laws. Second, students or parents can request a hearing at which a hearing officer or other impartial person or panel will render a decision about the existing dispute. Yet a third option is for the student or parent to file a complaint with the Office of Civil Rights (OCR) of the U.S. Department of Education.

Office of Civil Rights (OCR) Complaints

Any individual or organization who believes a school system or school official has violated students' or parents' rights under Section 504 or ADA may file a formal complaint with a regional office of OCR. The addresses of these offices may be found by contacting your school district, statewide Parent Training Information Center, or NICHCY (see Resources). The complaint may reflect alleged violations of the rights of individual students or parents, classes of individuals or parents, or the general practices of a local or state education agency. These complaints must be filed within 180 days of the alleged discriminatory action. OCR will then investigate the circumstances of the complaint and issue a Letter of Finding. The Letter of Finding will either conclude that no violation has occurred, or it will identify specific violations and the corrective actions that the school system must take. Only in extraordinary circumstances will OCR examine alleged violations of individual placement or other educational decisions, and these only when a child is excluded from services or the school system appears to be engaging in an ongoing pattern of discriminatory practices.

Judicial Action

A final alternative for students and parents is to seek enforcement of Section 504 and the ADA through court action. Parents and students who sue under

Section 504 and who prevail in their cases are entitled to corrective actions by the school system and to the reimbursement of all court-related expenses. Under some circumstances, students and parents may also receive monetary awards for compensatory damages due to claims of pain and suffering, emotional distress, mental anguish, and medical expenses—though such awards are seldom made by the courts. Finally, when parents take legal action solely under Section 504, they can immediately file suit in court without first having to follow an informal review process or due process procedure.

Because of the time, effort, strain, and costs of judicial action, this path should be your last alternative in trying to enforce your child's and your rights under Section 504 and the ADA. Nevertheless, the seriousness of the discriminatory action, the harm your child may endure, and/or the ineffectiveness of other remedies may all require this final action. It was for these reasons that Congress made this enforcement option available.

Section 504 and ADA: Two Critical Laws Complementing Special Education

Under the Individuals with Disabilities Education Act (IDEA), students whose disabilities meet certain narrowly specified criteria have been guaranteed a free appropriate public education in the least restrictive environment. Section 504 and the ADA add to these guarantees by ensuring that these students, as well as other students with disabilities not receiving IDEA protections, are not discriminated against in the provision of school programs and services.

By understanding the requirements school systems must meet in fulfilling their duties under Section 504 and the ADA, you can ensure that your child obtains the full educational benefits to which she is entitled. And those educational benefits will, in turn, promote the goals of Section 504 and the ADA by allowing your child to participate in, and contribute to, her community as fully as possible.

WHAT YOU CAN DO NOW

1. Call your state Parent Training and Information Center to discuss your specific questions and concerns.
2. Gather information about your child's rights under Section 504 and ADA using the links and phone numbers listed in the Resource section of this book.

16. LOOKING BACK AT THE SPECIAL EDUCATION MAZE

Does the Journey Ever End?

Parents have often been confused, frustrated, and generally perplexed in their attempts to understand how school officials make decisions about the education of their children. As parents talk with teachers and administrators and learn about evaluation and eligibility procedures, IEPs, learning disabilities, and due process hearings, they often feel that schools have built a complex special education maze through which only educators can find the way. Parents frequently have not known how to take the first step toward negotiating this maze.

This book has been written for parents—and their children. In the preceding pages you were introduced to the corridors of the special education maze—the cyclical process of referral, evaluation, eligibility, IEP, placement, checking up, and, when necessary, due process procedures. Understanding this process gives you insight into the entry points for the maze, the rules and regulations for traveling through the maze, and potential strategies for negotiating the maze. The end result of your journey, it is hoped, will be that your child receives a free, appropriate public education in the least restrictive environment.

Federal and state laws have created the legal basis for ensuring that children with disabilities receive a free, appropriate public education. Local school systems and their teachers and administrators have the potential knowledge, dedication, and resources to carry out these laws. You, as parents, however, possess the one additional ingredient needed to blend these laws and resources together to produce an effective education for your child. This ingredient is your unique knowledge of your child, what he knows, and how he learns. If this knowledge is not included in educational planning and programming for your child, the program ultimately developed may be inappropriate and, possibly, ineffective. Your child cannot afford to lose days, months, and years in the wrong program. You do not want this time to be lost, or you would not be reading this book.

Emphasis throughout this book is placed upon the importance of acquiring the skills, knowledge, and values essential for becoming effective educational advocates for your child.

Educational advocacy is a means for parents to participate intelligently and collaboratively in decisions affecting the education of their children with disabilities. Educational advocacy offers you an approach for ensuring that your unique knowledge of your child is reflected in the educational programs and the educational environment he encounters. Educational advocacy provides you with a plan of action for successfully negotiating the special education maze.

A New Experience with Each Trip through the Maze

The special education planning and programming cycle described in Chapter 2 is a recurring one. On a regular schedule, the educational goals, objectives, and services outlined in your child's IEP are reexamined and revised as needed. Each time you travel through the special education maze, whether it is for the annual review or the more extensive triennial evaluation, changes will have occurred:
- New school professionals may be working with your child.
- Laws, regulations, and policies may have shifted.
- Different strategies may now be in use by school officials to implement the rules of the maze.
- You have more experience and knowledge, and you will continue to learn with each cycle through the maze.
- Your child will have grown and gained skills, and may play an ever larger role in the meetings

The fact that each trip through the maze is a new experience has significant implications for parent educational advocates.

First, each time the cycle begins, you must gather new data about your child; analyze the data; organize it for purposes of making evaluation, eligibility, IEP, and/ or placement decisions; and prepare for and participate in the meetings where these decisions are made. All of this, of course, will be more easily accomplished when you have carefully checked up as your child progresses through the program.

Second, since laws, regulations, policies, and practices change rapidly in the special education field, you should check annually with your state and local education departments for any changes in these procedures that may have occurred since you last traveled the maze. Following this suggestion will ensure that you do not waste valuable time using outmoded procedures, and, more importantly, that you do not overlook any new rights or entitlements your child has been given over the years.

Third, because school personnel come and go as frequently as rules and regulations change, you should also continually update the Key People Chart found earlier in this book. By asking around, you should be able to learn something about the educational background and experience of these new people. And, by keeping your information about the professionals involved in your child's education up-to-date, you can help to foster the confidence and trust needed for successful collaboration.

Fourth, each year brings new problems and opportunities to local school systems. These problems and opportunities often are linked to changes in funding that may have either a positive or negative impact on educational programs. On the negative side, you might find fewer services, higher student/teacher ratios, and longer bus rides. On the positive side, some school systems are recognizing the value of strengthening the parent/professional partnership. One way they are doing this is by establishing parent resource centers in their school systems. Such centers offer training courses in educational advocacy for parents and provide information and referral to school and community services. Both positive and negative changes within local school systems will sometimes alter the ways in which school professionals view their duties for educating children with disabilities in accordance with federal and state law. By knowing the particular problems and opportunities confronting your school system, you will be better prepared to face any changes in strategy school officials may seek to implement.

Finally, since each trip through the maze is a new one, you will have to formulate new strategies and tactics to be sure they meet the changed conditions. Although you may have succeeded in obtaining an appropriate education for your child on one trip through the maze, past success does not promise continued success. Only thoughtful, careful, hard work can prepare you to be an effective educational advocate for your child. There is no substitute for diligent preparation for negotiating the maze.

Changing the Maze and the Rules of the Maze

You may find that no matter how skilled you become in negotiating the special education maze, your child's program never seems appropriate to meet his needs. Classes may be too large, related services unavailable, specialized instruction nonexistent, and transportation inconvenient. When these problems arise and due process procedures, short of court action, fail to correct them, educational advocacy has reached its limits of effectiveness. Legal and political advocacy must then be employed to bring about necessary changes.

Legal Advocacy

Legal advocacy is best used when school officials interpret the law one way and you interpret it another. Although hearing officers in due process hearings may agree with the interpretations of school officials, their word is not final. Only the courts can definitively answer questions about the interpretation of laws. Courts clarify the meaning of federal and state laws; courts rule authoritatively on whether state and local education policies and regulations conform to federal and state laws. When you feel that state laws conflict with federal laws and school officials will not change their procedures to meet your objections, the courts offer one alternative for changing both the system itself and the policies and regulations governing it.

Political Advocacy

Yet another option for altering the special education system is political advocacy. In this type of advocacy, groups lobby legislative, executive, and administrative bodies in an attempt to change specific government budgets, policies, and procedures. The Council for Exceptional Children, The Arc, and United Cerebral Palsy are just some examples of the many groups that engage in political advocacy. The distinguishing feature of political advocacy is its emphasis upon changing specific elements of the special education maze—for example, procedures for evaluation, criteria for eligibility, budgets appropriated for special education, and certain rules for special education, such as the rights of parents to participate in various meetings. In contrast to educational advocacy, where the advocate is concerned only with the welfare of one child, political advocacy seeks changes either in the overall process or its encompassing rules and regulations in order to benefit all children with disabilities.

Political advocacy may be essential when the process itself is being revamped or when the rules and regulations are viewed by some as inherently unjust or impractical. In these situations educational advocacy will prove insufficient and nothing short of political advocacy will assure a free, appropriate public education for children with disabilities.

In 2004, for example, Congress undertook the reauthorization of IDEA, considering major changes in requirements of the law. Many parent groups as well as special and general education professional associations became involved in providing information and suggestions as to how the law could be improved.

Legal and political advocacy have their places, but their effects are much less immediately effective as educational advocacy. In the short run, your child needs immediate services and educational programs that meet her unique needs. Educational advocacy, as outlined in this book, is designed to assist you in meeting these short-run educational needs. As you gain skill and experience in using legal, political, and educational advocacy, you learn the situations in which each is most effectively employed—and will use them accordingly. But in the last analysis, when the special education system and accompanying regulations have been changed by legal and political advocacy, success in negotiating the newly rebuilt maze ultimately depends upon every parent's abilities to serve as educational advocates for their own children.

Through the Maze with Others

At many points in the special education planning cycle you have been encouraged to ask a friend to assist and accompany you in advocating for your child. This is helpful in evaluation, eligibility, IEP/placement, and mediation or due process. The purpose of this suggestion is at least twofold. First, another person can enhance your effectiveness as an educational advocate by serving as a source of ideas and suggestions and as a second pair of eyes and ears. Second, another person can provide the personal and emotional support most parents need to cope with the stress of traveling through the special education maze.

While the help and assistance of one or two friends can make you a more effective educational advocate, the combined efforts and support of numerous other parents can increase your effectiveness even further. By forming a group of parents committed to educational advocacy for their children, you will immediately increase your collective knowledge of the local school maze and decrease the debilitating feeling of isolation so often caused by coping alone with the intricacies and frustrations of the maze.

How do you start your own groups of educational advocates? One good place to begin is by having a number of concerned parents study this book together. You may want to enlist the assistance of special education teachers, school psychologists, or other professionals who work with children with disabilities, to provide the group with expertise to explore selected topics in more depth—for example, evaluation, eligibility, IEPs, or due process procedures. But remember, this book was meant for you—the parent. The intent of the group study is to assist you as an educational advocate for your child. Any professional assistance you get should be oriented toward helping you incorporate your unique insights of your child into her special educational plans and programs.

Another step you can take is to contact the Parent Training and Information Center (PTI) or Community Resource Center in your state. These centers are funded by the U.S. Department of Education to provide training and information to parents of children with disabilities. Your state PTI can assist you with strategies for: participating in the educational decision-making process; communicating with teachers and other professionals involved in your child's education; and obtaining appropriate programs, resources, and services for your child. They can also help you locate strategies that research says are effective in educating children with disabilities. The Resource section at the back of the book tells you how to get in touch with your state's PTI.

In 1978, Winifred Anderson, Stephen Chitwood, and Deidre Hayden, the authors of the first edition of this book, founded one of the first Parent Training and Information Centers in the nation. This is now called The Parent Educational Advocacy Training Center (PEATC), in Virginia, and is funded in part by the U.S. Department of Education. PEATC has shown just how effective parent groups in educational advocacy can become. PEATC's current Executive Director, Cherie Takemoto, has joined the original writing team in this fourth edition.

PEATC has trained—directly and indirectly—thousands of parents to serve as educational advocates for their children. These parents come together for workshops focused upon the ideas discussed in this book. From these workshops, parents acquire insights into the special education process in their local school jurisdictions, skills in educational advocacy to work within that process, and a sense of identity and solidarity with other parents of children with disabilities.

By attending the course, parents make contact with other parents whom they can call upon for insights, knowledge, and the psychological and moral support needed to sustain them on their journeys through the maze. As these parents have gained proficiency as educational advocates, they have often reached out to help other parents who have not attended an educational advocacy course. This mutual support and assistance is essential if parents are to ensure the responsiveness of the system to their children.

By learning the basics of educational advocacy and speaking up for your child's rights, you can help forge a strong alliance between parents and school professionals. By banding together and speaking up for the rights of children with disabilities everywhere, parents throughout the United States can help make the promise of a free, appropriate public education for all children with disabilities a reality.

GLOSSARY

This glossary includes special education terms mentioned in the text, as well as words parents may find used in the school setting. It also defines the disabilities that qualify a child for special education services, but does not contain any other terms related to specific disabilities.

Academic Achievement: a child's performance in academic areas (such as reading or language arts, math, science, and history).

Accommodation: Supports that are provided to a child throughout the school day that do not significantly alter what is being taught or how the child participates in school activities. Examples of accommodations are preferential seating, extended time on tests, daily communication logs to share information between school and home, use of spell check and/or computer, enlarged print, and books on tape. *See also* **Reasonable Accommodation.**

Achievement Test: A test that measures a student's level of development in academic areas such as math, reading, and spelling.

Activity Center: A day program where staff members assist adults with disabilities with activities emphasizing community skill training (e.g., learning to use public transportation) and vocational skill development.

Adaptive Behavior: The extent to which an individual is able to adjust to and to apply skills to new environments, tasks, objects, and people.

Adaptive Physical Education: A physical education program that has been modified to meet the specific needs of a student with disabilities; e.g., inclusion of activities to develop upper body strength in a student with limited arm movement.

Administrative Review: A review process whereby disagreements between parents and school systems may be resolved by a committee of school system individuals not directly involved with the case. Also called a conciliatory conference.

Adult Day Programs: Programs in which adults with disabilities receive training in daily living skills, social skills, recreational skills and "pre-vocational" skills.

Advocacy: Speaking or acting on behalf of another individual or group to bring about change.

Advocate: A person who speaks or acts knowledgeably on behalf of another individual or group to bring about change.

Aged Out (Aging Out): Refers to students with special needs who have reached the maximum age limit mandated in their state for special education and related services.

Americans with Disabilities Act (ADA): An anti-discrimination law giving individuals with disabilities civil rights protections similar to those rights given to all people on the basis of race, sex, national origin, or religion.

Annual Goal: Statement describing the anticipated growth of a student's skill and knowledge written into a student's yearly Individualized Education Program.

Annual Review: A meeting held at least once a year to look at, talk about, and study a student's Individualized Education Program (IEP). The purpose of the review is to make decisions about changes in the IEP, review the placement, and develop a new IEP for the year ahead.

Appropriate: In free, appropriate public education provided by the Individuals with Disabilities Education Act (IDEA), "appropriate" refers to an educational plan that meets the individual needs of a student with disabilities.

Aptitude Test: A test that measures an individual's potential in a specific skill area, such as clerical speed, numerical ability, or abstract thinking.

Assessment: *See* Evaluation.

Assistive Technology: Any item, piece of equipment, or product system that is used to increase, maintain, or improve the functional capabilities of children with disabilities; e.g., augmentative communication boards, computer input devices, special switches.

At-Risk: Term used to describe children who are considered likely to have difficulties because of home life circumstances, medical difficulties at birth, or other factors, and who may need early intervention services to prevent future difficulties.

Audiologist: A professional nonmedical specialist who measures hearing levels and evaluates hearing loss.

Auditory Discrimination: The ability to identify and distinguish among different speech sounds; e.g., the difference between the sound of "a" in *say* and in *sad*.

Autism: A developmental disability significantly affecting verbal and nonverbal communication and social interaction, generally evident before age 3.

Behavior Disorders (BD): Disorders characterized by disruptive behavior in school, home, and other settings. They can include attention deficit hyperactivity disorder (ADHD), conduct disorder, difficulty learning, and inability to establish satisfactory relationships with others. Such behavior is considered inappropriate, excessive, chronic, and abnormal.

Behavioral Observation: A systematic way of observing, recording, and interpreting the behavior of a student as he/she works on the job in order to gain a broad picture of the student's interests and abilities. Part of a vocational assessment.

Blind (Blindness): Complete loss of sight. Educationally, individuals who are severely visually impaired, or have no vision and must learn to read by braille, are considered blind. See also **Legally Blind.**

Buckley Amendment: More commonly known name for the Family Educational Rights and Privacy Act of 1974. The law gives parents and students (over age 18) the right to see, correct, and control access to school records.

Career Education: A progression of activities intended to help students acquire the knowledge, skills, and attitudes that make work a meaningful part of life. Career education has four stages: 1) awareness/orientation, 2) exploration, 3) preparation, including vocational education, and 4) job placement/follow-up.

Carl D. Perkins Vocational and Applied Technology Education Act (1990): A federal law stipulating that students with disabilities be guaranteed the opportunity to participate in federally funded vocational programs that are equal to those afforded to the general student population.

Case Manager: *See* **Service Coordinator.**

Child Find: A state and local program mandated by the Individuals with Disabilities Education Act (IDEA) to identify individuals with disabilities between the ages of birth and twenty-one and to direct them to appropriate early intervention or educational programs.

Child Study Team or Screening Committee: A local school-based committee, whose members determine if a student should be evaluated for special education eligibility.

Cognition: A term that describes the process people use for remembering, reasoning, understanding, and judgment.

Communication Disorder: A general term for any language and/or speech impairment.

Community Participation: Activities by a person with disabilities within the community which contribute to the well-being and improvement of that community, such as volunteering at the hospital, planting trees, serving on the board of a nonprofit agency.

Competitive Employment: Everyday jobs with wages at the going rate in the open labor market. Jobs can be either on a part-time or full-time basis.

Compliance File: School records containing all reports of meetings, correspondence, and other contacts between parents and school officials.

Conciliatory Conference: *See* **Administrative Review.**

Confidential File: A file having restricted access and containing records of a child's evaluation and other materials related to special education (medical reports, independent evaluations, reports of eligibility meetings, etc.).

Confidentiality: The limiting of access to a child or family's records to personnel having direct involvement with the child.

Congenital: A term referring to a condition present or existing at birth.

Consent: Parental permission, usually given by signing a letter or form, agreeing to let the schools take an action which affects a child's education. Consent is required before a child can be evaluated or receive special education services under IDEA.

Contract Services: Services provided to students with disabilities by private service providers (private schools, institutions, therapists, etc.) when the school system is unable to provide the needed service.

Cumulative File: A file containing report cards, standardized achievement test scores, teacher reports, and other records of a student's school progress.

Deaf (Deafness): A hearing impairment so severe that an individual cannot process sounds even with amplification such as hearing aids.

Deaf-Blind: The combination of visual and hearing impairments causing such severe communication and other developmental and educational problems that a child cannot adequately be served in a special education program solely for deaf or blind children.

Developmental: Having to do with the steps or stages in growth and development before the age of 18.

Developmental Delay: Term used to describe slower than normal development of an infant or child in one or more areas.

Developmental Disability (DD): Any severe disability, mental and/or physical, which is present before an individual becomes eighteen years old, which substantially limits his activities, is likely to continue indefinitely, and requires lifelong care, treatment, or other services. Examples of developmental disabilities include Down syndrome, autism, and cerebral palsy.

Disability: A problem or condition which makes it hard for a student to learn or do things in the same ways as most other students. A disability may be short term or permanent.

Due Process: A system of procedures ensuring that an individual will be notified of, and have opportunity to contest, decisions made about him. As it pertains to early intervention (Part H) and special education (Part B) of IDEA, due process refers to the legal right to appeal any decision regarding any portion of the process (evaluation, eligibility, IEP or IFSP, placement, etc.).

Due Process Hearing: A formal session conducted by an impartial hearing officer to resolve special education disagreements between parents and school systems.

Early Intervening Services: Services intended to give struggling students needed support as soon as a student's needs become apparent.

Early Intervention: Providing services and programs to infants and toddlers (under age three) with disabilities in order to minimize or eliminate the disability as they mature.

Education of the Handicapped Act (EHA): *See* **Individuals with Disabilities Education Act (IDEA).**

Educational Advocate: An individual who speaks or acts knowledgeably for the educational needs of another.

Educational Diagnostician: A professional who is certified to conduct educational assessments and to design instructional programs for students.

Eligibility: The determination of whether or not a child qualifies to receive early intervention or special education services based on meeting established criteria.

Emotional Disorders (ED): Disorders characterized by their effect on an individual's emotional state. They may cause anxiety, such as separation anxiety, phobias, and post traumatic stress disorder. Other emotional disorders are affective or mood disorders, such as childhood depression, or bi-polar disorder.

Employability Skills: Personal habits and traits such as cleanliness, dependability, and punctuality that are necessary for successful employment; sometimes called "work adjustment skills."

Evaluation: The process of collecting information about a student's learning needs through a series of individual tests, observations, and talks with the student, the family, and others. Also, the process of obtaining detailed information about an infant or toddler's developmental levels and needs for services. May also be called **Assessment.**

Expressive Language: The ability to communicate through speech, writing, augmentative communication, or gestures.

Extended School Year: Special education provided during summer months to students found to require year-round services to receive an appropriate education.

Family Care: Care provided by individuals who are licensed by the state to provide family-like settings for adults with disabilities.

FBA. *See* **Functional Behavior Assessment.**

Fine Motor Skills: Body movements which use small muscles; for example: picking up a small object, writing, or eating.

Free Appropriate Public Education (FAPE): The words used in the federal law, the Individuals with Disabilities Education Act (IDEA), to describe a student's right to a special education program that will meet his or her individual special learning needs, at no cost to the family.

Functional Behavior Assessment (FBA): A process to determine the underlying causes or *functions* of a child's behavior that is keeping the child from learning or causing him to disrupt his peers' learning. For example, is the child using the behavior to get attention? To escape from a situation that he finds overwhelming? Included in the assessment is identification of when the behavior does and does not occur (what the antecedents are), what the child receives in return for the behavior (the consequences), and possible ways of replacing those behaviors.

Functional Goals: Goals that are designed to meet the needs of a child that result from the child's disability and enable the child to be involved in and make progress in the general education curriculum or meet the child's other educational needs resulting from his disability.

Functional Performance: How the child's disability affects his involvement and progress in the general education curriculum (i.e., the same curriculum used for children without disabilities). Or, for preschool children, how the disability affects the child's participation in appropriate activities.

Functional Vocational Evaluation. *See* **Vocational Assessment.**

General Education Diploma (GED): A method for obtaining a diploma for adults who did not complete high school. GED tests, which measure achievement in writing skills, social studies, science, literature, and mathematics, enable individuals to demonstrate that they have acquired a level of learning comparable to that of traditional high school graduates.

Goal: *See* **Annual Goal.**

Gross Motor Skills: Body movements which use large muscles; for example: sitting, walking, or climbing.

Habilitation: The process of helping an individual develop specific skills and abilities (e.g., dressing, eating, maneuvering a wheelchair) in order to become as independent and productive as possible.

Handicapped Children's Protection Act: The law providing for the reimbursement of reasonable attorneys' fees to parents who win their cases in administrative proceedings under IDEA.

Hard-of-Hearing: Impaired hearing which can be corrected sufficiently with a hearing aid to enable an individual to hear and process sounds.

Hearing Impaired: This term includes both individuals who are deaf and who are hard-of-hearing. The difference between deafness and hard-of-hearing is defined by amount of hearing loss.

Homebased Services: Early intervention services provided to a child and family in their own home.

Homebound Instruction: Educational instruction given in a student's home when he is unable to attend school for medical or other reasons.

IEP: *See* **Individualized Education Program.**

IFSP: *See* **Individualized Family Service Plan.**

I.Q.: See **Intelligence Quotient.**

Impartial Hearing Officer: Individual presiding over a due process hearing, appointed by the state education agency, and not connected in any way with either party in a dispute.

Inclusion: Ensuring that necessary supports and services are provided so that children with disabilities can participate with children who do not have disabilities in school, community, and recreation activities.

Independent Educational Evaluation: An evaluation/assessment of a student conducted by one or more professionals not employed by the school system. The person(s) doing the evaluation must be fully trained and qualified to do the kind of testing required.

Independent Living Skills: Basic skills needed by people with disabilities to function on their own, with as little help as possible. Skills include self-help (e.g., bathing, dressing), housekeeping, community living (e.g., shopping, using public transportation), etc.

Individualized Determination Plan: A written plan for each student who receives services, modifications, and accommodations under Section 504 of the Rehabilitation Act of 1973. In some schools, it is referred to as a "504 Plan."

Individualized Education Program (IEP): A written plan for each student in special education describing the student's present levels of performance, annual goals, specific special education and related services, dates for beginning and duration of services, and how the IEP will be evaluated.

Individualized Family Service Plan (IFSP): A written statement for each infant or toddler receiving early intervention services that includes goals and outcomes for the child and family. It also includes a plan for making the transition to services for children over age 2.

Individuals with Disabilities Education Act (IDEA): The authorizing federal legislation which mandates a free, appropriate public education for all children with disabilities. The law was formerly known as the Education for All Handicapped Children Act. **Part B** of the act refers to special education services for children age three through twenty-one. **Part C** refers to the early intervention program for infants and toddlers with disabilities from birth through age two and their families.

Infant Stimulation: A program designed to provide specific activities that encourage growth in developmental areas such as movement, speech and language, etc., in infants with developmental delays.

Intellectual Disability: A broad term describing delayed intellectual development resulting in delays in other areas, such as academic learning, adaptive behavior, communication, social skills, and physical coordination. This term is rapidly replacing the older term "mental retardation," which is an eligibility category used in IDEA.

Intelligence Quotient (I.Q.): A measurement of thinking (cognitive) ability that compares an individual with others in his age group.

Interagency Coordinating Council (ICC): Federal, state, or local group consisting of parents, advocates and professionals who serve in an advisory capacity to plan and implement early intervention services for infants and toddlers with disabilities and their families.

Intermediate Care Facility: Licensed facilities operating under strict regulations and providing intensive support for people with disabilities in the areas of personal care, communication, behavior management, etc.

Itinerant Teacher: A teacher who provides services to students in a variety of locations.

Job Coach: A service agency professional who works with an individual with disabilities at the job site, providing support by helping the employee to improve job skills, interpersonal relations, or any other job-related needs.

Lead Agency: State agency which has been designated by the governor to administer and implement a statewide comprehensive, coordinated, multidisciplinary, interagency service delivery system for infants and toddlers with disabilities and their families.

Learning Disability: A disorder in one or more of the processes involved in understanding or using language, spoken or written, resulting in difficulty with listening, thinking, speaking, writing, spelling, or doing mathematical calculations. This term does not include children with learning problems related to other disabilities such as mental retardation (intellectual disabilities).

Learning Style: The unique way that an individual learns best—for example, by playing games, imitating, reading a book, listening to a lecture, or handling materials. Most children learn through a combination of processes.

Least Restrictive Environment (LRE): Placement of a student with disabilities in a setting that allows maximum contact with students who do not have disabilities, while appropriately meeting the student's special education needs.

Legally Blind: An individual is considered to be legally blind if his vision, even with corrective lenses, is 20/200 or less, which means being able to see at 20 feet what a person with normal vision sees at 200 feet.

Mainstreaming: The concept that students with disabilities should be educated with nondisabled students to the maximum extent possible.

Major Life Activity: Such activities as caring for oneself, performing manual tasks, walking, seeing, hearing, speaking, learning, and working.

Mediation: A formal intervention between parents and personnel of early intervention or school systems to achieve reconciliation, settlement, or compromise.

Medicaid: A federal/state program that provides medical services primarily to individuals with low incomes.

Mental Retardation: An eligibility category used in IDEA. Although this terminology is still used in IDEA, most self-advocates, parents, teachers, and other professionals prefer the term intellectual or cognitive disability. *See* **Intellectual Disability.**

Minimum Competency: In order to receive a regular high school diploma, many states require students to pass a minimum competency test, demonstrating their academic skills to be at a state-defined level of achievement.

Modifications: Changes made to instruction or the curriculum that fundamentally changes what the child is expected to learn. Examples of modifications include providing instruction to the child at a different academic level or testing him on different knowledge or skills than other students in the class.

Multidisciplinary Evaluation: The testing of a child by a group of professionals, including psychologists, teachers, social workers, speech therapists, nurses, etc.

Multiple Disabilities: An educational label given to students having a combination of impairments such as mental retardation and blindness or orthopedic impairments and deafness which cause such educational problems that they cannot be accommodated in programs for any one impairment. This term does not include deaf-blind children.

Natural Homes: Places that are generally thought of as dwellings for people, such as apartments, houses, townhouses, trailers, etc.

Non-Categorical: Term relating to programs based on instructional needs rather than on categories of disabilities. Many states have only non-categorical programs; e.g., Maryland, Massachusetts, Minnesota, and others.

Nondiscriminatory Evaluation: An evaluation in which the materials and procedures used are not racially or culturally biased. In addition, an individual's disability must be accommodated such as by allowing more time, using a computer, etc.

Objective: An objective is a short-term step taken to reach an annual goal. IEP objectives are the steps between a student's present level of performance and an annual goal. IDEA previously required all IEPs to include objectives, but that requirement changed with the 2004 amendments.

Occupational Therapy (OT): Activities focusing on fine motor skills and perceptual abilities that assist in improving physical, social, psychological, and/or intellectual development; e.g., rolling a ball, finger painting, sorting objects.

On-the-Job-Training (OJT): Short-term training that enables a person to work on a job site while learning the job duties.

Orthopedic Impairment: A physical disability severe enough to affect a child's educational performance. Orthopedic impairments can be congenital, or caused by disease or injury.

Other Health Impairment (OHI): The term used in IDEA to describe conditions that adversely affect a child's educational performance and are not covered by other disability definitions (e.g., Learning Disabilities, Autism, etc.). This term is frequently used for medical conditions such as a heart condition, diabetes, cystic fibrosis, leukemia, etc. It also includes AD/HD and Tourette syndrome.

P.L. 101-476, P.L. 94-142, and P.L. 99-457: *See* **Individuals with Disabilities Education Act.**

Part B or Part C: *See* **Individuals with Disabilities Education Act.**

Physical Therapy (PT): Activities or routines designed to increase gross motor skills provided by a professional physical therapist.

Placement: The setting in which a child with disabilities is educated. Placement includes the school, the classroom, related services, community-based services, and the amount of time a student will spend with peers and others who do not have disabilities.

Postsecondary Education: Education programs for students who have completed high school, such as community and junior colleges, four-year colleges, trade and technical schools, and vocational programs.

Psychiatrist: A medical doctor with advanced training who specializes in the diagnosis and treatment of emotional, behavioral, and mental disorders.

Psychological Evaluation: The portion of a child's overall evaluation/assessment for special education that tests his or her general aptitudes and abilities, eye-hand coordination, social skills, emotional development, and thinking skills.

Psychologist: A professional, not a medical doctor, with advanced training in the study of mental processes and human behavior. A school psychologist conducts various evaluations, especially aptitude and ability tests, and may work with students, classroom teachers, parents, and school administrators on behavior assessments and behavior management programs.

Reasonable Accommodation: Changes a school is required to make to permit students with disabilities to participate in educational programs or extracurricular activities (for example, locating a classroom on the first floor if a higher floor is inaccessible to a student in a wheelchair). The concept also applies to the modification of job requirements and equipment for workers with disabilities. Generally, reasonable accommodations must be made if they do not impose an undue financial burden.

Receptive Language: The process of receiving and understanding written, gestured, or spoken language.

Reevaluation: *See* **Triennial Review.**

Referral: A formal notification to the early intervention system or local school that a child is experiencing learning or developmental difficulties and may require a full evaluation for early intervention or special education. A referral may be made by a family, teacher, or other professional.

Rehabilitation Act Amendments of 1992: Federal legislation that requires state vocational rehabilitation agencies to work cooperatively with local agencies, including schools, to create a unified system to serve people with disabilities.

Rehabilitation Act of 1973 (Section 504): A nondiscrimination statute. Section 504 of the Act stipulates that individuals with disabilities may not be excluded from participating in programs and services receiving federal funds. It also prohibits job discrimination against people with disabilities in any program receiving federal financial assistance.

Related Services: Those services a student must receive to benefit from special education; for example, transportation, counseling, speech therapy, crisis intervention, etc.

Residential Services: The placement of a student in a setting that provides educational instruction and 24-hour care.

Resource Room: A setting in a school where a student receives instruction for a part of the school day from a special education teacher.

Response to Intervention: A process schools may use to identify students with specific learning disabilities. It involves universal screening for learning difficulties, providing instruction and interventions matched to students' needs, frequent progress monitoring, and using data on students' responses to make educational decisions.

School-Based Screening Committee: *See* **Screening Committee.**

Screening: A brief examination of a child designed to pick up potential difficulties and to identify children who need further evaluation and diagnosis.

Screening Committee: A local school-based committee, whose members determine if a student should be fully evaluated for special education eligibility.

Section 504: *See* **Rehabilitation Act of 1973.**

Self-Advocacy: The abilities required to take primary responsibility for one's life and to make choices regarding one's actions free from undue interference. Also called **self-determination.**

Self-Contained Classroom: A classroom in which a group of students with disabilities receive their instruction with little or no interaction with nondisabled students.

Self-Determination: *See* **Self-Advocacy.**

Service Coordinator: Someone who acts as a coordinator of a child's and family's early intervention services and works in partnership with the family and other service providers.

Sheltered Workshop: A work setting in which employees with disabilities do contract work, usually on a piece-rate basis, such as preparing bulk mailings or refinishing furniture.

Social Worker: A professional who may provide services to the family including: arranging or attending parent-student conferences; providing family counseling, family education, information, and referral; writing a social-developmental history; and/or conducting a behavioral assessment. Social workers sometimes conduct parent education in the school and community.

Sociocultural Report: The portion of a child's overall evaluation/assessment for special education that describes a child's background and behavior at home and at school. It is usually completed by a social worker.

Special Education: Specially designed instruction to meet the unique needs of a child with a disability, as defined in the Individuals with Disabilities Education Act.

Special Education File: *See* **Confidential File.**

Special Needs: A term to describe a child who has disabilities, chronic illness, or is at risk for developing disabilities and who needs educational services or other special treatment in order to progress.

Specialized Nursing Homes: Licensed facilities operating under strict regulations and providing intensive support for people with disabilities in the areas of personal care, communication, behavior management, etc.

Specific Learning Disability (SLD): *See* **Learning Disability.**

Speech Impaired: A communication disorder involving poor or abnormal production of the sounds of language.

Speech-Language Pathologist: A professional who evaluates and develops programs for individuals with speech or language problems.

Speech Therapy: Activities or routines designed to improve and increase communication skills.

Standardized Tests: In a vocational assessment, standardized tests are used to predict how a student is likely to perform in jobs calling for certain interests and skills.

Student Progress Monitoring: A scientifically based practice used to assess students' academic performance and evaluate the effectiveness of instruction.

Substantially Limits (a major life activity): Refers to a disability that restricts the conditions, manner, or duration under which activities can be performed in comparison to most people, as defined by the Americans with Disabilities Act.

Supervised Living Arrangements: Homes or apartments for persons with disabilities that are managed by public or private agencies. Paid staff supervise the residents and assist them with budgeting, food preparation, transportation, etc.

Supplemental Security Income (SSI): A federal program administered through the Social Security Administration that provides payments to individuals who are elderly and/or have disabilities. Children may be eligible for SSI if they have disabilities and are from families with low income. In addition, children who are hospitalized for 30 days or more and have a disability expected to last 12 months or more may receive SSI.

Supported Employment: Paid employment for workers with disabilities in settings with people who are nondisabled. A job coach provides support by helping the employee to improve job skills, interpersonal relations, or any other job-related needs.

Trade and Technical Schools: Schools which prepare students for employment in recognized occupations such as secretary, air conditioning technician, beautician, electrician, welder, carpenter, etc.

Transition: The process of moving from one situation to another. Frequently used to mean moving from preschool programs into elementary school or from school to work and the community.

Transition Coordinator: School personnel chosen to manage transition services for students with disabilities.

Transition Planning: Careful preparation by the student, parents, educators, and other service providers, for the time when the student leaves high school. The plan is written in the Individualized Transition Plan.

Transition Planning Team: The people who are involved in transition planning for a student, including the student, parents, school personnel (teachers, guidance counselor, vocational coordinator, school administrator), adult service agency representatives (vocational rehabilitation counselor, independent living center staff).

Transition Services: A coordinated set of activities for a student that promotes movement from school to post-school activities, including postsecondary education, vocational training, integrated employment, continuing and adult education, adult services, independent living, or community participation.

Transitional Employment: A relatively short-term program designed to help an individual obtain a job, or to develop the work habits and learn the skills needed for a particular job.

Traumatic Brain Injury: An acquired injury to the brain caused by an external physical force causing a disability which affects a child's educational performance; e.g., cognition, memory, language, motor abilities.

Triennial Review: Every three years, a student in special education must be given a completely new evaluation/assessment to determine the student's progress and to make a new determination of eligibility for continued special education services.

Visual-Motor Integration: The extent to which an individual can coordinate vision with body movement or parts of the body; e.g., being able to copy words from the blackboard.

Visually Impaired: Having a mild to severe vision disorder, which adversely affects a child's educational performance.

Vocational Assessment (Evaluation): A systematic process of evaluating an individual's skills, aptitudes, and interests as they relate to job preparation and choice. Assessments include work sampling, standardized tests, and behavioral observation.

Vocational Education: Formal training designed to prepare individuals to work in a certain job or occupational area, such as construction, cosmetology, food service, or electronics. Also called vocational training and vocational program.

Vocational Rehabilitation: A comprehensive system that assists individuals with temporary or permanent disabilities in the areas of assessment, counseling, training, physical rehabilitation, and job placement.

Work Activity Centers: Programs for adults with disabilities providing training in vocational skills, as well as daily living skills, social skills, and recreational skills.

Work Adjustment Skills: See **Employability Skills.**

Work Sampling Test: The portion of a vocational assessment which tests a student's hands-on performance in certain simulated and actual work environments.

Work-Study Programs: Education programs in which the student receives employment training and earns credit toward graduation through employment.

RESOURCES

There have never been so many places to find information. Websites harbor wisdom from other parents and teachers, frank information from students and people with disabilities, information about special education and disability-related laws, and the latest research on a broad array of topics. They also lead you to print resources, including excellent books, articles, and fact sheets. This section lists some good places to start looking for information as you negotiate your own way through the special education maze.

The federal government has invested in places for parents and professionals to find reliable information that are easily accessed through the Internet. For those who would rather speak to someone in person, try:

- *Technical Assistance Alliance for Parent Centers*—888-248-0822;
- *The National Dissemination Center for Children with Disabilities* (*also known as NICHCY*)—800-695-0285 (voice or TTY)

Both groups can put you in touch with state and local Parent Centers who can help your find the information you need.

Especially for Parents

Parent Training and Information Centers and Community Parent Resource Centers
888-248-0822
www.taalliance.org

The U.S. Department of Education funds Parent Training and Information Centers (PTIs) and Community Parent Resource Centers (CPRCs) in each state to provide training and information to parents of infants, toddlers, children, and youth with disabilities and to professionals who work with children. This assistance helps parents to participate more effectively with professionals in meeting the educational needs of children and youth with disabilities. The Parent Centers work to improve educational outcomes for children and youth with all disabilities (emotional, learning, mental, and physical).

The Technical Assistance Alliance for Parent Centers is headed by the PACER Center in Minneapolis. At this site, you can find one of the approximately 100 parent centers in the United States that is closest to you. In addition to finding parent centers, the site contains information on IDEA, No Child Left Behind, Scientifically-Based Resources, a link to the over 50 centers funded by the US Department of Education as technical assistance and dissemination projects, and publications and national resources.

As mentioned previously, if you wish to speak to someone in person, you can call their toll-free number. They will also be able to give you the toll-free number for the state or community parent center nearest you where you can find out more about how things work at the state and community level in your area.

National Dissemination Center for Children with Disabilities
P.O. Box 1492
Washington, DC 20013
800-695-0285 (English/Spanish; voice/TTY)
www.nichcy.org

The National Dissemination Center for Children with Disabilities (also known as NICHCY) is a central source of information on disabilities, IDEA, No Child Left Behind, and research-based information. There is a searchable database of disability-related information, information from other centers funded by the U.S. Department of Education, and parent-friendly information on special education and instruction. NICHCY also has an E-Newsletter and a *Zigawhat* site for children and teens with disabilities.

NICHCY can also put you in touch with key organizations in your state including State agencies serving children with disabilities, state chapters of disability organizations and parent groups, parent training and information centers, and other useful associations and organizations.

Where to Find the Laws

Individuals with Disabilities Education Act (IDEA)

http://idea.ed.gov

The U.S. Department of Education has created a portal to find out more about the Individuals with Disabilities Education Act (IDEA). From this portal, visitors can find information specific to Part B—the Special Education provisions and Part C — Early Intervention for Infants and Toddlers with Disabilities.

This site was created to provide a "one-stop shop" for resources related to IDEA and its implementing regulations. The site has searchable versions of IDEA and the regulations, access to cross-referenced content from other laws such as the No Child Left Behind Act (NCLB) or the Family Education Rights and Privacy Act (FERPA), etc., video clips on selected topics, topic briefs on selected regulations, links to the Office of Special Education Program's (OSEP's) Technical Assistance and Dissemination (TA&D) Network and a Q&A Corner, where visitors can submit questions, and a variety of other information sources.

The search engine allows visitors to find relevant sections of the IDEA regulations, and OSEP-approved documents. Visitors can also locate state policies and procedures. Also available are model procedural safeguards, prior written notice, and IEP forms.

Family Education Rights and Privacy Act (FERPA)

Family Policy Compliance Office
U.S. Department of Education
400 Maryland Ave., SW
Washington, DC 20202-5920
202-260-3887
www.ed.gov/policy/gen/guid/fpco/index.html [complaints]
ww.ed.gov/policy/gen/reg/ferpa/index.html [regulations]

The Family Policy Compliance Office (FPCO) in the U.S. Department of Education enforces: the Family Educational Rights and Privacy Act (FERPA) and the Protection of Pupil Rights Amendment (PPRA). Parents and eligible students who need assistance or who wish to file a complaint under FERPA or PPRA should do so in writing to the Family Policy Compliance Office, sending pertinent information concerning any allegations through the mail, to the address above. For additional information or technical assistance, you may call the office.

Section 504 of the Rehabilitation Act

U.S. Department of Education
Office for Civil Rights

Customer Service Team
400 Maryland Ave., SW
Washington, DC 20202-1100
800-421-3481; 202-245-6840 (fax); 877-521-2172 (TDD)
OCR@ed.gov
www.ed.gov/about/offices/list/ocr/aboutocr.html [complaints]
www.ed.gov/policy/rights/reg/ocr/index.html [regulations]

The Office for Civil Rights(OCR) enforces several federal civil rights laws that prohibit discrimination in programs or activities that receive federal financial assistance from the Department of Education. Discrimination on the basis of race, color, and national origin is prohibited by Title VI of the Civil Rights Act of 1964; sex discrimination is prohibited by Title IX of the Education Amendments of 1972; discrimination on the basis of disability is prohibited by Section 504 of the Rehabilitation Act of 1973; and age discrimination is prohibited by the Age Discrimination Act of 1975.

These civil rights laws enforced by OCR extend to all state education agencies, elementary and secondary school systems, colleges and universities, vocational schools, proprietary schools, state vocational rehabilitation agencies, libraries, and museums that receive U.S. Department of Education funds. Areas covered may include, but are not limited to: admissions, recruitment, financial aid, academic programs, student treatment and services, counseling and guidance, discipline, classroom assignment, grading, vocational education, recreation, physical education, athletics, housing, and employment. OCR also has responsibilities under Title II of the Americans with Disabilities Act of 1990 (prohibiting disability discrimination by public entities, whether or not they receive federal financial assistance). More information on the ADA is available below.

Americans with Disabilities Act
U.S. Department of Justice
800-514-0301; 800-514-0383 (TDD)
www.usdoj.gov/crt/ada/adahom1.htm

The US Department of Justice manages the main portal for people interested in finding out more about the Americans with Disabilities Act (ADA). The site has links to the 10 agencies with some responsibility for enforcing ADA. Print copies of materials on the ADA are available by calling the toll-free numbers above. Regulations for the ADA can also be downloaded at the U.S. Dept. of Education site listed above.

Other Information from the Government

DisabilityInfo.Gov
www.disabilityinfo.gov

DisabilityInfo.gov is the federal government's one-stop website for people with disabilities, their families, employers, veterans and service members, workforce professionals, and many others. A collaborative effort among twenty-two federal agencies, Disabilityinfo.gov is intended to connect people with disabilities to the information and resources they need to actively participate in the workforce and in their communities.

In addition to education, topics include employment, benefits, housing, transportation, health, technology, community life, and civil rights. There are links to state and local resources on each topic. A search engine allows the user to enter key words in order to find topics of interest. Visit any of the nine subject areas at the top of this page to find disability-related resources, and then click on the State and Local Resources map to locate programs and information in your state.

Regional Resource & Federal Center Network (RRFC)
www.rrfcnetwork.org

The Regional Resource and Federal Centers (RRFC) Network is made up of the six Regional Resource Centers for Special Education (RRC) and the Federal Resource Center (FRC).

The six RRCs and the FRC are funded by the federal Office of Special Education Programs (OSEP) to assist state education agencies in improving education programs, practices, and policies that affect children and youth with disabilities. These centers offer consultation, information services, technical assistance, training, and product development.

The site is a portal to a massive amount of research-based information. Visitors can find their state special education and early intervention agencies, Parent Training and Information Centers, and National Dissemination Centers by going to the links on their home page. They can also find information briefs, papers, and handouts on a number of topics from very technical documents on State Performance Plans to easy-to-understand parent involvement information in multiple languages.

Other Good Sources of Information

All Kinds of Minds
1450 Raleigh Road, Suite 200
Chapel Hill, NC 27517
888-956-4637
www.allkindsofminds.org

A nonprofit institute that helps students who struggle improve their success in school and life. Their website provides resources to help parents, educators, and clinicians understand why a child is struggling in school and how to help each child become a more successful learner. The website includes a free monthly newsletter, articles, discussion groups, and a LearningBase and Parent Toolkit with practical strategies for supporting learning differences.

American Council of the Blind
1155 15th Street, NW, Suite 1004
Washington, DC 20005
202-467-5081; 800-424-8666
www.acb.org

The American Council of the Blind's membership consists of individuals who are blind, family members, and professionals. ACB advocates for civil rights, national health insurance, rehabilitation, eye research technology, and other issues that concern people who are blind.

American Foundation for the Blind
11 Penn Plaza, Suite 300
New York, NY 10001
212-502-7600
www.afb.org

The American Foundation for the Blind works to promote equality of access and opportunity to individuals who are blind or visually impaired. AFB Press, the publishing arm of this organization, produces the *Journal of Visual Impairment and Blindness* and many texts focusing on the topic of blindness and visual impairment.

The Arc
1010 Wayne Ave., Suite 650
Silver Spring, MD 20910
301-565-3842
www.thearc.org

A national organization of people with intellectual disabilities and their advocates. It publishes information on all types of developmental delays and has an extensive network of local affiliates which offer support, information, respite care, and other services.

ASPEN of America
(Asperger Syndrome Education Network of America)
P.O. Box 2577
Jacksonville, FL 32203-2577
904-745-6741
www.asperger.org
A national organization that provides information about Asperger's Syndrome to parents and professionals.

Autism Society of America
7910 Woodmont Ave., Ste. 300
Bethesda, MD 20814
800-328-8476; 301-657-0881
www.autism-society.org
The oldest membership organization for families of people with autism in the United States, the ASA is a good starting point for gathering information if you suspect that your child might have Asperger syndrome or another autism spectrum disorder. Acts as an information clearinghouse about autism and services for people with autism Publishes a bimonthly newsletter and coordinates a national network of affiliated state and local chapters.

CHADD
8181 Professional Place
Suite 150
Landover, MD 20785
800-233-4050; 301-306-7070; 301-306-7090 (fax)
ww.chadd.org
Children and Adults with Attention-Deficit/Hyperactivity Disorder (CHADD) is a national organization providing education, advocacy, and support for individuals with AD/HD. CHADD also publishes a variety of printed materials to keep members and professionals current on research advances, medications, and treatments.

The Council for Exceptional Children (CEC)

1110 North Glebe Road, Suite 300
Arlington, VA 22201
703-620-3660; 703-264-9494 (fax)
www.cec.sped.org

This is a membership organization for educators in the U.S. and Canada who are interested in the needs of children who have disabilities or are gifted. Their publication catalog offers a number of books and other materials on education-related topics.

Depression and Bipolar Support Alliance

730 N. Franklin St., Ste. 501
Chicago, IL 60601
800-826-3632
www.dbsalliance.org

The Alliance is a nonprofit organization whose mission is to improve the lives of people living with mood disorders. It offers information on research, contact information for local support groups, new publications, plus a bookstore related to depression and bipolar.

Epilepsy Foundation of America

4351 Garden City Drive
Landover, MD 20785-7223
800-332-1000; 301-577-2684 (fax)
www.efa.org

A national organization that works for the prevention and cure of seizure disorders and promotes independence and optimal quality of life for people with epilepsy. Services commonly provided in local communities are information and referral, counseling, patient and family advocacy, school alert, community education, support groups, and camps for children.

Family Village

www.familyvillage.wisc.edu

This website describes itself as "a global village of disability-related resources." It includes full text articles on specific disabilities, education issues, legal issues, recreation, and more, as well as opportunities to connect with others and extensive links to information, products, and resources.

International Dyslexia Association
Chester Building, Suite 382
8600 LaSalle Road
Baltimore, MD 21286
410-296-0232; 410-321-5069 (fax)
Voice Message Requests for Information: 800-ABCD123
www.interdys.org
   A nonprofit organization dedicated to helping individuals with dyslexia, their families, and the communities that support them. Provides a forum for parents, educators, and researchers to share their experiences, methods, and knowledge through periodicals and books; offers information and referral services.

Laurent Clerc National Deaf Education Center
800 Florida Ave. NE
Washington, DC 20002
202-651-5000
www.clerccenter.gallaudet.edu
   The Laurent Clerc National Deaf Education Center is supported by the U.S. federal government and disseminates information on model programs for education of deaf/hard of hearing children across the country.

LD Online website
www.ldonline.com
   Offers online articles, resources, and forums to help parents, teachers, and people with LD understand many different types of learning disabilities and learn strategies and information to help individuals with LD be more successful at home, school, and on the job.

Learning Disabilities Association of America
4156 Library Road
Pittsburgh, PA 15234
412-341-1515; 412-344-0224 (fax)
www.ldaamerica.us
   LDA is the largest nonprofit volunteer organization advocating for individuals with learning disabilities and has over 200 state and local affiliates in 42 states and Puerto Rico. The national office can provide publications and information on education, laws, and advocacy.

National Alliance on Mental Illness
Colonial Place Three
2107 Wilson Blvd, Ste 300
Arlington, VA 22201-3042
703-524-7600; 703-524-9094 (fax)
888-999-6264
www.nami.org

NAMI is the U.S.'s largest grassroots mental health organization dedicated to improving the lives of people with mental illness and their families. Their website has information on advocacy, programs, resources, and it lists all state contacts for child/adolescent network locations. There are links to many other good sites.

National Association of the Deaf
8630 Fenton St., Suite 820
Silver Spring, MD 20910
301-587-1788 V; 301-587-1789 TTY
www.nad.org

Promotes, protects, and preserves the rights and quality of life of individuals who are deaf and hard of hearing in the United States.

National Center for Learning Disabilities
381 Park Ave So, Ste 1401
New York, NY 10016
212-545-7510; 212-545-9665
888-575-7373
www.ncld.org

This parent-professional organization dedicated to working for the success of individuals with learning disabilities of all ages has a great website on learning disabilities organized by age group with resources, publications, advocacy, and online experts.

National Down Syndrome Congress
1370 Center Dr., Suite 102
Atlanta, GA 30338
770-604-9599; 800-232-6372
www.ndsccenter.org

A national organization of parents and professionals dedicated to improving the lives of people with Down syndrome and their families. Provides information and referral; holds conferences; advocates for issues of concern to members.

National Down Syndrome Society

666 Broadway, 8th floor
New York, NY 10012
212-460-9330; 800-221-4602
www.ndss.org

A national organization that works to promote a better understanding of Down syndrome. Sponsors scientific and educational research into Down syndrome, provides online and print publications, and operates a website with extensive links.

National Organization for Rare Disorders

www.rarediseases.org

The National Organization for Rare Disorders (NORD) is a federation of voluntary health organizations dedicated to helping people with rare "orphan" diseases and assisting the organizations that serve them. NORD is committed to the identification, treatment, and cure of rare disorders through programs of education, advocacy, research, and service.

NORD provides information about diseases, referrals to patient organizations, research grants and fellowships, advocacy for the rare-disease community, and Medication Assistance Programs that help needy patients obtain certain drugs they could not otherwise afford.

Online Asperger Syndrome Information & Support (OASIS)

www.udel.edu/bkirby/asperger

A useful website containing a wide variety of information and resources on Asperger's disorder.

Recording for the Blind and Dyslexic (RFB&D)

20 Rozel Rd
Princeton, NJ 08540
866-732-3585
www.rfbd.org

Recording for the Blind and Dyslexic (RFB&D) is a nonprofit agency providing recorded and computerized textbooks, library services, and other educational resources to people who cannot read standard print because of a visual, physical, or perceptual disability.

Spina Bifida Association of America
4590 MacArthur Blvd., NW, Suite 250
Washington, DC 20007-422
800-621-3141; 202-944-3285; 202-944-3295 (fax)
www.sbaa.org

A national voluntary health agency solely dedicated to enhancing the lives of those with spina bifida and those whose lives are touched by spina bifida. Members include people with spina bifida, family members, and professionals. Services include: toll-free information and referral service; a newsletter, legislative updates, pamphlets and other publications; information on clinics that specialize in spina bifida treatment and care; conferences; research; and advocacy.

TASH
29 W. Susquehanna Ave., Suite 210
Baltimore, MD 21204
410-828-8274; 410-828-6706 (fax)
www.tash.org

TASH is an international association of people with disabilities, their family members, other advocates, and professionals fighting for a society in which inclusion of all people in all aspects of society is the norm. Publishes a newsletter and sponsors conferences.

Tourette Syndrome Association
42-40 Bell Boulevard
Bayside, NY 11361
718-224-2999; 718-279-9596 (fax)
www.tsa-usa.org

TSA National is a must-have resource for families with Tourettes Syndrome. Committed to finding the cause and cure for TS and controlling the effects of TS, the TSA can link families with many resources in education, medical knowledge, counseling, research, science, advocacy, and fund raising. The website has state and local contact information and many helpful links.

United Cerebral Palsy
1660 L St., NW, Suite 700
Washington, DC 20036
202-776-0406; 800-872-5827
www.ucpa.org

UCP provides information about, and advocates for, individuals with cerebral palsy. Publishes *Washington Watch,* a newsletter with updates on disability policy and news; fact sheets and other publications can be downloaded from the website.

Woodbine House
800-843-7323; 301-897-3570

www.woodbinehouse.com

In addition to publishing books for parents and teachers about AD/HD, autism, Down syndrome, cerebral palsy, spina bifida, Tourette syndrome, and other childhood disabilities, Woodbine House has Resource Links to a variety of helpful organizations on its website.

Wrightslaw
www.wrightslaw.com

Parents, educators, advocates, and attorneys come to Wrightslaw for information about special education law, education law, and advocacy for children with disabilities. The site contains an Advocacy Library and Law Library. Topics include IDEA, No Child Left Behind, research-based education, and much more. Also check out their Yellow Pages for Kids directory and Best School Websites.

INDEX

About the Authors

Winifred G. Anderson is a special education professional whose work has been devoted to the relationships between families, children, and schools. She, along with Steve Chitwood, founded the Parent Educational Advocacy Training Center (PEATC), a training and information center for families and professionals who work with children and youth with disabilities located in Alexandria, Virginia. Prior to her work at PEATC she was a founder and director of Resurrection Children's Center, an inclusive early childhood school also in Alexandria. Ms. Anderson continues to write in the fields of special and adult education.

Stephen Chitwood is a professor Emeritus of Public Administration at The George Washington University in Washington, D.C., and former Director of the University's Center for Law Practice Strategy and Management. For fifteen years he served as a legal consultant for PEATC specializing in the educational rights of children with disabilities. As the parents of a child with special needs, he and his wife, Janet, worked for over twenty years to ensure their son received a free appropriate public education in the least restrictive environment.

Deidre Hayden has been involved with advocacy for children with disabilities and their families since 1979. She is a former Executive Director of PEATC and Matrix Parent Network and Resource Center in San Rafael, California, a model parent center providing parent-to-parent support, training, and information to families of children with disabilities from birth through young adulthood. While at Matrix, she served as Director, West Region Technical Assistance Center, providing technical assistance and support to federally funded parent centers in the West and Pacific Territories. She is currently the coordinator for the Special Needs Inclusion Project for the San Francisco Department of Children, Youth and Their Families.

Cherie Takemoto learned to be an advocate when her son, Pete, was born in 1988. She is PEATC's current Executive Director. Because children without parent advocates are the most vulnerable children of all, Ms. Takemoto strives to connect families with the knowledge and resources it takes to build a successful life for their children with disabilities. Her disability-related expertise includes early intervention, literacy, special education, transition, No Child Left Behind, parent involvement, and cultural competence. She served on the President's Commission on Excellence in Special Education that made many of the recommendations that were ultimately adopted in IDEA 2004, the recent reauthorization of the special education law.